The
Psychology of
Consciousness

SECOND EDITION

The Psychology of Consciousness

SECOND EDITION

ROBERT E. ORNSTEIN

THE LANGLEY PORTER NEUROPSYCHIATRIC INSTITUTE

THE INSTITUTE FOR THE STUDY OF HUMAN KNOWLEDGE

Harcourt Brace Jovanovich, Inc.

NEW YORK   CHICAGO   SAN FRANCISCO   ATLANTA

ISBN: 0-15-573082-7
Library of Congress Catalog Card Number: 77-71699
Printed in the United States of America

Illustration Credits appear on page 249.

COPYRIGHTS AND ACKNOWLEDGMENTS

For permission to use the selections reprinted in this book, the author is
grateful to the following publishers and copyright holders:

George Allen & Unwin, Ltd. for the selection from *The Persian Sufis* by
   Cyprian Rice. Reprinted by permission of the publisher, George Allen &
   Unwin, Ltd.

W. H. Allen & Co., Ltd. for the selection from *The Sufis* by Idries Shah,
   copyright © 1964 by Idries Shah. Reprinted by permission of the publisher, W. H. Allen & Co., Ltd.

Chatto and Windus, Ltd. for the selection, from *The Doors of Perception* by
   Aldous Huxley. Reprinted by permission Mrs. Laura Huxley and Chatto
   and Windus Ltd.

Curtis Brown, Ltd. for the selections from *The Exploits of the Incomparable Mulla
   Nasrudin* by Idries Shah, published by E. P. Dutton & Co., Inc., copyright
   © 1966 by Mulla Nasrudin Enterprises, Ltd. For the selection from *The
   Pleasantries of the Incredible Mulla Nasrudin* by Idries Shah, published by
   E. P. Dutton & Son, Inc., copyright © 1968 by Mulla Nasrudin Enter-
   prises, Ltd. For the selections from *Tales of the Dervishes* by Idries Shah,
   published by E. P. Dutton & Co., Inc., copyright © 1967 by Idries Shah.
   For the selection from *The Way of the Sufi* by Idries Shah, published by
   E. P. Dutton & Son, Inc., copyright © 1968 by Idries Shah. For the
   selections from *Caravan of Dreams* by Idries Shah, published by Penguin
   Books, copyright © 1968 by Idries Shah. All selections reprinted by
   permission of Curtis Brown, Ltd. No part of the works reprinted herein

Copyrights and Acknowledgments continue on page 249.

To the students who have developed a true psychology,
of consciousness

PREFACE

This is a textbook about consciousness, written for students of the human sciences. It is intended as a first book, requiring few or no prerequisites, to introduce the beginning student to research work and theories that bear on his or her own experience of the world. Psychology is, primarily, the science of human experience. Its researchers study secondary phenomena—such as behavior, physiology, and "verbal report"—as they relate to the central questions of consciousness. Too often psychologists have been guilty of becoming trapped by the ease of answering secondary questions and have turned away from the central questions of the discipline for the sake of convenience; for consciousness is difficult to study, since one's experience is not as observable to others as is one's behavior, physiology, or speech.

I suppose many who read this book have asked, "What is consciousness?" but still remain somewhat confused about the answer. In my own questioning I began to read contemporary psychology and philosophy, hoping to find an answer there. Instead I found a bewildering array of unconnected ideas, beginning with a definition of consciousness as "awareness of awareness," continuing with bizarre and facile cosmic blather, and ending with the conviction that the question is not meaningful. To ask "What is consciousness?" is not unreasonable, yet the question does not seem to be fully answerable in reasonable terms. So along with questions such as "What is life?" and "What is humanness?" it tends to be ignored among "hard-nosed" scientists.

After long study in many areas, I feel that this question *can* be answered, yet, unfortunately, not fully within the mode of reason. There is no way to simply write down the answer, as we might give a textbook definition. There is no place where the meaning of one's life is "written up." The answer is, at least in part, experiential and personal.

Then what is the purpose of *The Psychology of Consciousness?* I have tried to do two things at once in this book—to present what can be discussed scientifically, without pretending that such an approach is a complete answer, just as a biologist does not really answer the question, "What is life?" while studying life; and to point to a stream of knowledge directed to considering those questions of humanness, life, and consciousness that scientific method excludes, the esoteric traditions of the Middle and Far East. Seven hundred years ago Roger Bacon wrote, "There are two modes of knowing, those of argument and experience." They are complementary; neither is reducible to the other; and their simultaneous working may sometimes even be incompatible. One mode is rational and verbal—sequential in operation—the other is intuitive and spatial—diffuse in operation, less orderly than that of reason. The intuitive mode is one we often overlook in science as well as in society, education, and even in ourselves.

The Psychology of Consciousness is a look at a psychology that is in the process of formation, so its content is advanced but its writing is not. I present here a convergence of evidence from many sources: research on the functions of the two cerebral hemispheres in humans, and Eastern teaching stories that introduce each chapter; current scientific analyses of perception and cognition, and esoteric texts; research on control of involuntary functions in humans and animals, and reports on yoga. This is not a problem-solving, advanced scientific treatise, nor is it a step-by-step manual on how to get high or an apologia for such phenomena as astrology or witchcraft. The emphasis is on a synthesis of two major streams of knowledge, not on individual, unconnected states or techniques. This book is intended to redress an imbalance in textbooks, in that it attempts to treat responsibly many areas of concern not usually considered in psychology courses. A consideration of what lies behind "states of consciousness," meditation, techniques of mysticism and scientific investigation is what is most important and most needed at the moment, and will be of interest to the student as well as to the instructor.

This second edition of The Psychology of Consciousness is for the student and for the teaching situation. It has been developed with the cooperation of many instructors and students who used the first edition in classes and who have suggested useful changes.

ROBERT E. ORNSTEIN

CONTENTS

The
Psychology of
Consciousness

SECOND EDITION

1 Toward a Complete Psychology

Is There Any Number Higher Than 100?

A man, having looted a city, was trying to sell an exquisite rug, one of the spoils. "Who will give me 100 pieces of gold for this rug?" he cried throughout the town.

After the sale was completed, a comrade approached the seller, and asked, "Why did you not ask more for that priceless rug?"

"Is there any number higher than 100?" asked the seller.[1]

I t is easy to smile at the mistake of our friend the rugseller. Yet, we too are like him, for each day our own conceptions of what is possible limit awareness and action. This story reflects a process common both to everyday life and to scientific endeavor. Conceptions often act as barriers to understanding; they may conceal other possibilities, as the number 100 blocks higher numbers from view. To give an example: Once it was considered impossible for a man to run a mile in less than four minutes. The four-minute mile became a real barrier to many, as if effort of another order were required to run a mile in 3:59:99 instead of four minutes. Then one man broke this barrier, and quite soon many others were able to perform something once considered impossible. We seem to set limits on possibility and to work within these assumed limits.

A similar process limits ordinary consciousness. We screen out much of our surroundings because we do not believe that certain events occur. Once a friend unwittingly emphasized this to me by reversing an ordinary saying: "I'll see it when I believe it!" If an object or sensory input appears that does not fit our set of categories, we may ignore it. The psychologist Jerome Bruner and his associates carried out the following experiment, which demonstrated this phenomenon.

One assumption of our society concerns the suits of playing cards. Through years of experience, we have learned that spades and clubs are black, hearts and diamonds are red. Normally, each deck of cards we see confirms this assumption. Bruner asked his observers to look at some cards through a tachistoscope—a device that flashes visual materials on a screen for a brief period of time. Intermixed with the ordinary cards were several "anomalous" ones—a *red* ace of spades, a *black* four of hearts, for instance. Many of the observers in this experiment did not "see" the unusual cards as they were but "corrected" them, reporting a red six of spades as a six of hearts. Assumptions can limit the scope of awareness. At one point in the experiment, it was suggested to the observers that although hearts are usually red, this does not logically imply that they will *always* be red. With this new idea extending their category system, some observers were quickly able to see what was in front of them.[2]

Our ordinary assumptions about the nature of the world are generally useful to us. As we attempt to achieve stability in consciousness, we continuously "bet" about the nature of reality. We immediately assume that our rooms are "really" rectilinear, that a piece of coal is "really" black, that one person is intelligent, another aggressive. As Bruner's experiment and these examples suggest, our "assumptive world" is conservative. It is quite difficult to alter our assumptions even in the face of compelling new evidence. We pay the price of a certain conservatism and resistance to new information or knowledge in order to gain a measure of stability in personal consciousness.

Any organized community of people holds in common certain assumptions about reality. The structure of a given language is a set of common assumptions, shared for the convenience of transmitting information. The "four-minute mile" was another common assumption. In addition, each scientific community of physicists, mathematicians, psychologists, and others, shares an additional set of both implicit and explicit assumptions, termed a *paradigm* by Thomas Kuhn. The paradigm is the shared conceptions of what is possible, the boundaries of acceptable inquiry, the limiting cases.[3] It is the framework within which ideas are acceptable or not.

The scientific paradigm is analogous to the individual's assumptions about reality. Personal categories are by their nature conservative of effort. Given a stable category system, we need not measure the walls of every new room we enter to determine whether they are really rectilinear, or to inspect our friends at each meeting to determine whether they are really the same people we saw yesterday. In science, a paradigm allows a similar stability of knowledge, again, at the price of sensitivity to new input. If several researchers share a paradigm, it enables them to explore jointly one well-delimited area of inquiry and to coordinate effort. A shared paradigm allows them to communicate about an area in a specialized language as the residents of a particular town may have their own local phrases and jokes.

The development of a successful paradigm, then, enables a scientific community to maintain and share criteria for the selection of problems that might be amenable to solution. It allows a number of "local road maps" to be drawn up, tested, and validated by many independent researchers. But there is also a danger of parochialism. Just as the residents of a certain community may become smug about their town and consider it the "only" place in the world, so the scientists working within a successful paradigm may begin to lose sight of any possibilities beyond their own particular set of assumptions.

Psychology began as the science of consciousness and developed as a synthesis of natural philosophy and nineteenth-century science. One of its earliest practitioners, Gustav Fechner, invented the method of "psychophysics" in an attempt to correlate mental and physical events. Research on consciousness proceeded in the nineteenth century, spearheaded by a group at Cornell Unviversity under E.B. Titchener. This group sought evidence on consciousness through "introspection." Their research strategy was to have the observers attempt to analyze the contents of personal consciousness and to compare their analyses with that of others. But the observers did not often agree. Individual differences, and difficulties with verbal reporting of experience, were not taken into account. To remedy this lack of common ground, the introspectionists found it necessary to limit their field of inquiry. An observer in the act of introspection was "forbidden" to report seeing a book, for example. He or she was only allowed to report, say, a brown object, of a certain size and shape.

This and other limitations of the early mentalist approach soon led to a sterility in psychology. Controversies of only academic import (in the worst sense of the term) arose, due to these limitations on inquiry. One controversy, for instance, dealt with whether or not thoughts could occur without images. Psychologists drifted further and further away from their original concerns, until soon their questions were of interest only to them, and it was evident that the mentalist paradigm was more of a restriction than an aid.

John Watson opened the gates once again with his suggestion that psychology could study action, which was, after all, publically verifiable and testable by objective, impartial methods. This paradigm change allowed psychologists to study questions relevant to a wide range of mental and personal phenomena. For instance, Watson could include such phenomena as personality in his textbook, while Titchener could not.[4] This movement, called *behaviorism,* soon swept academic psychology. It was "objective" and "scientific" and encouraged the study of major problems that had been left out of the introspective paradigm.

Behaviorism stimulated an unusual amount of productive research, especially in the areas of learning and the motivation of behavior. But a problem arose that was similar to that of the mentalist approach: the scope of inquiry soon became unduly narrowed to processes that were amenable to ready solution by behavioristic methods. Psychologists began to ignore, and even to deny, the existence of phenomena that did not fit into the dominant scheme. Consciousness itself was ignored in research for many years; some even denied that it existed.* There was an almost fatal confusion of "behaviorism as a useful tool" with "behaviorism as the total extent of knowledge." "Objective," factual knowledge was emphasized, to the exclusion of any question not subject to a verbal, logical answer. The *reductio ad absurdum* of this position was that of *logical positivism,* which maintained that any question not amenable to a perfectly logical answer should *not even be asked.*

At about the same time, many disaffected psychologists found faith in a system called *psychoanalysis,* developed by Sigmund Freud in Vienna. Freud's work became a rallying point for many who were interested in "understanding" man, and as did behaviorism, it stimulated inquiry into new areas, such as the early determinants of behavior and the interpretation of dreams. But since this movement was dominated by a single authoritarian personality and its followers exhibited an almost religious zeal, the disadvantages of psychoanalysis were quickly in evidence: consciousness became identified with what could be verbalized, religious experience was reduced to neurosis, and the motivation for almost all behavior was analyzed to another *reductio ad absurdum*—the sexual etiology of action.

Much later, in the late 1950s and early 1960s, there was an attempt to correct the distortions of both behaviorism and psychoanalysis. This approach, known as *humanistic psychology,* focused on "growth," interpersonal processes, and new therapies. The early promise of this approach, as emphasized by Abraham Maslow and Carl Rogers, was never realized in the mainstream of psychology. Humanistic psychology became, unfortunately, a divisive force, for its practitioners often tended to degrade the usefulness of science and hence performed little research to support their ideas. A new dichotomy appeared—one that was less useful than most. In effect, psychologists were asked whether they were "humanistic" or "scientific." Psychologists failed to recognize that their discipline is *by definition* a

---

* It was sometimes jokingly said of John Watson that he thought no one conscious save himself.

scientific study of human concerns, and needs embrace both positions. The influence, then, of the humanists has not been as great as it might, had they contributed more to science.

The history of psychology parallels the workings of ordinary consciousness. We stabilize around a set of concepts (about cards, friends, the speed one can run) and hold them dear until we are overwhelmed by new evidence. Then our conceptions change once more to include new possibilities (a red ace of spades, for instance). Similarly, scientific knowledge progresses by a complementary functioning of paradigm build-up and paradigm change. A successful paradigm serves to create stable, conservative knowledge within the scientific community, until the restrictions of the paradigm become too great and it proves to limit research unduly.

Science as a mode of knowledge involves a *limitation* on inquiry. The essence of a good experiment is successful exclusion. One factor may be manipulated while a very few other processes are measured. If, for example, we wished to study the response of brain cells to visual stimuli, we would be considered slightly loony if we also monitored the blood flow to the feet, the temperature of the room, the phase of the moon, the current growth rate of mushrooms in Malaya, or any one of the millions of other available possibilities. But until recently in academic psychology, the limitations of the successful behavioristic paradigm outweighed the advances. For example, psychologists once tended to ignore some evidence (from sources as diverse as yoga and animal experiments) that man is capable of a high degree of self-mastery of his internal physiology. Further, we have not incorporated evidence that the linear, verbal-intellectual mode of knowing is not the only mode available to man.

The belief that all human knowledge is exclusively rational is incomplete. Even scientific inquiry, the most rational and logical of our pursuits, could not proceed without the presence of another type of knowledge. As an example: Two scientific researchers may meet and discuss their ideas. Perhaps an experiment will emerge, to be written up in a journal and still later in a textbook. Those writings are generally as orderly and well-reasoned as the scientist can make them. The *entire process,* however, is not exclusively linear and rational. Scientific investigators often act on personal knowledge, biases, hunches, and intuition. It is the genius of the scientific method that it translates the original, perhaps arational, idea into the rational mode and makes it explicit, so that other investigators can follow it.

The rational, verbal mode is primarily a method of analysis, testing, and communication. Experimental reports are made as explicit and logical as possible, so that any qualified reader can repeat the procedure. But this method of communication should not be misunderstood as implying that any given experiment was *conceived* in a linear and rational manner. We leave the scruffy aspects of our thought—the hunches, the insights—out of public scientific writing. And yet without these wonderings, these "nighttime" questions, many of us probably would not work in science at all. A researcher may spend time thinking, "What is the most important experiment to do?" or "How does this damn thing work?" and after much more of such scratching about, may try to perform an experiment that will aid his or her understanding. But the reliance on verbal rationality has caused many to feel that this method is the *only* way in which knowledge is gained, a conception that writers of textbooks often reinforce.

The scope of psychology as it has been defined in texts, in the teaching of psychology, and in the bulk of research reports has often been unduly limited to one *special* case of human abilities, one *special* method of study, one *special* manner in which consciousness can operate. Just as John Watson found it necessary to alter the paradigm of the introspectionists in order to open up inquiry, so we are faced with a similar situation today—a need to return to a psychology whose scope was well stated by William James: "Our normal waking consciousness, rational consciousness as we call it, is but one special type of consciousness, whilst all about it, parted from it by the filmiest of screens, there lie potential forms of consciousness entirely different."[5]

In performing scientific research, we are often unaware of the full effect of our tools, be they physical instruments or doctrines such as behaviorism. We often imagine that tools, like sensory organs, serve exclusively to extend awareness, but in fact we are wrong. Both serve to limit as well as extend. Abraham Maslow, commenting on the effect that strict behaviorism has had on psychology, wrote, "If the only tool you have is a hammer, you tend to treat everything as if it were a nail."[6] A corrective needs to be applied—one that can open up the scope of psychological inquiry to the relevant questions once again. Even if all the basic questions cannot be fully answered at the moment by available methods, the overall perspective of the field should not be lost. Part of the needed change involves the explicit recognition that, all too often, the *method* of psychology has itself become the goal. This confusion has led, in the past 70 years, to a "radical underestimation" of the possibilities, to use Jacob Needleman's phrase.[7]

Contemporary psychology has just recently progressed beyond the limited view exemplified by our rugseller. A new and extended conception of human knowledge and abilities is beginning to emerge, one that includes many capacities beyond the "normal" limits.

There are many recent developments that have begun to extend the scope of psychology. Psychologists are people of their culture, and our particular culture is in the midst of profound change. There exists a "countercultural" community opposed to science, exhibiting a tremendous distaste for rational thought and its products—logic, machines, computers, technology. And although science ought not to abandon summarily the tools that have been so brilliantly developed in the past century, this radical distaste does result from a certain excess within the scientific community and within modern psychology as well. Mainstream psychology has not been sufficiently concerned with consciousness, particularly the arational aspects. Some aspect of the complementary mode of knowledge, which is nonlinear, and personal in nature, could be incorporated into a more complete psychology, both on a personal and a scientific level.[8]

A second input comes from the widespread interest in consciousness-altering drugs, such as the psychedelics. These drugs have experientially demonstrated to many, as they did to William James, that ordinary consciousness is not the only way in which consciousness can operate.

Perhaps much more important, many "esoteric" disciplines have become popular in the United States in recent years. They range from the merely bizarre and degenerate to the accumulated work of thousands of years of personal investigation into the problems also studied by psychology. These more-developed disciplines include contemporary Sufism and a new understanding of classic mystic systems such as yoga and Buddhism. These disciplines have not yet been fully integrated into the West, although involvement with them has already shown many people that consciousness can be extended into areas beyond those defined as the current limits of contemporary psychology.

In concert with a shift in cultural interest, new areas of investigation open up to "legitimate" science as more and more sophisticated research tools are developed. A purely descriptive, behavioristic approach is no longer the sole option available to experimental psychologists. For instance, researchers in electrophysiology are able to detect subtle changes in brain and eye activity during sleep that signal the advent of dreaming. With this technological development, dreams can be researched objectively. Then, scientific psychology is able to admit the study of dreams, once that most private and "mentalistic" of phenomena, into the mainstream of science.

The problem goes deeper, however. Recently many writers, philosophers, and educators have observed that the contents of science have become extremely over-refined—more and more difficult for the public to understand, more and more remote from general concerns, more and more specialized and abstract. In psychology, the attempt at methodological refinement in the twentieth century has caused us to discard much of essential importance. Consider the process of refining wheat: refined wheat is much more easily packaged and stored than whole wheat and does not spoil as quickly. But refined wheat has lost much of the nutritional value of whole wheat—its essence. In psychology, we too have discarded much of the essence—consciousness—in the process of refining the methods.

I think it is necessary to continue to restore our psychological endeavors to completeness. However, the awareness of this necessity has been lacking in some recent efforts. The position of many involved in conventional scientific investigation is depicted in a famous story. Several blind men attempt to investigate an elephant. One who has the trunk says, "It is long and soft and emits air." Another, holding the legs, says, "It is massive, cylindrical, and hard." Another, touching the skin, "It is rough and scaly."

For a psychology of consciousness, the major import of this old story should be to make us recognize clearly that more than one way of knowing is possible. Each person standing at one part of the elephant can make his own limited, analytic assessment of the situation, but we cannot understand the nature of an elephant by combining "scalyness," "length," "softness," etc., in any conceivable proportion. Without the development of an overall perspective, we remain lost in individual investigations. Such a perspective is a province of another mode of knowledge and cannot be achieved in the same way that individual parts are explored. It does not arise out of a sum of independent observations.

The intent of this book is to document the existence in human beings of two major modes of consciousness: one is analytic, the other holistic. The first is analogous to the process of viewing in sequence the individual parts of the elephant, the second to viewing at once the whole animal. They are complementary; both have their functions. Another statement of the dichotomy of human knowledge is the "rational" and "intuitive" sides of man. In our intellectual history, many have separated these two modes of knowing into separate areas of specialization, into science and religion, for example. Those who use one approach have rarely commerced with the other. With the breakup of organized religion as a major cultural force, science has become the dominant influence in our culture. It is natural, then, that the textbook ideal of scientific knowledge has become a dominant mode of knowledge within our culture. This mode can be characterized as analytic, verbal, linear, and rational.

We deemphasize and even devalue the arational, nonverbal modes of consciousness. Much formal education consists predominantly of "readin', 'ritin', and 'rithmetic," and we are taught precious little about our emotions, our bodies, our intuitive capabilities. A strict emphasis on verbal, intellectual knowledge has screened out much of what is or could be appropriate for study in contemporary psychology—"esoteric" systems of meditation are much misunderstood; the experience of "nonordinary realities" is not studied because they do not fit into the dominant paradigm, and neither, of course, do phenomena named *paranormal*. Yet there are reports in popular and scientific circles of "paranormal" capacities—of yogis learning to control their hearts and metabolism, for instance, or of telepathy during dreams. These have not yet been fully explored, just as our friend at the beginning of the chapter was not able to conceive and use a number higher than 100.

Suppose there were two completely independent groups of investigators; one group (scientists) works exclusively during the day, the other (the mysterious "esoteric" psychologists) works exclusively at night, neither communicating well with the other. If those who work at night see faint starlight in the sky and concentrate on the movements of the stars, they may produce documents that predict the positions of the stars at any given time, which might be useful for navigation; but these writings would be totally incomprehensible to someone who experiences only daylight. The brilliance of the sun obscures the subtle light of the stars from view.

A modern scientific psychologist might read in an obscure, eso-teric book about the existence of these "points of subtle light" and attempt to locate them by his usual means of investigation—during the daytime. No matter how open and honest the investigator and how dutiful his observations, he will be unable to find the "subtle light" in the brilliance of the day. The failure of many scientific investigators to locate the "subtle light" will only strengthen their conviction that the "stars" do not exist. The methods of science, then, have largely focused on one mode of knowing—identified in this metaphor with daytime. Contemporary science has developed meth-odologies and techniques and discovered laws of nature that have proven essential to the development of our civilization, but which may be only a special case, as, say, Newtonian mechanics is to Einsteinian.

As the esoteric disciplines of other cultures become accessible to the West, they emerge as *psychologies* which have specialized in that inward, receptive space of the "night." Their sometimes misunder-stood techniques are exercises often designed to temporarily extend the perceptual functions of the human nervous system, in an analo-gous manner to turning off the brilliant light of the day until the faint stars are perceptible.

Until quite recently, communication between the two types of psychology has been very limited. Western science has tended to ignore, and even to deny, the existence of these "faint signals," since they are not visible under normal observation conditions. On the other side, certain "mystics," and others of the esoteric traditions, have compounded the problem by labeling ordinary consciousness an "illusion"—which it might be to a person who never enters the daylight. Then, of course, each side has its inevitable internal argu-ments and preoccupation with local color and methodology, be they commitment to a particular kind of meditation exercise with all its rituals or a maze-learning experiment with all its ritual and stylized behavior.

Communication has begun to open up in our culture, so that it now appears that neither view is complete: the day is incomplete without the night. Each is a special situation with its own laws.

This book is an attempt to redress the inbalance, to begin to integrate rational and intuitive approaches to knowledge and to consider the essential complementarity of these two modes of consciousness as they are manifest in science in general, in psychology in particular, and within each person psychologically and physiologically. A growing body of evidence demonstrates that each person has two major modes of consciousness available, one linear and rational, one arational and intuitive—one specialized for analysis, one for synthesis.

Our highest creative achievements are the products of the complementary functioning of the two modes. Our intuitive knowledge is never explicit, never precise, in the scientific sense. It is only when intellect can begin to process intuitive leaps, to explain and "translate" intuition into operational and functional knowledge that scientific understanding becomes complete. It is the function of the scientific use of our verbal intellect to fit intuition into the linear mode so that ideas may be explicitly tested and communicated in the proper manner. The linear, rational mode is not the only way in which we gain knowledge, but it is a way in which we can clarify and communicate that which we understand.

Current psychology is undergoing the first stirrings of a synthesis of the two modes. These may form the beginning of a more complete science of human consciousness, with an extended conception of our own capabilities. This "new" conception of human possibility is the ancient one of the traditional, esoteric psychologies aligned with the methods and technology of contemporary science.

It is time, once again, to extend the discipline of psychology and to return to its primary business—an examination of conscious experience, using the new tools that have been so painstakingly developed during this past century. It would be premature to try to delimit or obsessively and quantitatively define this new area. Rather, it is a time to redefine psychology itself and, once more, to extend the boundaries of our own possibilities.

FOR FURTHER READING

THOMAS S. KUHN. *The Structure of Scientific Revolutions.* Chicago: University of Chicago Press, 1962.

W. I. B. BEVERIDGE. *The Art of Scientific Investigation.* New York: Random House, 1950.

ABRAHAM MASLOW. *The Psychology of Science.* Chicago: Henry Regnery, 1966.

WILLIAM JAMES. "The Scope of Psychology." In *The Principles of Psychology,* Vol. 1, pp. 1–8. New York: Dover Publications, 1950. Original copyright, 1890. Reprinted in Robert Ornstein, ed. *The Nature of Human Consciousness.* San Francisco: W.H. Freeman; New York: Viking Press, 1973.

THOMAS R. BLACKBURN. "Sensuous-Intellectual Complementarity in Science." *Science* 172 (June 4, 1971): 1003–07. Reprinted in Ornstein, ed. *The Nature of Human Consciousness.*

DONALD HEBB. "What Psychology Is About." *American Psychologist* 29, no. 2 (February 1974): 71–79.

2 Two Sides of the Brain

Never Know When It Might Come in Useful

Nasrudin sometimes took people for trips in his boat. One day a fussy pedagogue hired him to ferry him across a very wide river. As soon as they were afloat, the scholar asked whether it was going to be rough.

"Don't ask me nothing about it," said Nasrudin.
"Have you never studied grammar?"
"No," said the Mulla.
"In that case, half your life has been wasted."
The Mulla said nothing.
Soon a terrible storm blew up. The Mulla's crazy cockleshell was filling with water. He leaned over toward his companion. "Have you ever learned to swim?"
"No," said the pedant.
"In that case, schoolmaster, *all* your life is lost, for we are sinking."[1]

The two characters in this story represent two major modes of consciousness: the verbal, rational mode is portrayed by the pedagogue, involved in and insisting on neat and tidy perfection; the other mode is represented by the boatman and the skill of swimming, which involves movement of the body in space—a mode often devalued by the neat, rational mind of the pedagogue.

In the ordinary meaning of the story, these two characters represent different types of people. The verbal-logical grammarian can also be the scientist, the logician, the mathematician, who are committed to reason and "correct" proof. The boatman, ungraceful and untutored in formal terms, represents the artist, the craftsman, the dancer, the dreamer, whose output is often unsatisfactory to the purely rational mind.

Yet other interpretations of this story are possible. These two characters can also represent major modes of consciousness that exist across cultures and that coexist within each person.

Try the following exercise: Close your eyes and attempt to sense each side of your body separately. Try to get in touch with the feelings of the left and the right side, their strengths, their weaknesses. When you are finished, open your eyes for a moment and reflect on one of these questions. Close your eyes and sense inside for the answer, then repeat the process with the next question.

1. Which side of you is more feminine?
2. Which is more masculine?
3. Which do you consider the "dark" side of yourself?
4. Which side is the "lighter"?
5. Which is more active?
6. Which is more passive?
7. Which side is more logical?
8. Which more "intuitive"?
9. Which side of you is more mysterious?
10. Which side is more artistic?

If you are right-handed, most likely you felt the right side of your body as more masculine, lighter, more active, and more logical, the left side as feminine, dark, passive, intuitive, mysterious, and artistic. The psychologist William Domhoff asked a large number of people to rate the concepts *left* and *right* on several dimensions. His sample regarded *left* as "bad," "dark," "profane," and "female," while *right* was considered the opposite.[2]

Jerome Bruner, who has contributed much to our understanding of individual consciousness, elegantly summarizes the interplay of the two modes. He relates them both to the current problem in psychology and science and to the two sides of the body.

Since childhood, I have been enchanted by the fact and the symbolism of the right hand and the left—the one the doer, the other the dreamer. The right is order and lawfulness, *le droit*. Its beauties are those of geometry and taut implication. Reaching for knowledge with the right hand is science. Yet to say only that much of science is to overlook one of its excitements, for the great hypotheses of science are gifts carried in the left.

Of the left hand we say that it is awkward, and while it has been proposed that art students can seduce their proper hand to more expressiveness by drawing first with the left, we nonetheless suspect this function. The French speak of the illegitimate descendant as being *à main gauche*, and, though the heart is virtually at the center of the thoracic cavity, we listen for it on the left. Sentiment, intuition, bastardy. And should we say that reaching for knowledge with the left hand is art? Again it is not enough, for as surely as the recital of a daydream differs from the well-wrought tale, there is a barrier between undisciplined fantasy and art. To climb the barrier requires a right hand adept at technique and artifice. . . .

One thing has become increasingly clear in pursuing the nature of knowing. It is that the conventional apparatus of the psychologist—both his instruments of investigation and the conceptual tools he uses in the interpretation of his data—leaves one approach unexplored. It is an approach whose medium of exchange seems to be the metaphor paid out by the left hand. It is a way that grows happy hunches and "lucky" guesses, that is stirred into connective activity by the poet and the necromancer looking sidewise rather than directly. Their hunches and intuitions generate a grammar of their own—searching out connections, suggesting similarities, weaving ideas loosely in a trial web. . . .

The psychologist, for all his apartness, is governed by the same constraints that shape the behavior of those whom he studies. He too searches widely and metaphorically for his hunches. He reads novels, looks at and even paints pictures, is struck by the power of myth, observes his fellow men intuitively and with wonder. In doing so, he acts only part-time like a proper psychologist, racking up cases against the criteria derived from a hypothesis. Like his fellows, he observes the human scene with such sensibility as he can muster in the hope that his insight will be deepened. If he is lucky or if he has subtle psychological intuition, he will from time to time come up with hunches, combinatorial products of his metaphoric activity. If he is not fearful of these products of his own subjectivity, he will go so far as to tame the metaphors that have produced the hunches, tame them in the sense of shifting them from the left hand to the right hand by rendering them into notions that can be tested. It is my impression from observing myself and my colleagues that the forging of metaphoric hunch into testable hypothesis goes on all the time. And I am inclined to think that this process is the more evident in psychology, where the theoretical apparatus is not so well developed that it lends itself readily to generating interesting hypotheses.

Yet because our profession is young and because we feel insecure, we do not like to admit our humanity. We quite properly seek a distinctiveness that sets us apart from all those others who ponder about man and the human condition—all of which is worthy, for thereby we forge an intellectual discipline. But we are not satisfied to forge distinctive methods of our own. We must reject whoever has been successful in the task of understanding man—if he is not one of us. We place a restrictive covenant on our domain. Our articles, submitted properly to the appropriate psychological journal, have about them an aseptic quality designed to proclaim the intellectual purity of our psychological enterprise. Perhaps this is well, though it is not enough.

It is well, perhaps because it is economical to report the products of research and not the endless process that constitutes the research itself. But it is not enough in the deeper sense that we may be concealing some of the most fruitful sources of our ideas from one another.[3]

The difference between the left and right sides of the body may provide a key to the understanding of the psychological and physiological mechanisms of the two major modes of consciousness. The study of the structure of the brain may provide the linkage. The cerebral cortex of the brain is divided into two hemispheres, joined by a large bundle of interconnecting fibers called the *corpus callosum*. The left side of the body is controlled mainly by the right side of the cortex, and the right side of the body by the left side of the cortex. When we speak of *left* in ordinary speech, we are referring to that side of the body and to the *right* hemisphere of the brain.

Both the structure and the function of these two "half-brains" underlie in some part the two modes of consciousness that coexist within each one of us. Although each hemisphere shares the potential for many functions and both sides participate in most activities, in the normal person the two hemispheres tend to specialize. The left hemisphere (connected to the right side of the body) is predominantly involved with analytic, logical thinking, especially in verbal and mathematical functions. Its mode of operation is primarily linear. This hemisphere seems to process information sequentially. Since logic depends on sequence and order, this mode of operation must of

Corpus callosum

Figure 2-1   The brain is divided in two hemispheres, connected by the corpus callosum.

necessity underlie logical thought. Language and mathematics, both left-hemisphere activities, also depend predominantly on sequence. If, for instance, any set of letters comprising a word were ordered in an alternate sequence, the letters would have no meaning.

If the left hemisphere is specialized for analysis, the right hemisphere (again, recall, controlling the left side of the body) seems specialized for synthesis. Its language ability is quite limited. This hemisphere is primarily responsible for orientation in space, artistic endeavor, crafts, body image, recognition of faces. It processes information more diffusely than does the left hemisphere, and its responsibilities demand a ready integration of many inputs at once. If the left hemisphere can be termed predominantly analytic and sequential in its operation, then the right hemisphere is more holistic and relational, and more simultaneous in its mode of operation.*

* This right-left specialization is based on right-handers. Left-handers, who are about 5 percent of the population, are less consistent; some have reversed specialization of the hemispheres, but some have mixed specialization, for example, language in both sides. Some are specialized in the same way as right-handers. And even in right-handers these differences are not binary, but are specializations of each "half-brain." At least in very young people, each side does possess the potential for both modes; for example, brain damage to the left hemisphere in young children often results in the development of language in the right side.

NEUROLOGICAL STUDIES
OF THE TWO HEMISPHERES

For over a century, neurological evidence of the differential specialization of man's two cerebral hemispheres has been slowly accu-
mulating. A very valuable part of this evidence has come from the
study of people whose brains have been damaged by accident or
illness and from the surgery performed on them. It is, then, in the
work of clinical neurology that the primary indications of our hemispheric specialization are to be found.[4]

In 1864, the great neurologist Hughlings Jackson considered the
left hemisphere to be the seat of the "faculty of expression" and
noted of a patient with a tumor in the right hemisphere, "She did not
know objects, persons, and places." Since Hughlings Jackson, many
other neurologists, neurosurgeons, and psychiatrists have confirmed
that two modes of consciousness seem to be lateralized in the two
cerebral hemispheres of human beings. In hundreds of clinical cases,
it has been found that damage to the left hemisphere very often
interferes with, and can in some cases completely destroy, language
ability. Often patients cannot speak after such left-hemisphere lesions, a condition known as *aphasia*. An injury to the right hemisphere may not interfere with language performance at all, but may
cause severe disturbance in spatial awareness, in musical ability, in
recognition of other people, or in awareness of one's own body. Some
patients with right-hemisphere damage cannot dress themselves
adequately, although their speech and reason remain unimpaired.

There is a tendency in clinical and neurological reports to term
the left and right hemispheres the *major* and the *minor,* respectively.
This seems more a social than a neurological distinction. The dominant or major mode of our culture is verbal and intellectual, and this
cultural emphasis can bias observations. If an injury to the right
hemisphere does not affect speech or reason, the damage has often
been considered minor. Injury to the left hemisphere affects verbal
functions; thus it has often been termed the "major" hemisphere.
However, the conception of the function of the two hemispheres is
changing, largely because of the superb work of Joseph Bogen and
the increasing evidence of the brain's lateral specialization.

Each hemisphere is the major one, depending on the mode of
consciousness under consideration. If one is a wordsmith, a scientist,

or a mathematician, damage to the left hemisphere may prove disastrous. If one is a musician, a craftsman, or an artist, damage to the left hemisphere often does not interfere with one's capacity to create music, crafts, or arts, yet damage to the right hemisphere may well obliterate a career. The position of the fussy pedagogue who devalues the nonverbal boatman becomes less and less tenable.

In more precise neuropsychological studies, Brenda Milner and her associates at McGill University in Montreal have attempted to correlate disorders in specific kinds of tasks with lesions in specific areas of the brain. For example, a lobectomy of the right temporal lobe severely impairs the performance of visual and tactile mazes, whereas left temporal-lobe lesions of equal extent produce little deficit. These researchers also report that lesions in specific areas of the left hemisphere are associated with specific kinds of language disorders: an impairment of verbal memory is associated with lesions in the anterior (front) left temporal lobe; speech impairment seems to result from lesions in the posterior (rear) left temporal lobe.[5] On less empirical grounds, the Russian physiologist A. R. Luria has reported that mathematical function is also disturbed by lesions of the left side.[6] Milner and her associates also report that the recognition of musical pitch seems to be in the province of the right hemisphere.

The clinical neurological research is intriguing, correlating the different functions of the hemispheres that are impaired by brain damage. More intriguing still is the research of Roger Sperry of the California Institute of Technology and his associates, notably Joseph Bogen and Michael Gazzaniga. The two cerebral hemispheres communicate through the corpus callosum, which joins the two sides anatomically. Professor Sperry and his colleagues had for some years experimentally severed the corpus callosum in laboratory animals, which allowed the hemispheres to be trained independently. This research led to the adoption of a radical treatment for severe epilepsy in several patients of Drs. Philip Vogel and Joseph Bogen of the California College of Medicine.[7]

This treatment involved an operation on humans similar to Sperry's experimental surgery on animals—a severing of the interconnections between the two cerebral hemispheres, effectively isolating one side from the other. The hope of the researchers was that when a patient had a seizure in one hemisphere, transmission of the seizures between hemispheres would be lessened. In many cases, the severely disturbed patients were improved enough to leave the hospital.

In day-to-day living, these "split-brain" people exhibit almost no abnormality, which is somewhat surprising in view of the radical surgery. However, Sperry and his associates developed several ingenious and subtle tests that showed that the operation had clearly separated the specialized functions of the two cerebral hemispheres.

If, for instance, the patient held a pencil (hidden from sight) in his right hand, he could verbally describe it, as would be normal. But if the pencil was in his left hand, he could not describe it at all. Recall that the left hand informs the right hemisphere, which possesses only a limited capability for speech. With the corpus callosum severed, the verbal (left) hemisphere is no longer connected to the right hemisphere, which communicates largely with the left hand; so the verbal apparatus literally does not know what is in the left hand. If, however, the patient was offered a set of objects—a key, a book, a pencil, and so on—and was asked to select the previously given object with his left hand, he could choose correctly, although he still could not state verbally just what he was doing. This situation closely resembles what might happen if I were privately asked to perform an action and you were expected to discuss it.

Normally, when we wish to inquire about the consciousness of another person, we allow the verbal apparatus to determine it—we reduce "consciousness" to that which a person can report. The preceding example is a primary indication that doing so can be a fundamental error in the study of consciousness. We are aware of more than we can discuss.

Another experiment tested the lateral specialization of the two hemispheres, using split visual input. The right half of each eye sends its messages to the right hemisphere, the left half to the left hemisphere. In this experiment, the word *heart* was flashed before the patient, with the *he-* to the left of the eyes' fixation point, and *-art* to the right. Normally if any person were asked to report this experience, he or she would report having seen *heart*. But the split-brain patients responded differently, depending on which hemisphere was responding. When the patient was asked to name the word just presented, he or she replied, "art," since this was the portion projected to the left hemisphere, which was answering the question. When, however, the patient was shown two cards—one with the word *he*, the other with the word *art*—and asked to point with the left hand to the word he or she had seen, the left hand pointed to *he*. The simultaneous experience of each hemisphere seemed unique and independent of each other in these patients. The verbal hemisphere gave one answer, the nonverbal hemisphere another.

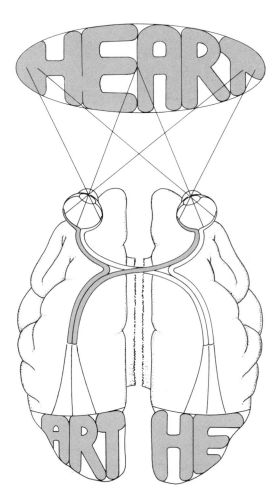

Figure 2-2 A simplified diagram of visual input to the two hemispheres of the brain. Images in the left visual field are projected to the right hemisphere; images in the right visual field, to the left hemisphere. This schematic drawing illustrates one experiment performed on split-brain patients. Note that the corpus callosum is cut. The *HE* and *ART* projections are, of course, fanciful, not anatomically correct.

In several tests it was found that the left hemisphere is superior for verbal tasks, and the right for spatial. A common test of spatial mentation requires the construction of a two-dimensional geometric figure using a set of cubes, each face painted with a different color or combination of colors. The patient's left hand could perform this task quite well; the right hand could not. Professor Sperry shows an interesting short film of the right hand attempting to solve the problem and failing, whereupon the patient's left hand cannot restrain itself and "corrects" the right—in the same way that one individual cannot refrain from telling another the answer to a problem after watching that person make several mistakes.

Although many have reported these differences in abilities, we should not conclude that the specialization of the hemispheres is for one type of *information* or another; rather it is the cognitive mode that differs.

Most right-handed people write and draw with the right hand, but many can also write and draw to some extent with their left. After surgery, Dr. Bogen tested the ability of the split-brain patients to write and draw with either hand. The right hand retained the ability to write, but it could no longer draw very well. It seemed to have lost the ability to work in a relational, spatial manner.[8]

In the illustrations in Figure 2–3, the left hand (right hemisphere) can no longer write, while the right hand can. In copying the geo-

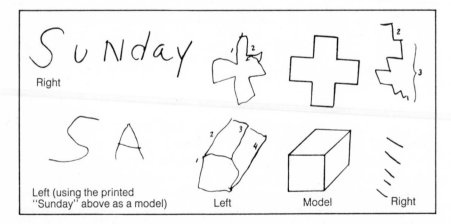

Figure 2–3 The response of a split-brain patient to the request to write *Sunday* and to copy the two figures.

| Design | Left hand | Right hand |

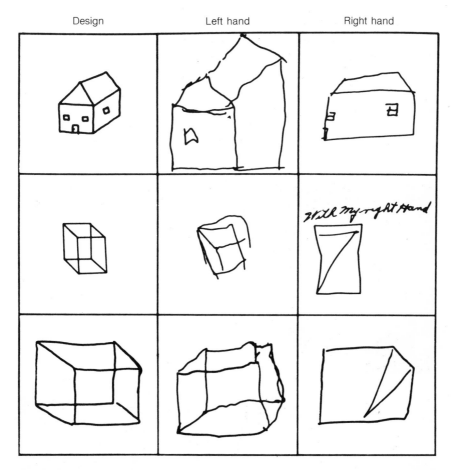

Figure 2-4 The left hand of this split-brain patient (who is right-handed) is still able to reproduce the three-dimensional designs. The right hand cannot copy the designs but retains the ability to write.

metrical figures, the left hand certainly conveys the relationship of the parts, even though the line quality may be poor. Note the right hand's performance: the cross contains the correct elements, yet the ability to link the disconnected elements is lacking. And no one, save the most analytic, could consider a cube a set of corners!

More recent tests of hemisphere functioning confirm that the right hemisphere is superior at part-whole relations, which might indicate that it is responsible for the "cognitive map" of the world that each of us has. Robert Nebes tested this in Sperry's lab, requiring the split-brain patients to match arc segments of circles with the completed circles. The right hemisphere proved superior in generalizing from the segment to the whole.[9]

In another experiment in Sperry's lab, the split-brain patients were shown faces that were divided in such a way that the left hemisphere would "see" only half a face, the right another. When the patients were asked to point to the face they had seen (with either hand), they pointed to the one shown to the right hemisphere. When

Figure 2-5 A composite figure presented to the split-brain subjects for identification with comparison faces.

asked to verbally choose the face, they chose the face shown to the left hemisphere.[10]

The split-brain surgery most dramatically delineates the two major modes of consciousness that seem normally to coexist within each person. Recent research with experimental split-brain monkeys indicates that the two hemispheres can function simultaneously as well as independently. At the same moment, a split-brain monkey can be trained on one learning problem with one eye-brain pair (the optic chiasm in monkeys is severed as part of the experimental procedure), and a second problem with the other eye-brain pair.[11] Sperry writes of the effect of the operation on humans: "Everything we have seen so far indicated that the surgery has left each of these people with two separate minds, that is, with two separate spheres of consciousness."[12]

The recognition that we possess two cerebral hemispheres that are specialized to operate in different modes may allow us to understand much about the fundamental duality of our consciousness. This duality has been reflected in classical as well as modern literature as reason versus passion, or mind versus intuition. Perhaps the most famous of these dichotomies in psychology is that proposed by Sigmund Freud, the split between the "conscious" mind and the "unconscious." The workings of the "conscious" mind are held to be accessible to language and to rational discourse and alteration; the "unconscious" is much less accessible to reason or to the verbal analysis. Some aspects of "unconscious" communication are gestures, facial and body movements, tone of voice.

There are moments in each of our lives when our verbal-intellect suggests one course, and our "heart," or intuition, another. Because of the surgical separation of the hemispheres, the split-brain patients provide a clear example of dual response in certain situations. In one experimental test, Sperry attempted to determine whether the right hemisphere could learn to respond verbally to different colors. Either a red or a green light was flashed to the patient's left visual field—which is received on the right half of the retina and sent to the right hemisphere (see Figure 2-2). Sperry then asked the split-brain patients to guess verbally which color was flashed to them. Since the left hemisphere controls the verbal output and the color information was sent to the right hemisphere, it was expected that the patients would not be able to guess correctly other than by chance, no matter how many guesses were allowed. The side that was guessing, after all, was disconnected from the side that knew the answer.[13]

After a few trials, however, the patients' scores improved whenever the examiner allowed a second guess. The following process occurred: If a red light was flashed and the patient guessed correctly by chance, the trial was terminated. If the patient guessed incorrectly, he might frown, shake his head, and then "correct" his answer verbally. The right hemisphere had seen the light, then heard the left make an incorrect answer. Having no access to verbal output, the right hemisphere used the means at its disposal and caused a frown and a head-shake, which informed the left hemisphere that its answer was incorrect.

In a loose way, the responses of the two hemispheres could be analogous to the conflict between the "conscious" and "unconscious" processes that Freud described. In the split-brain patients, the verbal, rational processing system, disconnected from the source of information, was countermanded by gestures and tone of voice, in the same way that a person may insist that he or she is *not* angry, yet simultaneously indicates exactly the opposite feeling with tone of voice and facial expression.

A similar situation occurred when emotion-laden information was given to the right hemisphere while the verbal hemisphere remained unaware of it. In the course of a series of otherwise dull laboratory tests, a photograph of a nude woman was shown to the right hemisphere of a patient. At first, the woman viewing the pinup on the screen said that she saw nothing, then immediately flushed, alternately squirmed, smiled, and looked uncomfortable and confused. But her "conscious" or verbal half was *still* unaware of what had caused the emotional turmoil. All that was accessible to the verbal apparatus was that *something* unusual was occurring in her body. Her words reflected that the emotional reaction had been "unconscious," unavailable to her language apparatus. To paraphrase her, What a funny machine you have there, Dr. Sperry.[14]

In this instance a clear split was observed between the two independent consciousnesses, which are normally in communication and collaboration. In such an experiment with split-brain patients, we can accurately localize the split of information in the system. A similar process, although much more difficult to localize precisely in an area of the brain, may underlie the classic Freudian symptoms of repression and denial, both situations in which the verbal mechanism has no access to emotional information in other parts of the system. In less pathological instances, when we perform an action "intuitively," our words often make no sense, perhaps because the action has been initiated by a part of the brain little involved in language.

THE TWO HEMISPHERES IN NORMAL PEOPLE

These spectacular split-brain and lesion studies are not the only evidence for the physiological duality in consciousness. In general, great caution should be exercised in drawing inferences to normal functioning from pathological and surgical cases alone. In dealing with these cases we must remember that we are investigating disturbed, not normal, functioning and the connection to normal functioning may be a bit tenuous. In cases of brain damage, it is never fully clear that one hemisphere has not taken over a function from the other to an unusual degree because of the injury. In the case of the surgical patients, they are by definition quite atypical, due to their epilepsy. It is necessary to seek out evidence from normally functioning people, even if that evidence is necessarily more indirect, since we don't go poking inside the brains of our friends. In this, we are fortunate that recent research with normal people has confirmed much of the neurosurgical explorations. The evidence comes from many sources—tests of vision, eye movements, reaction time, ear preference, and electrical signs of brain asymmetry.

If the right hemisphere operates predominantly in a simultaneous manner, it could integrate diverse input quickly. This mode of information-processing would be advantageous for spatial orientation, when the person must quickly integrate visual, muscular, and kinesthetic cues. In a carefully controlled experiment with normal people, the right hemisphere was found to be superior to the left hemisphere in depth perception.

When a tachistoscope is used to introduce information to only the right hemisphere and either a nonverbal or a verbal response is required, the nonverbal response comes more quickly than the verbal one. A verbal response requires the information to be sent across the callosum to the left hemisphere, which takes some time. This indicates that the normal brain does indeed make use of the lateral specialization, selecting the appropriate area for differential information-processing.[15]

The ears, as well, differ: the right ear informs primarily the left hemisphere, the left ear the right hemisphere. If verbal material is presented to both ears simultaneously in what is called *dichotic listening*, the right ear (left hemisphere) is superior. The left ear (right hemisphere) is often so for music.

Another experiment that confirms the differential specialization of the two hemispheres uses eye movements as an indicator. Ask some friends a question such as, How do you spell Mississippi? The chances are that they will shift their gaze off to one side while reflecting. Marcel Kinsbourne of Duke University, and Katherine Kocel, David Galin, and I of the Langley Porter Neuropsychiatric Institute, have found that the direction a person gazes in is affected by the kind of question asked. If the question is verbal-analytical (such as, Divide 144 by 6, and multiply the answer by 7), more eye movements are made to the right than if the question involves spatial mentation (such as, Which way does the Indian face on the nickel?).[16]

Kinsbourne has performed another experiment that deserves special mention. Ask a friend to balance a wooden dowel on the index finger of each hand, one hand at a time. Generally, the preferred hand is more adept at this balancing. Ask the person then to speak while balancing this dowel, and time the length of the balancing. In Kinsbourne's experiment, the balancing time of the right hand decreased, as would be expected, since the addition of a task interferes with performance in most situations. But the balancing time of the left hand *increased* with concurrent verbalization.[17]

The right hand, recall, is controlled predominantly by the left hemisphere. When the left hemisphere is engaged in speech, its control of the right hand suffers. While the left hand is balancing, the left hemisphere may still intrude on its performance. When the left hemisphere is occupied in speech, it no longer seems to interfere with the left hand and the balancing time improves.

Brain Studies of Normal Functioning

But it remains important to develop a method for studying normal people, doing normal activities, since the reaction time, the dichotic listening, and the binocular disparity situations are quite special laboratory situations, and not terribly representative of ordinary activity. Also, it is one thing to demonstrate that one hemisphere *can* perform an action, and another to demonstrate that normal people make use of this specialization. For instance, is the language ability of the right hemisphere used in ordinary situations?

For this reason David Galin and I began a research project in which we recorded the brain's electrical activity from both cerebral hemispheres while people were performing both verbal and spatial tasks. We used an electrode helmet that covered the areas of the brain from which we recorded, as illustrated in Figure 2–6. The voltages that appeared at the scalp were minuscule, millionths of a volt. They were classified according to frequency. The delta (δ) rhythm was 1–3; theta (ϑ), from 4–7; alpha (α), 3–13; and beta (β), above 13. The findings are these: when a person is writing, more alpha rhythm appears in the right hemisphere than in the left, and while arranging blocks, more alpha is present in the left hemisphere than in the right (Figure 2–7). This indicates that we turn off the hemisphere not involved in the situation. Alpha rhythm is taken conventionally as a sign of this idling.

But how do these two modes interact in daily life? My opinion, and that of David Galin, is that in most ordinary activities we alternate between the two modes, selecting the appropriate one and inhibiting the other. It is not at all clear how this process occurs. Do the two systems work continuously in parallel and merely alternate control of the body, or do they truly time-share the control? Clearly, each of us can work in both modes—we all speak, we all can move in space, we all can perform both at once. Yet in skiing, for instance, an attempt to verbally encode each bodily movement would lead to disaster. The two modes of operation *complement* each other but do not readily substitute for one another. To describe a spiral staircase, for example, most would begin with words, then switch to gestures. One cannot ride a bicycle purely from verbal instruction.

This lateral specialization of the brain seems to be unique to humans and is related to the evolution of language. There is no evidence that the two cerebral hemispheres of other primates are so specialized, although it would be reasonable to assume some evolutionary precursor of man's hemispheric asymmetry. Jerre Levy-Agresti and Roger Sperry have suggested that humans have evolved in this manner because the information-processing that must underlie language, mathematics, and "rational" thought is not readily compatible with the mode of information-processing that underlies relational perception, orientation in space, and what our verbal intellect can only term *intuition*.[18]

Figure 2-6 In this experiment the subject is arranging the blocks to match the pattern on the card while the electrical activity of her brain is being recorded. The cap contains the EEG electrodes and is connected to a small computer that analyzes the EEG.

Figure 2-7 EEGs over the left hemisphere (T_3) and over the right (T_4) recorded during two cognitive tasks. Note the increase in alpha (the high-voltage sinusoidal rhythm) in the left hemisphere during the block design and the reverse during the writing of the letter.

Within each person the two polarities exist simultaneously as two semi-independent information-processing units with different specialties. There is some preliminary evidence that the modes of physiological organization may be different in the two hemispheres. Josephine Semmes of the National Institute of Mental Health has found that damage to the left hemisphere results in quite localized disturbance of function, whereas damage to the right interferes less focally with performance. Semmes and her co-workers studied 124 war veterans who had brain injuries. They tested the effects of brain injury on simple motor reactions, somatosensory thresholds, and object discrimination—testing each hand-hemisphere pair separately. Studying the right hand, they found that injuries in quite specific areas of the left hemisphere interfered with performance of specific tasks, but no such focus of localization could be found with right-hemisphere lesions.[19] This evidence seems to indicate that the left hemisphere is more anatomically specialized for the discrete, focal information-processing underlying logic, and that the right hemisphere is more diffusely organized, which is advantageous for orientation in space and for other situations which require simultaneous processing of many inputs.

TWO MODES OF CONSCIOUSNESS

The polarity and the integration of these two modes of consciousness, the complementary workings of the intellect and intuition, underlie our highest achievements. Some persons, however, habitually prefer one mode over the other, for example, our pedagogue at the beginning of this chapter. The exclusively verbal, logical scientist manifests a similar dominance, often forgetting, or even denying, that he or she possesses another side and finding it difficult to work in the areas of the right hemisphere—in art, crafts, dance, sports. But this other mode, although less logical and clear, is important for creativity, and perhaps for survival: "combinatory play" was Einstein's phrase. "Have you ever learned to swim?" asks the boatman.

This duality in human consciousness has long been recognized in other cultures. For instance, the Hopi Indians of the American Southwest distinguish the function of the two hands, one for writing, one for making music. The French words for law, that most linear and rational of human pursuits, is *droit*, which literally means "right." For the Mojave Indians, the left hand is the passive, maternal side of the person, the right, the active father. William Domhoff concludes his interesting survey of the myth and symbolism of *left* and *right* by noting that the left is often the area of the taboo, the sacred, the unconscious, the feminine, the intuitive, and the dreamer. And we find that the symbolism of the two sides of the body is quite often in agreement with these ideas. In myth, the feminine side is most often on the left, the masculine on the right.[20]

The only scientific evidence we have of this right-left duality deals with dreaming, and the evidence is not too strong. In a report on three cases, Humphrey and Zangwill have found that damage to the right parietal lobe of the brain seems to interfere with dreaming. Bogen notes that his split-brain patients tend to report the absence of dreams after surgery, perhaps because of the disconnection of the verbal output from the right hemisphere. In a study of normal subjects, Austin reports that people who tend to specialize in analytic thinking (convergers) are less likely to recall dreams than those with the opposite bias (divergers), whom he characterizes as more imaginative and more able to deal with the nonrational.[21]

In Vedanta, the duality in consciousness is said to be between intellect (Buddhi) and mind (manas). Such a distinction may be hard for people with Western education to state clearly, for when we say, "This person has a fine mind," we are usually referring only to the verbal and intellectual portion of the mind.

The complementarity of these two modes of consciousness is a central consideration of this book, as they are manifest within each person, between different persons, within different disciplines such as scientific inquiry (psychology in particular), and in the organization of cultures. In his review on the "other" side of the brain, Joseph Bogen clarified the concept by presenting a set of dichotomies between the two modes of consciousness. Following him, I present one such table, but only for purposes of suggestion and clarification in an intuitive sort of way, not as a final categorical statement of the conception and not always with referral to the brain. Many of the poles are, of course, tendencies and specialization, not at all binary classifications. Examination of the table may also make the day-night metaphor I am using a bit clearer.

THE TWO MODES OF CONSCIOUSNESS: A TENTATIVE DICHOTOMY

Who Proposed It?

Many sources	Day	Night
Blackburn	Intellectual	Sensuous
Oppenheimer	Time, History	Eternity, Timelessness
Polanyi	Explicit	Tacit
Levy, Sperry	Analytic	Gestalt
Bogen	Propositional	Appositional
Lee	Lineal	Nonlineal
Luria	Sequential	Simultaneous
Semmes	Focal	Diffuse
I Ching	The Creative: heaven, masculine, yang	The Receptive: earth, feminine, yin
Many sources	Verbal	Spatial
Many sources	Intellectual	Intuitive
Vedanta	Buddhi	Manas
Jung	Causal	Synchronicity
Bacon	Argument	Experience

Many different occupations and disciplines involve a concentration in one of the major modes of consciousness. Science and law are heavily involved in linearity, duration, and verbal logic. Crafts, the "mystical" disciplines, music, are more present-centered, aconceptual, intuitive. A complete human consciousness involves the polarity and integration of the two modes, as a complete day includes day and night.

The first chapter of this book restated the idea that even scientific knowledge, largely a linear and rational pursuit, also relies heavily on intuition for completeness. In *The Art of Scientific Investigation*, W.I.B. Beveridge stresses the need for the development of the intuitive side in scientists. He defines intuition in science as "a clarifying idea which comes suddenly to mind." Intuitive knowledge complements the normal, rational scientific knowledge, much as the paradigm change is the complement to the normal progress of scientific thought.[22]

According to Beveridge, intuitions have most often come to scientific investigators when the normal rational processes were temporarily suspended. The French mathematician Poincaré, after dismissing his work from his "rational" mind, went for a drive in the country. "Just as I put my foot on the brake, the idea came to me." Many others have stressed this point, that reason in science must be complemented by the "other" mode. Albert Einstein, for instance, said of his own creative processes, "The really valuable thing is intuition." The realm of the paradigm *maker* is the "other" side of science. The complete scientific endeavor, then, involves working in both modes.

To take a similar example quite close to hand: In the writing of this book, I have had one vague idea after another at different times: on the beach, in the mountains, in discussion, even while writing. These intuitions are sparse images—perhaps a connection that allows a new gestalt to form—but they are never fully clear, and never satisfactory by themselves. They are incomplete realizations, not a finished work. For me, it is only when the intellect has worked out a form for these glimpses that the intuition becomes of any use to others. It is the very linearity of a book that enables the writer to refine his own intuitions and clarify them, first to himself, and then, if possible, to the reader.

The process of building a house provides another example. At first, there may be a sudden inspiration of the gestalt of the finished house, but this image must be brought to completion slowly, by linear methods, by plans and contracts, and then by the actual construction, sequentially, piece by piece.

The idea of the complementarity of two major modes of consciousness is hardly new. It antedates systems such as the *I Ching* and is found in many forms of philosophical, religious, and psychological endeavor. It was emphasized in physics by Robert Oppenheimer and in metaphysics by many. What is new now is a recognition that these modes operate biologically as well as mentally and culturally. With a recognition of the biological basis of the dual specializations of consciousness, we may be able to redress the imbalance in science and in psychology. This balance has in recent years swung a bit too far to the right, to a strict insistence on verbal logic that has left context and perspective undeveloped and has ignored the existence of many basic human questions.

FOR FURTHER READING

MICHAEL S. GAZZANIGA. "The Split Brain in Man." *Scientific American,* August 1967, pp. 24–29.

DOROTHY LEE. "Codifications of Reality: Lineal and Nonlineal." *Psychosomatic Medicine* 12, no. 2 (1950): 89–97.

ARTHUR DEIKMAN. "Bimodal Consciousness." *Archives of General Psychiatry* 25 (December 1971): 481–89.

JOSEPH E. BOGEN. "The Other Side of the Brain: An Appositional Mind." *Bulletin of the Los Angeles Neurological Societies* 34, no. 3 (July 1969): 135–62.

G. WILLIAM DOMHOFF. "But Why Did They Sit on the King's Right in the First Place?" *Psychoanalytic Review* 56 (1969–70): 586–96.

All the preceding have been reprinted, in whole or in part, in Robert Ornstein, ed. *The Nature of Human Consciousness.* San Francisco: W.H. Freeman; New York: Viking Press, 1973.

JEROME BRUNER. *On Knowing: Essays for the Left Hand.* New York: Atheneum, 1965.

ROGER W. SPERRY. "The Great Cerebral Commissure." *Scientific American,* January 1964, pp. 142–52.

ROGER W. SPERRY. "Lateral Specialization in the Surgically Separated Hemispheres." In Frances O. Schmidt and Fredric Worden, eds. *The Neurosciences: Third Study Program.* Cambridge, Mass.: M.I.T. Press, 1974.

ROBERT ORNSTEIN, ed. *Symposium on Consciousness.* New York: Viking Press, 1976.

3 "Ordinary" Consciousness: A Personal Construction

Seeing Double

A father said to his double-seeing son, "Son, you see two instead of one."
   "How can that be?" the boy replied. "If I were, there would seem to be four moons up there in place of two."[1]

W e should begin the study of the nature of consciousness with our own. Consider your normal consciousness, and reflect for a moment on its contents; you will probably find it a mixture of thoughts, fantasies, ideas, and visual, auditory, olfactory sensations of the external world. Objects appear, such as trees, books, chairs. We are aware of people, as bodies in space, as personalities, as voices. We move in tridimensional space and actively manipulate perceived objects—we may turn the page of a book, sit in a chair, speak to someone, listen to a lecturer. Normally, our personal consciousness conveys a version of an external reality and this transformation can be considered successful to the extent that it enables us to survive.

But although in our own personal experience we are sure that the world we contact has some "objective" physical validity, we usually go a bit further. At each moment of each day, we make the same mistake as does the double-seeing son—we consider that our own personal consciousness *is* the world, that an outside "objective" reality is perfectly represented in our experience. After all, trees have substance, a movement affects the world. Most people never realize there is an issue here, since for ordinary purposes the "reality" of our experience is unchallenged.

Some of the early film cartoons portrayed such an understanding. A little man at a switchboard in the brain projected physical "pictures" of the world on a consciousness screen. The pictures, of course, were a perfect reflection of the external world.

Even a moment's reflection, though, will confirm that our general idea of a personal consciousness as a perfect mirror of an external reality cannot be true. If there were a consciousness screen, who could see it? Does the little man (or woman) have another one inside? And in addition, we do sometimes experience things that are *not* physically present. We hallucinate, daydream, imagine. And most consistently, we distort images that are present as well. Each night we dream and experience events and objects that we produce totally by ourselves.

Consider also the enormous variety of physical energies that we contact at each moment of our lives. The air, or more properly, the atmospheric environment, conveys energy in the electromagnetic band: visible light, X-rays, radio waves, infrared radiation. In addition, there is present the mechanical vibration of the air, containing the information of sound; the constant energy from the gravitational field; pressure on the body; gaseous matter in the air. We also generate our own internal stimuli—thoughts, internal organ sensations, muscular activity, pains, feelings, and much more. These processes are always occurring simultaneously and continue as long as we are alive; yet we are certainly not aware of *each* process at *each* moment. Our personal consciousness, then, cannot fully represent the external world or even our internal world but must consist of an extremely small fraction of the entire ''reality.'' We do not even possess the sensory systems to perceive many forms of available energy, such as ultraviolet radiation.

Many questions arise once we realize that our personal consciousness is extremely limited. How do we manage to maintain a relatively stable personal consciousness in the face of all the stimuli that impinge on us? What is the nature of our experience of the world? Why is it necessary for our personal consciousness to be so limited?

Personal consciousness is outward oriented, involving action, for the most part. It is most likely to have evolved for the primary purpose of ensuring individual biological survival, for which active manipulation of discrete objects, sensitivity to threatening organisms or forces that pose a threat, and separation of oneself from others would have been useful. Our biological inheritance determines that we *select* the sensory personal consciousness from the mass of information reaching us. This is done by a multilevel process of filtration, for the most part sorting out survival-related stimuli. From this, we are ultimately able to *construct* a stable consciousness in coordination with the filtered input.

If we can realize from the outset that our ordinary consciousness is something we must of necessity construct or *create* in order to survive in the world, we can understand that this consciousness is only *one* possible consciousness. And if this consciousness is a personal construction, then each person can alter his or her consciousness simply by *changing the manner of construction*. The psychologist William James compared this process to that of a sculptor carving a statue out of marble. The process largely involves many levels of selection and consequent limitation, yet each individual sculptor's statue is unique, as is each person's consciousness.

We see that the mind is at every stage a theatre of simultaneous possibilities. Consciousness consists in the comparison of these with each other, the selection of some, and the suppression of others, of the rest by the reinforcing and inhibiting agency of attention. The highest and most celebrated mental products are filtered from the data chosen by the faculty below that, which mass was in turn sifted from a still larger amount of yet simpler material, and so on. The mind, in short, works on the data it received much as a sculptor works on his block of stone. In a sense, the statue stood there from eternity. But there were a thousand different ones beside it. The sculptor alone is to thank for having extricated this one from the rest. Just so the world of each of us, however different our several views of it may be, all lay embedded in the primordial chaos of sensations, which gave the mere *matter* to the thought of all of us indifferently. We may, if we like, by our reasoning unwind things back to that black and jointless continuity of space and moving clouds of swarming atoms which science calls the only real world. But all the while the world we feel and live in will be that which our ancestors and we, by slowly cumulative strokes of choice, have extricated out of this, like sculptors, by simply rejecting certain portions of the given stuff. Other sculptors, other statues from the same stone! Other minds, other worlds, from the same monotonous and inexpressive chaos! My world is but one in a million, alike embedded and alike real to those who may abstract them. How different must be the world in the consciousness of ants, cuttle-fish, or crab![2]

How, then, do we interact with the external chaos and "make sense" out of it? Each of us selects and constructs a personal world in several simultaneous procedures. Sense organs gather information that the brain can modify and sort. This heavily filtered input is compared with memory, expectations, body movements, and preparations for motor output until, finally, our consciousness is constructed as a "best guess" about reality. These "best guesses" are the formations of our assumptive world; they offer stability at the cost of exclusion.

THE SENSES AS DATA REDUCTION SYSTEMS

We normally consider that the senses are the "windows" to the world—that we "see with our eyes" and we "hear with our ears." But such a view, though it certainly explains part of our situation, is not entirely the case, for a primary function of sensory systems (considered as whole systems) is to discard "irrelevant" information, such as X-rays, infrared radiation, or ultrasonic waves. Aldous Huxley most elegantly stated this idea. In *The Doors of Perception*, Huxley quotes C.D. Broad:

The function of the brain and nervous system is to protect us from being overwhelmed and confused by this mass of largely useless and irrelevant knowledge, by shutting out most of what we should otherwise perceive and remember at any given moment, leaving only that very small and special selection that is likely to be practically useful.

And then Huxley comments:

According to such theory each one of us is potentially Mind at Large. But insofar as we are animals our business is at all costs to survive. To make biological survival possible, Mind at Large has to be funneled through the reducing valve of the brain and nervous system. What comes out at the other end is a messy trickle of the kind of consciousness which will help us to stay alive on the surface of this particular planet. To formulate and express the contents of this reduced awareness man has invented and endlessly elaborated those symbol-systems and implicit philosophies that we call languages. Every individual is at once the beneficiary and the victim of the linguistic tradition into which he has been born—the beneficiary inasmuch as language gives access to the accumulated records of other people's experience, the victim insofar as it confirms him in the belief that reduced awareness is the only awareness, and as it bedevils his sense of reality, so that he is all too apt to take his concepts for data, his words for actual things. That which, in the language of religion, is called "this world" is the universe of reduced awareness expressed and, as it were, petrified by language. The various "other worlds" with which human beings erratically make contact are so many elements in the totality of awareness belonging to Mind at Large. Most people most of the time know only what comes through the reducing valve and is consecrated as genuinely real by their local language. Certain persons, however, seem to be born with a kind of bypass that circumvents the reducing valve. In others temporary bypasses may be acquired either spontaneously or as the result of deliberate "spiritual exercises" or through hypnosis or by means of drugs. Through these permanent or temporary bypasses there flows, not indeed the perception "of everything that is happening everywhere in the universe" (for the bypass does not abolish the reducing valve which still excludes the total content of the Mind at Large), but something more than, and above all something different from, the carefully selected, utilitarian material which our narrow individual minds regard as a complete, or at least sufficient, picture of reality.[3]

Consider the most important avenue of personal consciousness, the eye. It responds to radiant electromagnetic energy in the visible spectrum. If we consult a chart of the electromagnetic spectrum, we

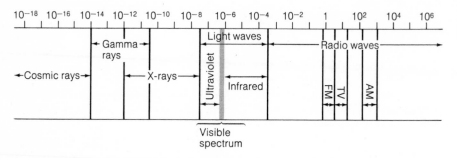

Figure 3-1 The electromagnetic spectrum

note that the "visible" spectrum is but one tiny aspect of the energy band. The entire spectrum ranges in wavelength from less than one billionth of a meter to more than a thousand meters; yet we can "see" only the tiny portion between 400 and 700 billionths of a meter. In addition to electromagnetic energy, many other forces arrive at the eye—pressure, mechanical vibrations in the air, gaseous matter, and so on—but the eye is "by design" ignorant of these.

We could not possibly experience the world as it fully exists, from microscopic phenomena and infrared radiation to phenomena of the universe and high-frequency radiation—we would be overwhelmed. We are restricted by our physical evolution to only a few sensory dimensions. If we do not possess sensory systems for a given energy form, or if an object is out of our range or too quick, it is not part of our personal world and consciousness. It is almost impossible for us even to imagine an energy form or an object outside our normal receptive range. What would infrared radiation or an X-ray "look" like? What is the "sound" of a one-cycle note? Or, as in Zen, what would be the sound of one hand clapping? These questions may be difficult to grasp and, as I said, impossible to imagine. The problem may be easier to identify if we descend a bit on the evolutionary scale and examine an animal whose sensory systems, evolved for its own survival, in its own evolutionary niche, limit information even more than do ours, an organism that ignores dimensions of the external world that are a part of human experience.

Perhaps the clearest relevant research has been on the visual system of the frog. The eye of the frog was studied by Jerome Lettvin and his associates Maturana, McCulloch, and Pitts at the Massachusetts Institute of Technology. They followed the same theoretical approach as did Aldous Huxley, that sensory systems serve mainly for data *reduction*.[4]

The M.I.T. researchers devised an experiment in which visual stimulation could be offered to one eye of an immobilized frog. The frog was so situated that its eye was at the center of a hemisphere seven inches in radius. Small objects could be placed in different positions on the inner surface of this hemisphere by means of magnets, or they could be moved around in the space inside the hemisphere. The investigators implanted microelectrodes into the frog's optic nerve to measure, as they expressed it, "what the frog's eye tells the frog's brain"—the electrical impulses sent to the brain by the eye. Since the frog's eye is somewhat similar to our own, these investigators hoped that electrical recordings from the optic nerve would discriminate the different kinds of "messages" that the eye sends to the brain and reveal the relationship of the evoked patterns of electrical activity to the different objects displayed on the hemisphere.

There are literally an infinite number of different visual patterns that one could present to a frog—colors, shapes, movements, various combinations of these—a choice from the richness of the human visual world. However, in presenting many different objects, colors, and movements to the frog, the investigators observed a remarkable phenomenon: from all the different kinds of stimulation presented, only four different kinds of "messages" were sent from the retina to the brain. In other words, no matter what complexity and subtle differences are present in the environment, the frog's eye is "wired up" to send only a very few different messages. The frog's eye presumably evolved to *discard* the remainder of the information available.

The structure of its eye limits the frog's awareness to only four different kinds of visual activity. Lettvin and his co-workers termed the four related systems *sustained contrast detectors, moving-edge detectors, net dimming detectors,* and *net convexity detectors.* The first provides the general outline of the environment; the second responds to any significant movement in the environment; the third seems to enhance response to a sudden decrease in light, as when a large enemy is attacking. These systems have presumably evolved to extract information relevant to survival and to discard the rest, in the manner described by Huxley.

The fourth type of "message," conveyed by the net convexity detectors, is the one most obviously related to the frog's biological needs and is the most interesting system. The net convexity detectors do not respond to any general change in light or to contrast; they respond only when small dark objects come into the field of vision and move quite close to the eye. It is quite clear, then, how the frog gets its food, how it can see flying bugs even with its limited visual system. The frog has evolved its own subsystem, which is "wired up" to ignore all "irrelevant" information and to notice only that of bugs flying close to it—a very specialized "bug-perceiving" subsystem.

So, out of the complexity and richness of the information presented to its eye, the frog seems to select only four different classes of phenomena. Higher-level animals exhibit similar selectivity, but in a much more complicated way. This type of electrophysiological analysis has been extended to cats and monkeys by David Hubel and Torsten Weisel at Harvard University, and now by many other investigators, who have determined that different cells in the cortex of cats and monkeys respond to different types of sensory stimulation. Certain cells detect edges and corners, others respond directly to movement on the retina, and so on. Although vision has been the sensory system most often studied (since it is relatively easy to record from the visual system and to specify the stimulus dimension), one would also expect other sensory modalities to show the same kinds of relationships.

By their physiological design, then, the sensory systems function to reduce the amount of "useless" and "irrelevant" information reaching us and to serve as selection systems. The information input of the senses seems to be gathered for the primary purpose of biological survival. The frog is a clear physiological demonstration of this highly evolved selective system.

All human beings are similarly evolved to select certain common aspects of the physical universe: we possess eyes that receive radiant electromagnetic energy, ears that receive mechanical vibrations, a nose, touch sensors, and taste. It is easy to assume that these exhaust the extent of the "real," "known" world. After all, there is "consensual validation"—friends agree that there is a tree "out there," a bird singing, a dinner on the table. It is important to realize that this kind of validation is limited to the con-sensual—with the senses. Our human "agreement" on the nature of external reality is subject to *common* shared limitations that have presumably evolved to ensure the biological survival of the race. All humans may agree on certain events only because we are all similarly limited in our very structure as well as in our culture. Like the double-seeing son, it is very easy for us to confuse our common agreement with an external reality. If everyone "saw" double, for instance, we would believe that two moons existed, or we would simply have a doubled system of numbering. Perhaps we do. As can well be imagined given the limited nature of our senses, our agreement covers but a small portion of what actually exists, as the noontime is only a part of an entire day-night cycle.

HIGH-LEVEL SELECTIVITY AND "TUNING"

Ascend the evolutionary ladder from the frog, and consider more advanced organisms. The avenues of sensation become more complex, multimodal. More important, though, the *flexibility* of the sensory systems themselves becomes much greater because of the increasing programmability of the central nervous system. To make use of familiar machine analogies, the sensory systems of some animals are like permanently wired-up, simple machines. In a mousetrap or a pencil sharpener, or even in a telephone or an automobile, a change in one part throws everything else out of adjustment, since the machine has no built-in capacity for internal reorganization. In the more complicated animals, including humans, the nervous systems seem to be more computer-like—machines, to be sure, but ones that can alter the relationship between input and performance by a change in the program. The higher mammals can be regarded as machines that are capable of reprogramming themselves in accordance with alterations in the external environment. This is not to say that there are no limits to their performance. Even the most sophisticated current computer has its physical limitations. No matter how the computer alters its own programs, it will never learn to fly all by itself—it has no wings. But a computer can alter itself within the limits of its own physical structure, as can we.

We can personally experience this computer-like, higher-level selectivity and tuning. At a gathering where several people are talking at the same time, close your eyes and listen to one person speaking, then tune him or her out and listen to another person. Perhaps you will be surprised at how easy it is to tune your attention in this way. In fact, we have little reason to be surprised at this ability, since we tune ourselves continuously to suit our needs and expectations, but the surprise comes because we are not usually *aware* of such self-tuning. The selection process is programmable, within the fixed sensory limits. When we perspire during the summer, we like the taste of foods that are more salty than usual. We don't consciously think that we need salt and that we should take more salt in our foods; we simply *like* foods that at other times we would consider quite oversalted. We also continuously "set" ourselves to see objects. For example, the character in the middle of Figure 3-2 can be seen either as a number or as a letter, depending on the context.

Many contemporary psychologists have investigated this human programmability. Some have used the tachistoscope, which allows figures to be presented for short and measurable periods of time. One interesting series of experiments with the tachistoscope demonstrated that we recognize familiar objects or words in less time than unfamiliar ones. It takes more time to recognize the nonsense word *merrof* than the word *former,* and still more to recognize *efrmro,* even though they each contain the same letters. A coherent sentence is recognized much more quickly than is a random sequence of words. Our past experience "tunes" us to have some idea of what to expect, and we need much less information to construct the experience. Jerome Bruner calls this "going beyond the information given."

One naive view of the brain and nervous system has stimulated some useful research in psychology. (Remember that the lens of the eye reverses the light from left to right and from up to down.) A

Figure 3-2

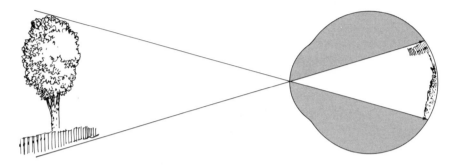

Figure 3-3   The lens of the eye reverses the input of the retina surface.

common question reflects this view: "If the eye reverses the visual world, then why do we see the world right-side up when the image on the retina is upside down?" The answer, of course, is that "right-side up" and "upside down" have no real biological meaning. The idea of perceiving "right-side up" presupposes that we see *what exists.* Yet since we do not directly view an external reality, the question is meaningless. All that is required in order for us to "see" is for a *consistent* relationship to exist between the external object and the pattern of excitation on the retina. In man, this pattern can be "upside down," "reversed," or any other constant transform of the stimulus.[5]

If the visual world of a goldfish is inverted by surgical rotation, it never adapts to the alteration in input, swimming in circles forever. It may even starve, unable to reach food.[6] In contrast, if a human being's or monkey's visual world is optically altered, adaptation is quite quick. Since we do not surgically experiment on people, the alterations are done with lenses. After a period of adjustment, a man can pedal a bicycle through a crowded town wearing specially designed inverting lenses.[7] The naive view cannot be correct. We *never* see the world "right-side up"; we select from the input and construct a personal consciousness from what we have selected. So if the visual input is inverted, there is of course an initial disturbance in the input and output systems of the brain. The normal and consistent relationship between external objects and the pattern of sensation on the retina is upset. It takes some time for us to learn the new calendars of correspondences. In reaching toward an object, we may move in the wrong direction initially, then overreach, then hit it. But gradually, in the same manner as we first learned to see, we begin to learn the newly appropriate correspondences between input and objects. The consistency of the selection is once again restored, we are able to ride a bicycle with visual information inverted, and we presumably see objects "right-side up."

Our eyes are also constantly in motion, in large eye movements (saccades) as well as in eye tremors (nystagmus). We blink our eyes almost every second, move our eyes around, move our heads and bodies, and follow moving objects. The view of an object is never constant, and the very receptive fields on the eyes change all the time; yet our visual world remains quite stable. If we walk around a horse, for instance, our image of the animal is constantly changing—we sometimes see the tail, sometimes the back or a side, a three-quarter view or a straight front view—yet we always see the *same* horse. If we were to "see" an "image" on our retina, the interpretation of this constantly changing visual world would be quite different each second; sometimes we would "see" one object, then another, sometimes we would experience a blur due to the eyes moving, sometimes a bit of darkness due to blinks. But we do not. The horse is seen, not the blinks, movements, or pieces. We must then *construct* a personal consciousness from the selected input and in this way achieve a stability of awareness out of the rich and continuously changing flow of information reaching our receptors.[8]

AUTOMATIZATION

If at each moment we were aware of each quantum of energy reaching us, we would probably be overwhelmed by the flood of irrelevant information. We might not be able to discriminate enough to notice impending dangers, such as a tree about to fall, an animal, or a truck approaching. Because we must discriminate between continuous, "safe" stimuli and new survival-related occurrences, we have evolved sensory systems that respond primarily to alterations in the external environment. The cells in the visual cortex and the retina, for example, are specialized to detect *changes* in input and to ignore constancies (see Figure 3–4).

To take another example. There is a spot in our visual field that we can never "sense" because of the anatomy of the eye (see Figure 3–6). At the exit of the optic tract, no light energy can stimulate the retina. There is a "hole" always present in our world; the exercise in

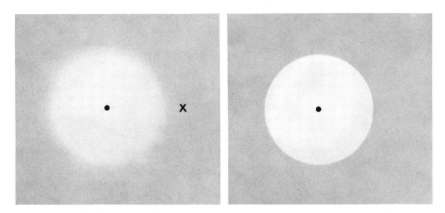

Figure 3-4 Look steadily at the left dot; the light circle disappears. You can make it reappear by looking at the X. The right-hand circle will not disappear if you stare at it, although it is as light in the center as the other circle. The visual system, like other sensory systems, is maximally sensitive to sharp changes.

Figure 3–5 merely makes it explicit. But since this gap in perception is always present, we *never* notice it, because we are specialized to notice change.

Further back in the central nervous system, higher levels of brain organization allow us to respond automatically, "unconsciously," to the more complex constancies of the environment. Consider several examples of such constancies: if you were to say the word *need* over and over to yourself one hundred times, it becomes strange, loses meaning, and no longer seems like the same word. The mere repetition of a stimulus can alter consciousness.

While learning a new skill, such as skiing or playing the piano, we are somewhat painfully aware of the many complex postural adjustments and motor movements. As we progress and the skill becomes "automatic," the movements no longer enter consciousness. Compare

Figure 3-5 To find the blind spot, close your right eye and stare at the circle. Hold the book 10 to 12 inches from the eye, and move it toward you or away until the square disappears. Notice that this "hole" is *always* present in your visual world.

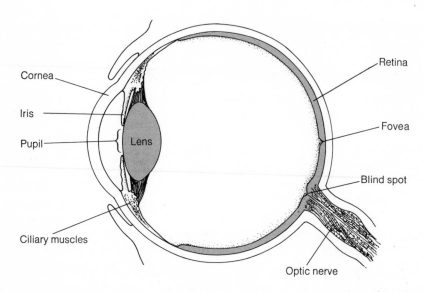

Figure 3-6   The blind spot is formed by the exit of the optic nerve from the retina.

the first time you tried to drive a car with your experience after you had learned.

After you have learned to drive, when you travel along a road for the first time, everything appears quite new and interesting—a red house, a big tree, the road itself—but gradually, as you drive the same route over and over, you become accustomed to everything on the way. You stop "seeing" the trees, the bridges, the corners, and so on. You have become somewhat *automatized* in your response to them.

When you enter a room in which a fan is creating a buzzing sound, you are aware of the sound for the first few moments, but then it disappears from awareness; you have stopped "*paying* attention" to it.

We quickly adapt to the constancies of the world; hence, we constantly need new stimulation. When we buy a new phonograph record, we often play it over and over again for a brief initial period, then leave it on the shelf unplayed. We get bored with it; the record no longer seems "new"; it is out of our awareness, on automatic. Most consumer products are periodically changed slightly (automobiles, for instance), so that we begin to notice them once again, and presumably buy them.

In psychology and physiology, the phenomenon we have been

describing is termed *habituation*. It is one of the physiological components of the *orienting reaction* to new stimuli, the reaction that is
involved in our registering of input information. The physiological
indicators of this reaction often include a blocking of the alpha
rhythm of the electroencephalogram, an increase in heart rate, and a
drop in skin resistance. Suppose we measure the resistance of the
skin, for example, and repeat a click every five seconds. The first click
will cause a sharp drop in skin resistance. The second click will cause
a smaller drop, the third still less, until, depending on the parameters
of the particular experiment, the skin resistance no longer drops with
each click. The response of the skin to this stimulus has "habituated."
After we hear the sound of a clock ticking, when the sound ceases, we
no longer show the orienting, or registering, reaction. This physiological process is not merely a simple one in which the threshold for
stimuli entering into awareness is raised, thus tuning the click out.
Our nervous system is capable of a more sophisticated selective
tuning. It is true that if we substitute a louder click, we will begin to
hear it again. But if we substitute a *softer* one, the orienting reaction
also returns, and we will hear it again. If we change the interval
between the clicks—if a click appears a little later than we expect, or
a bit sooner—the click returns to awareness, and the orienting reaction reappears.

Karl Pribram has pointed out another example of this phenome-

Figure 3-7 The response of a spinal cord neuron under constant stimulation. Note
the decrease in firing rate of the neuron, which is called *habituation*.

non, which he termed the "Bowery El" effect. An elevated railroad once ran along Third Avenue in New York City. At a certain time late each night, a noisy train ran. The train line was torn down some time ago, with some interesting aftereffects. On subsequent nights, many people in the neighborhood began to call the police quite late to report "something strange" occurring—unusual noises, suspected thieves or burglars were reported. The police determined that these calls took place at about the time the former late-night train would have passed these peoples' houses. What they were "hearing," of course, was the *absence* of the familiar noise of the train. We have such an experience, although often a much simpler one, whenever a noise that has been continuing suddenly stops.[9]

If we view the same object over and over again, we begin to look at it in the same way each time. We do this with the constancies of our world, ordinary surroundings such as the pictures in our house or the routes we drive every day. Charles Furst has studied the effect of repeated viewing of the same picture on the way we look at it. He found that eye movements tend to become more and more stereotyped as the same visual stimulus is presented. When we see a new image, our eyes tend to move in a new pattern around it, but as we see it again and again—as we see the rooms in our house—we tend to look in a fixed way at the same portions of it and ignore or tune out the rest.[10] The "Bowery El" effect, the "Furst" effect, and other studies on habituation suggest that we tune out the recurrences of the world by constructing a "model" of the external world within our nervous system and testing input against it. We somehow can program, and continuously revise or reprogram, our models of the external world. If the transformed input information and our internal model agree, as they do most often for the constancies of the world, the input remains out of consciousness. If there is any significant disagreement, if the new information is recognizably different, slower, softer, louder, different in form or color, or even *absent*, we become aware of it once again. This programming forms an additional active selection process imposed on the data that pass through the relatively fixed reducing valves of the sensory systems. In everyday situations there is more flexibility than in laboratory demonstrations; much more discrepancy can be tolerated, although the extent depends upon the situation.

OUR ASSUMPTIVE WORLD

Perhaps the clearest and most striking trend in the psychology and physiology of perception in the past few years has been the increasing understanding of the interactive and constructive nature of ordinary awareness. One of the leaders in this field of investigation, Jerome Bruner, has emphasized that perception involves acts of categorization.[11] As we mature, we attempt to make more and more consistent "sense" out of the mass of information arriving at our receptors. We develop stereotyped systems, or *categories,* for sorting input information. The set of categories we develop is limited, much more limited than the wide variety of potential occurrences. Simple categories may be "straight," or "red," or "loud." More complex ones may be "English," "interesting," or "in front of." In social situations, the categories may be stored as attributed personality traits. If we categorize a person as "aggressive," we might then consistently tend to sort all his or her actions in terms of this category.

Our own previous experience with objects and events strengthens the category systems as it does a scientific paradigm. We expect cars to make a certain noise, traffic lights to be a certain color, food to smell a certain way, and certain people to say certain things. But what we actually experience, according to Bruner and others, is the *category* that is evoked by a particular stimulus, *not* necessarily the occurrence in the external world.

The anomalous-card experiment that Bruner and his associates carried out was an attempt to demonstrate the effects of our well-learned categories on the contents of awareness. Our past experience with playing cards evokes in us an assumed relationship between the colors and the forms of playing cards. The import of these and others of Bruner's demonstrations is that at each moment we construct a model of the world, expect certain correspondences of objects, colors, and forms to occur, and then experience our categories.

THE TRANSACTIONALISTS

About the time Jerome Bruner was studying the effects of categories on the contents of awareness, another group of psychologists, led by Adelbert Ames, was exploring the basic nature of awareness. Ames characterized ordinary awareness as a "transaction" between the perceiver and the environment. In spite of the overflow of information available to our sense organs at any given time, *relevant* information is often lacking. Color information, for instance, is directly present on our retina, but we cannot determine tridimensionality directly. We cannot immediately know whether a room is "really" rectangular or not, or whether a given chair is physically closer than others, since we do not possess a direct monocular sense of distance. Perceptible dimensions and interposition are, however, usually associated with closeness of objects. If we assume that two objects we are looking at are the same size, then the one that looks larger would be closer to us. If one object is interposed on another, we usually assume that the interposed object is closer, as in Figure 3–8. That is, if we are trying to determine closeness, we "bet" that the "larger" object or the interposed object is the closer.

However, this "bet" is not a conscious process of correction. We *directly experience* these objects as closer. The Ames group set out to demonstrate the nature of the "bet" we make with the environment.[12]

By manipulating "unconscious inference," as Helmholtz called it,

 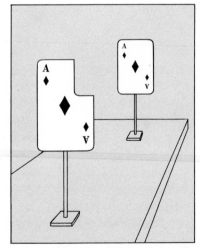

Figure 3–8 Normally, if we were to look at the picture on the left, we would assume that the smaller card, due to interposition, is closer to us and that the larger one is farther away. But our assumptions are not always correct, as shown in the picture on the right.

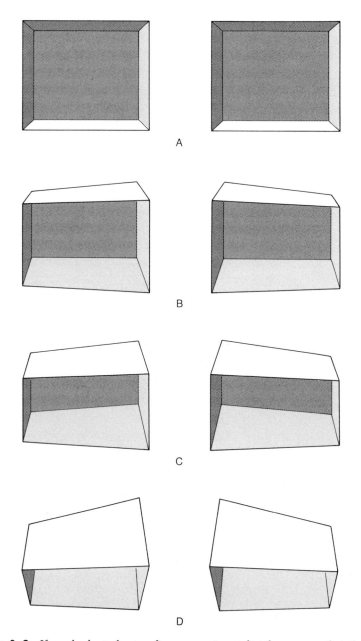

Figure 3-9 If we look at the top figures, we immediately assume that they are rectilinear. However, many shapes can give rise to the impression of rectilinearity, as this drawing illustrates: as the front of each box is tilted downward, we can see that they are not rectilinear at all.

Figure 3-10 In one of these pictures the dog appears to be large, due only to our assumptions; in another, the boy seems to have grown. But these size changes are a consequence of the shape of the room and the nature of our own constructions.

we can become aware of the bets or, in Bruner's term, the categories that constitute our awareness. To give another example: When we see a line drawing of a room, as in Figure 3–9, we "bet" that in a top view it would be shaped like a rectangle. But a rectangle is only one of the many possible forms that could be derived from the two-dimensional drawing. One side may not be parallel with the other. We bet that the room is rectangular because almost all the rooms in our experience have been rectangular. But if the room is in fact not rectangular, our bet causes us to "see" objects or people in the room in a very strange way (see Figure 3–10).

HOW THE BRAIN CONTROLS ITS INPUT

Since we can tune ourselves in terms of our category systems, there must be physiological mechanisms that allow tuning to take place. Karl Pribram and Nico Spinelli have set out to demonstrate a physiological analog of this process. They recorded from cells in the frontal cortex of the brain while stimulating the retina and showed that the patterns in which the receptive fields of the retina respond to external stimuli can be altered by the brain. That is, the way in which stimuli are received, even on the retina itself, can be reprogrammed from moment to moment, and this ability can be demonstrated physiologically.[13] These and other experiments demonstrate that the motor-output system of the brain (efference) has an effect on the input (afference); the brain "selects its input."

If the output of the brain in some way determines conscious experience, how does this occur? We do know that if a monkey or a cat is deprived of visual experience in early infancy (by simply rearing it in the dark), it will not fully learn to see.[14] Is this due to simple degeneration of the visual system or to something more complex?

To test this question, Richard Held raised kittens in the dark, save for an hour or so each day when they were given visual experience.[15] One group was allowed to roam around a tunnel more or less normally (see Figure 3–11). Others were treated similarly except that they were carried passively in a "gondola" attached to the active kittens. The active ones learned to see normally, the passive ones did not. Held's ingenious experiment demonstrates that passive regis-

Figure 3-11 Two kittens harnessed together in a "gondola." They were raised in darkness, save for three hours per day in this room. One kitten walked, the other was carried. Their visual experience was similar, yet the "passive" kitten could hardly see, while the active one exhibited normal vision.

tration of input within a sensory system is not sufficient to develop a fully operating consciousness. The input information must in some way be correlated with the organism's motor output, including muscle movements.

THE MOTOR THEORY OF CONSCIOUSNESS

The investigation of the active role of the brain's output in determining the contents of awareness has been a recent major trend in the psychophysiology of perception. The work of Bruner and the transactionalists demonstrates this active role on a psychological level; that of Pribram and Spinelli on the physiological. Some investigators have been explicitly concerned with how the relationship between the input processing and the output systems of the brain affect the contents of awareness. There is a personal demonstration we can attempt: Close one eye, and push the other eye gently from the outside corner. The visual world seems to shake a bit and jump about discontinuously. Yet, if we were to move our eye in the normal manner over the same space, the world would not seem to shake. The difference between these two situations indicates that in constructing our awareness we must also take our own movements (motor output of the brain) into account and correlate them with the continuous changes in input information. If we did not possess continuous fleeting records of our efference (in this case, our eye movements), the visual world would be constantly jumping around.

Some researchers have even argued that consciousness depends solely on the output of the brain, no matter what the input is that keys off a given output. In this view, we consider that the brain is largely specialized to make motor movements, be they of the tongue, as in speech, of the eye, or of the large muscles of the body. If the brain's activity is largely to regulate motor output, then, as Roger Sperry writes:

Insofar as an organism perceives a given object, it is prepared to respond with reference to it. This preparation-to-respond is absent in an organism that has failed to perceive. In the case of the triangle, a person who perceives it, is ready to point to it, to outline it with his finger, to show its location and orientation in space, to pick it up, describe it, etc. Animals lacking the verbal and symbolic capacities of man illustrate the principle more simply. The perceiving animal is able to avoid or to approach the triangle, to run under it or up one edge of it, to leap to a corner of it or to pick it up in its mouth by one of the points, etc. The presence or absence of adaptive reaction potentialities of this sort, ready to discharge into motor patterns, makes the difference between perceiving and not perceiving.[16]

If this approach is viable, then many or most of the perceptual demonstrations and illusions can be most parsimoniously understood as shifts in preparation to respond. Leon Festinger and his associates have elaborated on this useful idea and have provided a direct demonstration of it. By changing a person's preparation-to-respond to a given stimulus, perception changed, although the stimulus did not.

In one of the experiments, observers were asked to view a straight line and convey their impression of it. Normally a straight line yields preparations to respond by moving the eyes in a straight line. If a wedge prism on a contact lens is placed over the eye of the observer, the retinal image of the straight line is altered from this $+$ to this $\{$ and the perception at first alters accordingly.

A wedge prism on a contact lens has interesting properties. Its maximum point of deflection is at the point of regard, so that if one is looking at the middle of the line the image appears as above. If one looks at the top of the line the image is like this $\{$, and at the bottom, $\{$. Therefore, the point of maximum deflection is the point at which one is looking, and to view the line, one has to make *straight* (not curved) eye movements.

After viewing the line, what happens to the observer's perception? It becomes straight! The observer "sees" the preparation-to-respond, not the curved retinal image.[17]

The contention that awareness depends solely on output regardless of input is consistent with Bruner's contention that the category activated will determine awareness. For example, if you are "ready" to see a black ace of spades or a red ace of hearts when a red ace of spades is shown, you will see one of the two choices you have set for yourself. Or if you are "ready" to make a straight eye movement in response to a curved line, you will see the curved line as straight.

TRANSITORY CHARACTERISTICS OF PERSONAL CONSCIOUSNESS

The very physiology of the senses and central nervous system in large part determines the characteristics of our personally constructed worlds. There are, however, further limitations on our perceptions. We are each subject to moment-to-moment changes in our personal worlds. We each have a specific personal history and have undergone training that can partially program consciousness (schooling, jobs, special interests, and so on). Moreover, all of us, within a given culture, share a set of "unconscious" assumptions given us by the very organization of the culture and by our possession of a common language.

Individual consciousness is not wholly stable: Biases and as-sumptions shift, as do needs and intents. We are sometimes hungry, sometimes full, sometimes sexually attracted, sometimes sated, sometimes tired, sometimes alert. Consciousness is necessarily con-structed differently on these occasions. When hungry, we seem to notice food, aromas, and restaurants more than when we are full. When we are interested in those of the opposite sex, we perceive them differently from when we are not. Awaiting the arrival of a friend, we may immediately tune ourselves to notice anyone who remotely resembles him or her. The thirteenth-century Persian poet Jallaludin Rumi noted this phenomenon when he wrote: "What a piece of bread looks like depends on whether you are hungry or not."

For this area, as for many other important dimensions of personal consciousness, some of the most relevant psychological experiments have been performed by Jerome Bruner and by the transactionalist group. In one experiment, Bruner studied poor and well-to-do chil-dren. Noting that need may alter the characteristics of consciousness, Bruner found that children from poor homes tended to think a given coin larger than their more fortunate peers did. In addition, the poor children thought nickels were worth more than dimes.[18] What money looks like depends on whether you are poor or not.

Albert Hastorf and Hadley Cantril studied an event at a Prince-ton-Dartmouth football game. A football game is a suitable place to observe the transitory influences on consciousness caused by the extreme biases that may be called up by an emotional involvement with one side or the other. In this particular game, the star quarter-back of the Princeton team was injured. Hastorf and Cantril asked two groups of spectators to record their experiences at the game on a questionnaire. The Princeton fans reported undue violence and aggressions directed unfairly toward their quarterback; the Dart-mouth fans experienced the game as rough, but fair.[19] What an injury looks like depends on whether you are from Princeton or not.

The contents of consciousness vary, and expectations are transi-tory and fleeting. They move from one idea, object, or image to another; yet it is always the *same consciousness* that flows from experi-ence to experience. More than any other factor, our thoughts are the foundation of normal consciousness. We maintain and refresh our personal construction through our continued thoughts. William James presents the most suitable metaphor:

Consciousness then does not appear to itself chopped up in bits. Such words as "chain" or "train" do not describe it fitly, as it presents itself in the first instant. It is nothing jointed, it flows. A "river" or a "stream" are the metaphors by which it is naturally described. *In talking of it thereafter, let us call it the stream of thought, of consciousness, or of subjective life.*[20]

ENDURING CHARACTERISTICS OF PERSONAL CONSCIOUSNESS

Each person is an individual with a unique family history, training, profession, and unique personal interests. These background factors continuously influence the differences in our personal consciousnesses. Any given moment of our experience is infinitely rich in itself; but this richness will be perceived variously, depending on the perceiver. Consider a scene in a park on a Sunday afternoon: An artist walking through might note the quality of the light, the colors of the leaves on the trees, the geometric forms of the landscape. A psychologist might notice the people present, their mannerisms, interactions, speech patterns. A physician, looking at the same people, might notice not their interactions but their body structures and their health. A botanist might ignore the people to focus on the flowers. One woman may remember words, another gestures. One man may be fascinated by a particular smell in the air, while another may be too immersed in his own thoughts and fantasies to register anything about the external environment.

Entire lives can be spent directing personal consciousness to one small portion of the world. One person's attention can be occupied by sailboats, becoming an expert on the winds, rigging, hull design; another is concerned with taste and smell, learning to discriminate a 1947 red Bordeaux wine from a 1949 of the same chateau.

It seems that one of the most basic differences between individuals is between those who tend to employ the linear, verbal mode and those who are less verbal and more involved in spatial imagery. The scientist, the writer, the mathematician, are examples of the culturally "dominant" verbal-rational mode. The visual artist, the craftsman, the musician, the teacher of body movement, may be examples of another mode. Of course, each of us works in both modes: almost everyone speaks and reads; we all move in three-dimensional space. However, some people are more specialized in one mode of operation than others, which often makes communication difficult between, say, husband and wife, if one is a scientist, the other an artist.

CULTURAL CHARACTERISTICS

The primary motivation in life is biological survival, both of the individual and of the species. To survive individually, man adopts a mode of active manipulation of the external environment. This mode could be considered an *analytic* position toward the world, involving an attempt to separate oneself from other people, living organisms, and objects. At times this separation may be essential for an individual's survival. If many of our ancestors had put up no boundaries between their personal identity and the remainder of creation when, say, a wild animal approached, the race might not have survived.

This mode of individual survival is *active*, geared to the consciousness of external events, to analysis, and to linearity. With *linearity*, I refer largely to the consciousness of events enduring in time, in sequence—of causes and effects. Such linearity is essential in the development of an organized culture. It is necessary for planning into the future, for taking the lessons of past history into account.

Language and science can be considered quite refined aspects of this mode. Their sequential structure allows us to dissect, discriminate, and divide the external environment into consistent segments that can be actively manipulated. They enable us to record experience cumulatively, to transmit information at a distance, and even to partake of the wisdom of those long dead.

To possess a language is to employ a set of ready-made categories that must help shape individual consciousness. Contemporary Americans possess only a few words for snow, the Eskimo many. We use one word for love, the mystic many. According to Benjamin Lee Whorf, language is an organ of the mind.[21] Within a linguistic community, the common language provides an almost unconsciously agreed-on set of categories for experience and allows the speakers of that language to ignore experiences excluded by the common category system—as our eye allows us to perceive radiant electromagnetic energy in the band between 400 and 700 billionths of a meter but forces us to ignore everything else. "Is there any number higher than 100?"

SCIENCE AS A MODE OF KNOWING

Personal consciousness is a continuous process of selection and construction, at each stage more and more conservative, more and more limiting. As a refinement of the active, personal mode, science is one of the most restricted and sure forms of knowledge available to man. Our sensory systems limit; our central nervous system limits; our personal and cultural categories limit; language limits; and beyond all these selections, the rules of science cause us to further select information that we can consider to be true. By a slow, conservative process of construction, science gradually builds a stable knowledge. Science is, with law, the very highest development of the analytic mode, meticulously charting causes and effects, radically restricting the conditions of observation in order to attain precision. It constitutes another highly specialized development of consciousness, at once its most conservative, yet its most reliable.

Most Western cultures are fundamentally based on this active, linear mode—the way of language, science, and history. Ours is so thoroughly based on linearity that many have almost forgotten that other constructions of individual consciousness, other cultural styles, are even possible. Again, the study of others can make these differences more clear.

The anthropologist Dorothy Lee studied the people of the Trobriand Islands and reports that their lack of linearity is evident even in language. In lieu of a sequential construction, the Trobrianders have a total present-centeredness, in which every action exists only in the present. Lee contrasts our dominant mode with this alternative.

The line is found or presupposed in most of our scientific work. It is present in the *induction* and *deduction* of science and logic. It is present in the philosopher's phrasing of means and ends as lineally connected. Our statistical facts are presented lineally as a *graph* or reduced to a normal *curve*. And all of us, I think, would be lost without our diagrams. We *trace* a historical development; we *follow* the course of history and evolution *down* to the present and *up* from the ape. . . .

When we see a *line* of trees, or a *circle* of stones, we assume the presence of a connecting line which is not actually visible. And we assume it metaphorically when we follow a *line* of thought, a *course* of action, or the *direction* of an argument: when we *bridge* a gap in the conversation, or speak of the *span* of life or of teaching a *course*, or lament our *interrupted* career. . . .

But the Trobrianders do not describe their activity lineally; they do no dynamic relating of acts; they do not use even so innocuous a connective as *and*. Here is part of a description of the planting of coconut. "Thou-approach-there coconut thou-bring-here-we-plant-coconut thou-go thou-plant our coconut. This-here-it-emerge sprout. We-push-away this we-push-away this-other coconut-husk-fiber together sprout it-sit together root." We who are accustomed to seek lineal continuity, cannot help supplying it as we read this; but the continuity is not given in the Trobriand text; and all Trobriand speech, according to Malinowski, is "jerky", given in points, not in connecting lines.[22]

THE PROCESS OF PERSONAL CONSCIOUSNESS

Our normal personal consciousness is not a complete, passive registration of the external environment; rather, it is a highly evolved, selective, personal construction constrained primarily for individual biological survival. But if this consciousness is something we each personally construct, how is it that many people seem to agree quite well on the nature of events? Personal consciousness has been called an illusion in the yogic tradition. This may be far too strong a condemnation, but to adopt it for a moment, we could say, Yes, personal consciousness may be an illusion, in Huxley's sense, in that only a measly trickle of the available external information is ever present in an individual's consciousness. But if personal consciousness is an illusion, it is a *constrained* illusion. The constraints are that we select the *appropriate* survival-related objects and events to be the contents of personal consciousness. Alternative "illusions" have (presumably) disappeared in the course of biological evolution. Further, the constraints make "consensual validation" possible. All humans have evolved with identical sense organs, which select only *certain aspects* of the flux of available stimulation, as well as higher-level similarities.

Let us trace this process: The sensory organs discard most of the input information reaching us. The brain further limits input by selectively inhibiting sensory activity, sending down efferent signals that can modify stimulation even in the receptor itself. Our senses and central nervous system select by responding primarily to changes. We quickly learn to "habituate" to the constancies of the world. Further, we sort the input into categories that depend on transitory needs, language, our past history, our expectations, and our cultural biases. Finally, we must *construct* a stable consciousness in terms of our motor output as does James's sculptor.

We do not, for instance, "see" with our eyes. More properly, the eyes participate in the entire process of visual experience. There is no "image" or "copy" of the external world on the retina, nor is one transmitted to the brain to be seen by a little man.

The experience of an infant is, according to William James, a "blooming, buzzing, confusion." It is so partly because the infant lacks a suitable category system in which to sort experience consistently. As we learn to construct a socially acceptable personal consciousness we learn to consistently associate, say, the experience of light and color with the appearance of external objects. As we mature, this correlation is increased. Whenever a particular pattern of excitation is produced in the nervous system, we become more and more likely to be "conscious" of, or ready to respond to, light energy from external sources. Our world becomes relatively stable; we become able to avoid danger successfully and to manipulate objects. We survive.

But it is quite important here to consider that light is a dimension of human consciousness. In physical fact, the only difference between "visible light" and the nearby portions of the electromagnetic spectrum is in wavelength. Nothing sacred occurs in nature between the electromagnetic wavelengths of 390 and 400 billionths of a meter, yet we can perceive one and not the other. It is only the receptive characteristics of our eyes that give a special place to a wavelength of 400 billionths of a meter, but not to one of 390.

Furthermore, we do not even require the presence of external light to "see." If "seeing" is a certain pattern of excitation in the central nervous system (be it a mixture of input and output or, simply, readiness to respond), then anything that produces this pattern will result in visual experience. Obviously, the vast majority of visual experiences occur in the normal way: light strikes the eye, which then transmits electrophysiological impulses through the optic tract to the brain, contributing to the construction of a certain visual experience. However, this system can be interrupted at several points. Close your eyes and press your eyeball for a moment. You will probably experience a greenish flash of light. No light energy but merely the pressure of the finger was transmitted to the retina. Yet we have "tricked" the visual system, causing the retina to fire by means of pressure rather than stimulation by light. *Any* stimulus that causes the retina to fire will give rise to the experience of light, be it pressure or some more subtle form of electrical or chemical stimulation.

Wilder Penfield, among others, has demonstrated that the experience of vision can also be evoked by electrical stimulation of the central nervous system. Penfield performed brain surgery on patients with epilepsy and as part of this procedure, electrically stimulated various areas of the brain; his patients often reported conscious experiences without other input.[23] Many surgeons have found that electrical stimulation of the occipital cortex usually leads to the experience of vision. We can understand, then, that seeing is a process that takes place not *in* our eyes but rather *with the help of* our eyes. It is constructed in the brain, determined by the output systems of the brain.

At other times, hallucinations may be caused by unusual functioning of the nervous system if the brain is stimulated by drugs that alter the normal relationships between external input and consciousness. Also, we dream each night and enter visual worlds that do not exist outside personal consciousness. Similar analyses would hold for other senses as well. Ordinary consciousness, then, is each individual's own private construction. Alfred North Whitehead wrote:

Nature gets credit which in truth should be reserved for ourselves, the rose for its scent, the nightingale for his song, and the sun for its radiance. The poets are entirely mistaken. They should address their lyrics to themselves and should turn them into odes of self-congratulations on the excellence of the human mind. Nature is a dull affair, soundless, scentless, colorless, merely the hurrying of material, endlessly, meaninglessly.[24]

The poet T.S. Eliot, similarly: "We are the music while the music lasts."

THE NATURE OF ORDINARY INDIVIDUAL CONSCIOUSNESS

Ordinary consciousness is an exquisitely evolved personal construction, "designed" for the primary purpose of individual biological survival. Sense organs and the brain serve to select aspects of the environment most relevant for survival. Our ordinary consciousness is object-centered; it involves analysis, a separation of oneself from other objects and organisms. This selective, active, analytic construction enables us to achieve a relatively stable personal world in which we can differentiate objects and act upon them. The concept of causality, linear time, and language are the essence of this mode.

And yet this individual, active mode is not the only mode in which consciousness can operate, as the daylight hours do not constitute an entire day. If ordinary consciousness is a personal construction, then other constructions and other consciousnesses are potentially available to us. William James (as usual) put it best:

Our normal waking consciousness, rational consciousness as we call it, is but one special type of consciousness, whilst all about it, parted from it by the filmiest of screens, there lie potential forms of consciousness entirely different. We may go through life without suspecting their existence; but apply the requisite stimulus, and at a touch they are there in all their completeness, definite types of mentality which probably somewhere have their field of application and adaptation. No account of the universe in its totality can be final which leaves these other forms of consciousness quite disregarded. How to regard them is the question—for they may determine attitudes though they cannot furnish formulas, and open a region though they fail to give a map. At any rate, they forbid a premature closing of our accounts with reality.[25]

FOR FURTHER READING

W. H. ITTELSON and F. P. KILPATRICK. "Experiments in Perception." *Scientific American*, August 1951, pp. 50–55.

ULRIC NEISSER. "The Processes of Vision." *Scientific American*, September 1968, pp. 204–214.

ALBERT H. HASTORF and HADLEY CANTRIL. "They Saw a Game: A Case Study." *Journal of Abnormal and Social Psychology* 49 (January 1954): 129–34.

WILLIAM JAMES. "The Stream of Consciousness." In *The Principles of Psychology*, Vol. 1, pp. 224–90. New York: Dover Publications, 1950. Original copyright, 1890.

ALDOUS HUXLEY. *The Doors of Perception*. New York: Harper & Row, 1954.

BENJAMIN LEE WHORF. *"Language, Mind, and Reality."* In *Language, Thought, and Reality: Selected Writings of Benjamin Lee Whorf*. Edited by J.B. Carroll. Cambridge, Mass.: M.I.T. Press, 1951.

Selections from all the preceding have been reprinted in Robert Ornstein, ed. *The Nature of Human Consciousness*. San Francisco: W.H. Freeman; New York: The Viking Press, 1973.

ROGER W. SPERRY. "Neurology and the Mind-Brain Problem." *American Scientist* 40, no. 2 (April 1952): 291–312.

LAWRENCE DURRELL. *The Alexandria Quartet: Justine, Balthazar, Mountolive, Clea.* New York: E.P. Dutton, 1960. A series of novels that explore consciousness as a personal construction.

4 The Study of Alterations in Consciousness

The Sultan Who Became an Exile

A sultan of Egypt, it is related, called a conference of learned men, and very soon—as is usually the case—a dispute arose. The subject was the Night Journey of the Prophet Mohammed. It is said that on that occasion the Prophet was taken from his bed up into the celestial spheres. During this period, he saw paradise and hell, conferred with God 90,000 times, had many other experiences—and was returned to his room while his bed was yet warm. A pot of water which had been overturned by the flight and spilled was still not empty when the Prophet returned.

Some held that this was possible, by a different measurement of time. The sultan claimed that it was impossible.

The sages said that all things were possible to divine power. This did not satisfy the king.

The news of this conflict came at length to the Sufi Sheikh Shahabudin, who immediately presented himself at Court. The sultan showed due humility to the teacher, who said: "I intend to proceed without further delay to my demonstration: for know now that both the interpretations of the problem are incorrect, and that there are demonstrable factors which can account for traditions without the need to resort to crude speculation or insipid and uninformed 'logicality.'"

There were four windows in the audience chamber. The sheikh ordered one to be opened. The sultan looked out of it. On a mountain beyond he saw an invading army, a myriad, bearing down on the palace. He was terribly afraid.

"Pray forget it: for it is nothing," said the sheikh.

He shut the window and opened it again. This time there was not a soul to be seen.

When he opened another of the windows, the city outside was seen to be consumed by flames. The sultan cried out in alarm.

"Do not distress yourself, sultan, for it is nothing," said the sheikh. When he had closed and again opened the window, there was no fire to be seen.

The third window being opened revealed a flood approaching the palace. Then, again, there was no flood.

When the fourth window was opened, instead of the customary desert, a garden of paradise was revealed—and then, by the shutting of the window, the scene vanished as before.

Now the sheikh ordered a vessel of water to be brought, and the sultan to put his head into it for a moment. As soon as he had done so the sultan found himself alone on a deserted seashore, a place which he did not know.

At this magic spell of the treacherous sheikh he was transported with fury, and vowed vengeance.

Soon he met some woodcutters who asked him who he was. Unable to explain his true state, he told them that he was shipwrecked. They gave him some clothes, and he walked to a town where a blacksmith, seeing him aimlessly wandering, asked him who he was. "A shipwrecked merchant, dependent upon the charity of woodcutters, now with no resources," answered the sultan.

The man then told him about a custom of that country. Every newcomer could ask the first woman who left the bath-house to marry him, and she would be obliged to do so. He went to the bath, and saw a beautiful maiden leaving. He asked her if she was married already: and she was, so he had to ask the next, an ugly one. And the next. The fourth was really exquisite. She said that she was not married, but pushed past him, affronted by his miserable appearance and dress.

Suddenly a man stood before him and said: "I have been sent to find a bedraggled man here. Please follow me."

The sultan followed the servant, and was shown into a wonderful house in one of whose sumptuous apartments he sat for hours. Finally four beautiful and gorgeously attired women came in, preceding a fifth, even more beautiful. The sultan recognized her as the last woman whom he had approached at the bath-house. She welcomed him and explained that she had hurried home to prepare for his coming, and that her hauteur was only one of the customs of the country, practiced by all women in the street.

Then followed a magnificent meal. Wonderful robes were brought and given to the sultan, while delicate music was played.

The sultan stayed seven years with his new wife, until they had squandered all her patrimony. Then the woman told him that he must now provide for her and their seven sons.

Recalling his first friend in the city, the sultan returned to the blacksmith for counsel. Since the sultan had no trade or training, he was advised to go to the marketplace and offer his services as a porter.

In one day he earned, through carrying a terrible load, only one-tenth of the money which was needed for the food of the family.

The following day the sultan made his way to the seashore again, where he found the very spot from which he had emerged seven long years before. Deciding to say his prayers, he started to wash in the water; he suddenly and dramatically found himself back at the palace, with the vessel of water, the sheikh and his courtiers.

"Seven years of exile, evil man!" roared the sultan. "Seven years, a family and having to be a porter! Have you no fear of God, the Almighty, for this deed?"

"But it is only a moment," said the Sufi master, "since you put your head into this water."

His courtiers bore out this statement.

The sultan could not possibly bring himself to believe a word of this. He started to give the order for the beheading of the sheikh. Perceiving by inner sense that this was to happen, the sheikh exercised the capacity called *Ilm el-Ghaibat:* The Science of Absence. This caused him to be instantly and corporeally transported to Damascus, many days' distance away. From here he wrote a letter to the king:

"Seven years passed for you, as you will now have discovered, during an instant of your head in the water. This happens through the exercise of certain faculties, and carries no special significance except that it is illustrative of what can happen. Was not the bed warm, was not the water jar empty in the tradition?

"It is not whether a thing has happened or not which is the important element. It is possible for anything to happen. What is, however, important, is the significance of the happening. In your case, there was no significance. In the case of the Prophet, there was significance in the happening."[1]

It is now more than eighty years since William James summed up the potential of changes in consciousness, yet the scientific study of the possible alterations in human consciousness still evokes many misguided ideas and unfortunate opinions. Currently, many people are interested in changing consciousness, extending consciousness, or even "getting high" without considering what changing consciousness *might mean* or what the significance of any change in consciousness might be.

Others reject the idea of alterations in consciousness immediately. For them, a true and agreed-on "common sense" reality exists, and anyone deviating from their version of the external reality is either foolish or "insane." Our ideas, in fact, about the nature of mental disturbances have more than a little to do with our ordinary concept of consciousness. If an agreed-on and unchanging external reality exists, then anyone whose experience differs would be deviant and could justifiably be ignored, or even suppressed.

Yet, we have just reviewed evidence that demonstrates that our "normal" consciousness is not stable and is not unitary at all. Both the mode and the contents of ordinary consciousness alter radically due to situational factors like hunger and other needs, and to more enduring factors such as a person's language, training, and profession. There is, then, *no* stable and fixed "normal" consciousness from which all other "states" depart. Instead we should consider the differing continua of experience that vary on one scale of arousal from sleep to full awakening, on another scale from linearity to simultaneity, and also from internal control to external—as the day slowly alters from darkness, to dawn, to brilliance, to dusk, and to dark again. It is because of the complexity of our own individual experience that such confusions occur and that there is so little scientific agreement or progress in the study of alterations in consciousness.

It is not impossible, as we have seen, to dramatically "alter" consciousness. Those who do so may be at times unclear or confused about what is occurring, but they are not automatically "insane."

To the scientific-minded psychologist, the question of alterations in consciousness calls forth the fundamental difficulties of the study of private experience, difficulties that have restricted the study of consciousness.

Training in scientific knowledge includes special ways of formulating conceptions, proper methodology, and communication. The fundamental tenets of science are that observations be made as honestly and rigorously as possible, with repeatable methods, and that these observations be communicated so that the same phenomena can be observed by other people. This is a small problem if we are interested in observing the effect of sunlight on the growth of plants or of a new hormone on the organ systems of a laboratory animal. Although it might well take a few years to learn to read such a report (in, say, a technical journal) the operations and the phenomena remain available to those interested and willing to commit the time and funds. Even at the twin outer reaches of contemporary physics—the analysis of the subatomic building blocks of matter and the study of the expansion of the universe—the same phenomena are publicly available to those who are interested—although after years of specialized training, of course.

Yet, in the scientific analysis of the psychology of consciousness—both "normal" and "altered"—the situation differs fundamentally. *I, or any other investigator, can never have the same access to your consciousness as do you.* A person's consciousness is not publicly available. We are, of course (most of the time!) personally pleased that others do not have the same access to our experience as do we, but to scientists of consciousness this is cause for dismay. Since the fundamental data are not publicly available, two research strategies are employed.

The first is to attempt to analyze the contents of one's own direct experience, since the researcher is the only possible source of evidence for his or her private experience. This method, controlled systematic introspection, was used in psychology at its outset but did not yield much useful research evidence, since the observers rarely could agree on the contents of their consciousness. It also seems that with this approach too little attention is given to the problems of bias, needs, training, and individual differences.

The assumption that a verbal report can adequately index consciousness has additional difficulties. Ordinarily when we are interested in assessing whether a friend is "conscious" of something, our efforts to discover his or her experience are almost always verbal. We might ask, Did you see that? or Did you hear that? or Do you know that? or a similar question. If a person replies negatively, we ordinarily assume that he or she was not "conscious" of the event or is deceiving us. This is, of course, the same difficulty that psychologists and philosophers have had in restricting their analysis of consciousness to what is termed *verbal report*—people may experience something, yet this experience may not translate well into a verbal report. One cannot, then, invariably reduce consciousness to what can be expressed verbally.

It is rarely reported, though, that the esoteric psychologists attempt to analyze the content of experience in a similar way: there are striking similarities between Titchener's introspection procedures and the practices of classic Zen meditation. In both, for instance, one is instructed not to confuse the experience percept with the inferred external occurrence. In introspectionist terms this is a *stimulus error*; in Zen, it is *conceptualizing*, rather than experiencing. The attempt in esoteric tradition has been to circumvent, or at least reduce, the biases and distractions of personal experience through procedures that undo or countermand these transient effects.

The second major approach to the study of alterations in consciousness, and to psychology in general, has been to focus attention on secondary phenomena, on publicly observable events such as speech, behavior, or physiological processes.

Other scientists have suggested that since external *behavior* is publicly observable, psychology might well focus on it. Although this approach does not *necessarily* limit the scope of psychological inquiry, in practice this has been the case. The *"empty organism"* approach fostered by behaviorism tended to ignore the existence of consciousness, to direct inquiry away from it, and to reduce direct experience to its indicators.

In order to provide a more sensitive index of alterations in consciousness, some psychologists have turned to the study of ongoing physiological processes. This approach has the advantage of providing a continuous record of biological functions that correlate with, and may underlie, certain processes directly related to consciousness, such as brain waves. The dual structure of the cerebrum, for instance, tells much about the divisions of consciousness. The physiology of the ascending reticular activating system yields information on the nature of arousal and vigilance. The structure, as well as the underlying physiology, has an increasingly important place in the study of alterations of consciousness.

If we record a brain rhythm and check whether its occurrence coincides with a certain experience (which in practice is rather difficult to do), we can use the physiological process as an external indicator of the private experience. Like markers on the road, these indicators are useful but should not be confused with the major focus of interest—that is, consciousness cannot be reduced to these indicators and is more than just the sum total of these physiological processes. The meaning of a written message is not reducible to an analysis of the chemical composition of the ink.

ALTERED STATES OF CONSCIOUSNESS

Consciousness alteration techniques have been available for millennia—from the time of ancient Egypt, through the use of coffee in the Middle Ages, to our current preoccupation. Indeed, this preoccupation seems almost paramount of late—an interest in "consciousness" seems almost always to indicate an interest in "altered states of consciousness."

The idea of discrete "altered states of consciousness" is valid within a limited range, for instance, a comparison between deep sleep and wakefulness. But since ordinary consciousness is *continuously in alteration*, the idea of numerous discrete "states" of awareness is probably not productive as a scientific concept, much as the idea of an objective, discrete time existing independently of the organism proved less useful than the idea of a *time as experienced* that undergoes many alterations within each person.* Indeed, the concept of a "new state of consciousness" seems less useful to researchers than it is to promoters; for example, the new "altered state" the devotees of transcendental meditation claim to have discovered in their analysis of meditation. They point to the meditator's decreased sensory responsivity, transient EEG and EMG changes, and decreased oxygen consumption, plus a supposed experience of "transcendence," as evidence of the altered state. Yet, these data are more appropriately described in objective terms, without the label of "state." This label is merely a construct in Bruner's sense, a convenient device for identifying an experience or a cluster of experiences, but a label that may persist at the expense of accuracy.

Nonetheless, major alterations in consciousness do occur and should not be ignored due to the problems of studying them. In this

*See Chapter 5 for a full discussion of time.

chapter we consider four areas of consciousness alteration: the first, and most important, the major variation we all experience as we sleep and dream. The others are examples of transient alterations in consciousness: alterations by other people, in hypnosis; by pharmacological means, with drugs; and by sensory isolation.

MAJOR ALTERATIONS IN CONSCIOUSNESS

Dreams

Each night we sleep, and occasionally, some of us remember our dreams. But do we all dream? Are our dreams similar each night? If it is difficult to know another's waking experience, how can we know even when another person is dreaming. In dreams we lose even the common indicators of speech and action. Until recently we have had to rely on the word of the dreamer—as experience was remembered. If he or she reported dreaming, who was to contradict this report?

Since dreams have always been considered of great importance and significance, their inaccessibility to others has been a great problem. The Bible contains several instances of prophetic dream interpretation, as in the story of Joseph and the grain. When Francis of Assisi visited the Pope to convince him of his genuineness, he was at first rebuffed, until the Pope dreamt of a sign that made him believe Francis. For the most part, however, people seem to dream about objects and events in their lives. Local culture, local events and happenings seem to be part of most dreamers' experience. One's culture and language, as well as objects, seem to shape one's dreams.

Sigmund Freud held that dreams are "the royal road to the unconscious," a direct link to subterranean thought processes—"repressed" desires or hostilities. He felt that an analysis of dream content would enable a person to consider these aspects of the self in full consciousness. His "psycho-analysis" consisted in part of attempts to analyze the contents of dreaming sleep. Whether this "therapy" actually aided people or whether it only allowed them the opportunity to discuss items and ideas not usually discussed, there is no doubt that Freud and his followers did much to focus the attention of psychiatrists on dreaming.[2]

Yet, why do we dream, and what occurs when we do? It is the consensus of investigators that sleeping and dreaming are part of a process evolved to aid the survival of mammals during the night, although we are not actually attending to the environment. If, sometime, you spend an evening alone outdoors, far from civilization, you will soon note that devoid of cultural trappings people are almost helpless at night. Strange and unexplained movements, noises, and animals take on a threatening aura. We might imagine that it would be best to remain as still and as quiet as possible. Sleep enables us to do this at the time of our maximum vulnerability.

Yet until recently, what happens to our consciousness and physiology during sleep has been a mystery. Is sleep a state of complete relaxation that banishes fatigue? Recent physiological and psychological research indicates quite the opposite—that sleep is a very active state.

In studies conducted at the sleep lab of the University of Chicago in the early 1950s, Aserinsky and Kleitman noticed that sleepers regularly moved their eyes at discrete periods during the night.[3] If sleepers were awakened during these "rapid eye movements," they almost unanimously reported dreaming. With more precise investigation, Aserinsky, Kleitman, Dement, and others determined that these rapid eye movement (REM) periods almost always signified dreaming. These REMs offered a converging index of the internal occurrence of dreams. With this index, many complex questions could be studied. Does everyone dream? All the subjects who have slept in the lab, even those who did not report dreams, have had REM periods regularly throughout the night and when awakened during or immediately after a REM period, described a dream (even though they may not have remembered it in the morning). More important, the REM period also demarcates significant changes in EEG and motor activity that occur in phase throughout the night. At first it was thought that we only dream during rapid-eye-movement sleep, but there have been reports of significant amounts of mental experiences within the other sleep stages, yet they are not as strong as those that occur during REM. Physiologically, though, the REM state is unique: although the eyes move, all other motor output to the limbs is prevented from reaching its destination. If this did not occur, we would all be sleepwalkers, following imaginary objects around!

Figure 4-1 Sleep stages are studied by placing electrodes on the skull, near the eyes, and over the heart and recording the subject's brain waves, eye movements, and heart activity through the night, as in these photographs from the Dartmouth Sleep Laboratory.

STAGES OF SLEEP

Awake

Stage 1 (descending).

Stage 2

Stage 3

Stage 4

Stage REM

REMs—Left eye

REMs—Right eye

100uv

2 sec.

Figure 4-2 The EEG from waking through the stages of sleep. Note that in REM the EEG shows high-voltage waves, indicating many rapid eye movements, but that otherwise it is similar to that of Stage 1.

Indeed, animals who have brain lesions designed to test this function often behave as if, say, they were chasing another animal, although they are quite asleep.

If we are deprived of dreaming, we tend to have our dreams during the day: first as daydreams, then as hallucinations, then as more extreme difficulties. "The madman is a waking dreamer," wrote Immanuel Kant.

Sleep and dreams are certainly a most common and yet dramatic alteration of consciousness. Sleeping is almost instantaneous, and dreams are often fully orchestrated, elaborate hallucinations that *each of us experiences every night.* The study of dreams involves a convergent operation, using both self-report and external indicators of private events. It also confirms the motor theory of consciousness, since the contents of dream consciousness are associated with the occurrence of eye movements, and it provides us with our most direct experience of the mode of the night.

Hypnosis

Two hundred years ago Anton Mesmer began his explorations in "animal magnetism," in which he would attempt to influence the course of a person's experience by the transmission of an unknown "force." Although the idea of this sort of "force" is not popular, the phenomena that Mesmer uncovered remain in hypnosis. There is nothing very magical nowadays in hypnotic induction: the person is encouraged to relax and to yield his or her normal volitional control over to another. Not all people are hypnotizable, and a scale of hypnotic suggestibility has been developed.[4]

Is hypnosis a "state" of consciousness, like sleeping or dreaming? Probably not, for if one hypnotizes and instructs a person to behave and experience as if he were alert, then to all outward signs he will appear alert. If one is instructed to relax, then the outward signs and inward experience will be as if relaxed. Hypnosis is not a unitary or consistent state as is dreaming sleep.

The most important aspect of hypnosis research is to indicate that we are far more capable of controlling our experience and physiology than is commonly thought. A study of hypnotized college students found they were able to alter their skin body temperature in the manner of yogis.[5] Pain thresholds are reported to be raised during hypnosis, and memory increased. The hypnotic induction seems to be one of many ways people can allow themselves to explore areas of their consciousness, such as a deep trance or a "mystic experience" that the normal constraints of life do not allow. If hypnotic consciousness is developed within, if it could possibly be integrated into a coherent system and lifestyle, these experiences may have further uses. If not, they remain unconnected, as were those of the king in exile in the story that begins this chapter.

A striking finding was reported recently by Ernest Hilgard of the laboratory of hypnosis research at Stanford University. It is often reported that pain thresholds are lowered through hypnosis, yet for an analysis of consciousness this raises a major question: Is the pain completely inaccessible to consciousness, or, rather, is the pain not attended to as usual? The latter seems the case. In an ingenious procedure Hilgard elicited two different reports of pain experience. The first was done by ordinary verbal means and showed a consistent absence of pain. In the second, a "hidden observer," communicating by automatic writing (or by automatic talking) reported increased pain *at the same time*. This split indicates the large control we possess over consciousness, at least over our criteria for reporting events, although it is necessary for us to devise such a study to see this control.[6] We say, for instance, that we "pay attention."

Hypnosis, like meditation, biofeedback, and systems such as autogenic training, indicates our great potential for conscious regulation, here attained by suggestion. Still, even today most of us do not believe in these capacities. Our perspective is often too similar to the Royal College of Physicians of England in the 1850s, when Esdaile demonstrated hypnotic anesthesia for amputation of a gangrenous limb. After he had performed the operation and the patient was awake and obviously not in pain, the physicians (who possessed no reliable anesthetic) discounted the "anomalous" information in front of them. One reported that Esdaile had hired a "hardened rogue" to undergo the operation for a fee. As we have seen, it is often difficult for people to change their categories of possibility, even in the face of direct evidence.

Sensory Deprivation and Isolation

If the ordinary functions of consciousness are to consider changes in the environment, then the absence of such changes may cause consciousness to alter. For centuries techniques to eliminate awareness of these changes have been known: mystics remove themselves to a cave or to the desert, or they perform repetitive movements or sounds to minimize changes.

Recently these situations have been duplicated in the laboratory in a variety of situations. The isolation rooms may be primarily anechoic, or even hydrohypodynamic, but the purpose is to keep perceived changes to a minimum.

In early experiments in sensory deprivation, subjects reported unusual experiences, temporal disorientation, hallucinations, and extreme psychological pathology. Yet those bizarre results are somewhat dependent on the expectations of the subjects and of the experimenter. Martin Orne and his associates have conducted research in which they vary the preliminary instructions but keep the experiment itself constant. They used a "social isolation" situation in which

Figure 4-3 The subject sensorily isolated by goggles, pads, and other attenuators.

the subject was confined in a normal room (with adequate illumination) for four hours. One group was merely told they were controls, but another was given medical release forms, shown emergency trays, and given other indications that the situation might be perilous. The latter group reported more restlessness and dullness and minor effects of disorientation.[7]

More recently researchers have found the "disorienting" effects of sensory deprivation and isolation to be potentially beneficial.[8] Sensory isolation has been used for relaxation and in smoking-control clinics. The radical shift in the environment may cause consciousness to change in line with expectations. There may be both pathology and benefit in boredom, depending to a large degree on what we expect from it, and more generally, on what we expect from any alteration in consciousness.

DRUG-INDUCED ALTERATIONS IN CONSCIOUSNESS

One of the most popular means of inducing alterations is through the ingestion of drugs. The effects of drugs are not only pharmacological but also social. Drugs can also express one's desire for change, both in oneself and in society. But, the benefits of taking drugs may pass if they are unsupported by the perspective and context provided in, say, the esoteric traditions, and the drug's negative aspects may be quite great, in terms of both physiology and psychology. The most popular drugs used in our culture are coffee, tobacco, and alcohol, with marijuana as a recent addition. More exotic and more troublesome to manage in our society are the opiate narcotics such as opium, morphine, and heroin; barbiturate tranquilizers such as phenobarbitol, Librium, and methaqualone; the central stimulants such as the amphetamines; and the "psychedelic" drugs such as mescaline and LSD.

In spite of the dissimilarity of these drugs, most drug taking follows a general pattern, largely one of expectation. In most cases social and recreational drugs are introduced into a culture by an avant-garde minority who are primarily interested in their effects on consciousness. This occurred, for example, with the use of coffee in Egypt and in England, with tobacco in the West (after the discovery of its use by Indians), with alcohol, with opiates, and with "psychedelics." As Brecher points out in an excellent review in *Licit and Illicit*

Drugs, the pattern is similar: The drug is first confiscated and condemned but finally co-opted by the culture.[9] Most Americans do not realize, for instance, that nicotine withdrawal, as Brecher documents, is as difficult as heroin withdrawal, and perhaps as dangerous. Yet heroin is quite illicit; cigarettes are readily available. The user of heroin must, therefore, traffic in the underworld, where many other factors influence the use of the drug. The drug may be impure and of an uncontrolled dosage; the supply may be unreliable and often unsanitary. The user may have little or no means of controlling the dosage. The drug may be quite costly and he or she may be forced to extreme means to obtain the dosage, including criminal means.

Since we are considering these drugs as they are used to *change consciousness*, the social aspects are quite relevant. As these drugs are used, they all take maximum advantage of the placebo effect. Jerome Frank, for instance, points out that with appropriate expectations an emetic drug, which is taken for constipation, will cause constipation.[10] Tobacco can be either a relaxant or a stimulant, depending on the needs of the person. Each drug, of course, has a specific pharmacological action, but the drugs also all share a certain mild cautomatization of experience, in which, like hypnosis, people organize so that consciousness can change.

Sedative Drugs: Alcohol

Alcohol is consumed in vast quantities in most civilized countries and is used socially, recreationally, and medically—as well as for psychological support by some users. It is probably the most severe drug of abuse in our society. Most experts agree that "alcohol addiction, unlike morphine addiction, is utterly destructive to the human mind,"[11] and similarly to the body, through irreversible brain and liver damage. Large proportions of the arrests in the United States are for drunkenness. Still, the drug is used by most without difficulty.

Alcohol is a depressant. Yet, it often produces euphoria in small doses, probably because in small doses it primarily depresses inhibitions. As with other sedatives, alcohol displays a continuum of action, summarized in Figure 4–4.

In certain cultures throughout the world alcohol is employed in religious rituals as a "sacred" drug, although it is also the subject of

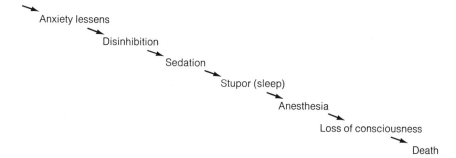

Anxiety lessens

Disinhibition

Sedation

Stupor (sleep)

Anesthesia

Loss of consciousness

Death

Figure 4-4 The continuum of action of alcohol and other sedatives

prohibition. In our society it is such a standard drug that a group of researchers meeting to discuss the problems of drug abuse might well serve martinis and wine at their dinner without a second thought.

Sedative Drugs: Barbiturates

Barbiturates act in the same manner as does alcohol and their effects add to any alcohol ingested, making the combination extremely dangerous. Like alcohol, barbiturates are commonly used in our society, and they can cause both psychological and physiological dependence. These drugs, sold under trademark names, provide an example of the shift from internal to external control of our conscious state. In medical and quasi-medical situations these drugs have become a substitute for training to relax at will. Barbiturates are often introduced as an external tranquilizer. They often act as a placebo; many people, for instance, report relief from stress immediately after the administration of such a drug, even though it has not had time to act.

Stimulants: Caffeine

Coffee and tea are so widely used that it is difficult for us to consider them drugs. But they are, and have been for centuries, employed to change consciousness. These drugs have been considered of such immense value that wars have been fought to ensure their supply. The "lift" and clear thinking they supply were first used by the Sufis of Egypt to enable them to remain awake during rituals. Coffee was later banned in several countries with the same repercussions as our contemporary difficulties with marijuana. The *Encyclopaedia Britannica* quotes an early Arabic writer:

The sale of coffee has been forbidden. The vessels used for this beverage . . . have been broken to pieces. The dealers in coffee have received the bastinado, and have undergone other ill-treatment without even a plausible excuse; they were punished by loss of their money. The husks of the plant . . . have been more than once devoted to the flames, and in several instances persons making use of it . . . have been severely handled.

Again, if a drug is given great attention, and is distributed with great expectations and with appropriate ritual, its effect on us will be great. If the same drug is routinely dispensed by vending machines in polyethylene cups at regular intervals, its effect on our experience will be lessened.

Stimulants: Nicotine

Tobacco was introduced to the West in the sixteenth century, when Columbus found Indians smoking rolled tobacco leaves and inhaling the smoke. Settlers in the New World learned to smoke, and when asked about their "disgusting habit," they replied that they found it impossible to give up. The nicotine in tobacco is physiologically addicting and is the main reason for its continued use. Tobacco is used as either a relaxant or a stimulant, depending on the circumstances. Its use is quite widespread now, and we do not consider its effect a "drug-induced state of consciousness," again, because its use is so common.[12]

Amphetamines

Although caffeine and other drugs are central stimulants, people take the stronger central stimulants, such as amphetamines, in large doses to induce a feeling of well-being, or inject it into their veins for a euphoric "rush." This feeling is the primary motivation for those who use these drugs for consciousness alteration. Central stimulants heighten people's sensitivity to weak stimuli, deautomatize their awareness to some extent, and produce exhilaration for brief periods, but this is often followed by depression. The drawbacks to amphetamine use are due, again, to often extreme dosage and the method of injection, as well as to the social—often criminal—milieu of the drugs' availability.

Opiates

Long used in east and northeast Asia to induce extraordinary, dream-like experiences, the opiates have recently become a major drug in the West. Opium is the basic derivative of the poppy. Morphine, used primarily for pain relief, is stronger than opium, and heroin is, in turn, stronger than morphine. "Street" heroin, however, is diluted to below the strength of opium. People may use this drug for several reasons: they may be introduced to morphine as a pain killer and become addicted to it, they may be part of a subculture where its use is widespread, or they may be new "middle-class" users of a generation not part of the "underground dope scene."

The primary effect of opiate drugs on consciousness seems to be an intoxication euphoria that is especially likely when the drug is injected. However, the drawbacks of these drugs are immense: they are addicting and, much worse, they are illegal in most cases. This illegality often forces the user to enter the world of the "pusher," one in which great sums of money are needed a to supply a habit; this, in turn, may force the user to follow a criminal career. This is undoubtedly the worst social effect of the drug. Most experts agree that heroin in controlled dosages does not cause any major biological damage, as does continual overdose of alcohol or tobacco, and opium addicts can be maintained (as in England) with little or no difficulty.

THE "PSYCHEDELIC" DRUGS

Psychedelic means "mind expanding" or "mind manifesting." This is not a strictly descriptive term but rather is frankly promotional. It is used to describe drugs such as marijuana, LSD, psilocybin, mescaline, and so on. These drugs have attained great popularity in terms of their supposed "mystic" nature and, hence, the promotion. It is by no means clear how they work biologically, especially in the case of

LSD, of which a dose of less than 100 millionths of a gram is likely to have significant psychological effects. People take these drugs exclusively to affect consciousness.

Marijuana is reported to enhance the appreciation of music and other sensory pleasures, to aid in sleep and in relaxation, and to increase appetite. At strong levels of intoxication people get easily sidetracked and forget their thoughts. Its use is spreading in western Europe and America as a replacement for alcohol.

The effect of LSD and similar drugs, such as mescaline, is much more striking; yet, the effect seems quite dependent on the taker's expectations. These drugs are used in developed religious rituals by American Indians, and in undeveloped rituals by people seeking a radical restructuring of consciousness. Albert Hoffman, the discoverer of LSD, had no expectations and thus provides perhaps the clearest recorded summary of the experience:

After 40 minutes, I noted the following symptoms in my laboratory journal: slight giddiness, restlessness, difficulty in concentration, visual disturbances, laughing. . . . Later: I lost all count of time, I noticed with dismay that my environment was undergoing progressive changes. My visual field wavered and everything appeared deformed as in a faulty mirror. Space and time became more and more disorganized and I was overcome by a fear that I was going out of my mind. The worst part of it being that I was clearly aware of my condition. My power of observation was unimpaired. . . . Occasionally, I felt as if I were out of my body. I thought I had died. My ego seemed suspended somewhere in space, from where I saw my dead body lying on the sofa. . . . It was particularly striking how acoustic perceptions, such as the noise of water gushing from a tap or the spoken word, were transformed into optical illusions. I then fell asleep and awakened the next morning somewhat tired but otherwise feeling perfectly well.[13]

These drugs seem to work largely by causing a radical disruption of "normal" consciousness and perhaps unusual randomness of neuronal activity. When this is done, new insights may occasionally result, but they rarely prove of lasting use or significance, since they are brought about quickly and with little of the preparation and surrounding support that can cultivate insight into lasting change.

As with the sultan who became an exile, alterations in consciousness brought about by hypnosis, fasting, drugs, sensory deprivation, or in dreams may fascinate the person who experiences them. To psychologists these alterations indicate that awareness has many more possibilities than is normally thought. To those schooled in esoteric traditions, more expert in these areas, these experiences may be interesting, but the question is whether they are significant for the development of the person's consciousness or are sidetracks.

FOR FURTHER READING

CHARLES TART. "State Specific Sciences." In *States of Consciousness*. New York: Dutton, 1975.

WILLIAM C. DEMENT. *Some Must Watch While Some Must Sleep*. San Francisco: W. H. Freeman, 1974.

ERIKA FROMM and RONALD E. SHOR. *Hypnosis: Research Developments and Perspectives*. Chicago: Aldine, 1972.

EDWARD M. BRECHER. *Licit and Illicit Drugs*. Boston: Little, Brown, 1972. (An excellent overview of the social problem of drugs.)

ROBERT M. JULIEN. *A Primer of Drug Action*. San Francisco: W.H. Freeman, 1975.

CARLOS CASTANEDA. *The Teachings of Don Juan*. Berkeley, Calif.: University of California Press, 1968.

CARLOS CASTANEDA. *A Separate Reality*. New York: Simon & Schuster, 1971.

JOHN ZUBEK. *Sensory Deprivation: Fifteen Years of Research*. New York: Appleton-Century-Crofts, 1969.

5 The Temporal Dimensions of Consciousness

Moment in Time

"What is Fate?" Nasrudin was asked by a scholar.

"An endless succession of intertwined events, each influencing the other."

"That is hardly a satisfactory answer. I believe in cause and effect."

"Very well," said the Mulla, "look at that." He pointed to a procession passing in the street.

"That man is being taken to be hanged. Is that because someone gave him a silver piece and enabled him to buy the knife with which he committed the murder; or because someone saw him do it; or because nobody stopped him?"[1]

ike the scholar in the story, we live our daily lives in a realm of causality, with a past and a future, in the province of the clock. The clock is an embodiment of linearity and sequence. Inside a clock, rotations of a wheel, vibrations of a tuning fork or crystal, or other similarly precise repetitive processes are mechanically translated into movements of an external indicator. These yield seconds, then minutes, then hours, as the movements sum. For any ordinary purpose, the more constant the internal mechanism of the clock the better, for one hour must be defined as the equal of any other in a linear time system, otherwise a consistent sequencing of events could not be maintained. According to the clock, one event follows another, one hour follows another, in a strict unchanging sequence; eight o'clock always follows seven and precedes nine. Spring is followed in time by summer. The consistent linear sequence of time is so much a given part of our ordinary consciousness that it seems a bit strange to examine it; we might even wonder whether time could operate in any other manner.

But consider, for a moment, this normal "sense" of time. Our normal consciousness consists of objects and people, who can only exist in time. Our experiences seem to follow each other linearly, as do the hours of the clock. We notice our friends growing up and growing old "in time." To paraphrase Benjamin Lee Whorf, our experience consists of a stream of duration, which carries us out of the past and into the future. The normal modality is linear; it includes a past, present, and future and consists of a sequence of enduring events, one following another.

This mode of temporal experience forms a basis of our personal and cultural life. The clock of hours, minutes, and seconds allows us to "time" meetings and races, to arrive at the moment when an event such as a lecture is to begin. This linear concept of time allows us to plan for a future, to arrange actions well in advance, to coordinate our individual and social lives with those of others. All in all, it forms an integral part of the sustaining, invisible fabric of normal life and normal consciousness. This mode of time is as much a necessary dimension of ordinary consciousness as is vision. Words must follow a recognizable sequence to make sense; causes must precede effects for science to exist; if 5,000 people are to appear on schedule, the concept *three o'clock next Thursday* must have some real meaning.

Although the linear mode of temporal experience is necessary for the functioning of our daily lives, this mode does not, therefore, exhaust the possibilities. In Chapter Two we noted that the contents of normal consciousness are a personal construction; so now we must consider the possibility that the normal mode of experiencing time is only one particular personal construction of reality. There is nothing sacred about our clock. Many civilizations have existed without the clock as we know it.

The question here is not whether the clock, and the linear, sequential, enduring time that goes with it, are "successful" in terms of survival. They are. Indeed, they have become *necessary* for the functioning of a complex technological society. Nevertheless, other modes of experiencing time are available to us.

Each person, each day, may move in and out of linear and nonlinear modes of experience. Let us resume the metaphor of two modes of consciousness, identified with the day and the night: It is the *daytime* that is governed by the clock and by linearity. The clock is quite important in our jobs, in our studies, in coordination of action. Clock time is an important element in the active mode of consciousness. To perform successful manipulative action, precise and sequential concept of time is very helpful. In work or at school, it is quite important whether we arrive at 9:00 a.m. or 9:17. In the former case we are "on time"; in the latter we are "late."

The precise timing of events underlies scientific inquiry. It necessarily governs any inference we make about causality. The more linear and objective the endeavor, the smaller the basic unit in which sequential time is measured. In scientific inquiry, the second is defined as "1,192,631,700 cycles of the frequency associated with the transition between the two energy levels of the isotope cesium 133."[2] The smallest sequential unit of our ordinary day is a second, unless we are "timing" a race, where we may use a stopwatch to measure hundredths of a second or perhaps employ an even more sophisticated electronic counter. But many other cultures less technically advanced and linearly organized than ours do not break time into such small units. One Indian culture uses the "time to boil rice" as the smallest basic unit. The Trobrianders and the Hopi Indians of the Southwest do not even seem to employ the linear construction. Theirs is a continuous mode of simultaneity and present-centeredness, the mode of the night.

Our *nighttime* existence is less "in time" than our daytime existence. To most people it usually matters much less whether it is 4:00 A.M. or 4:17 A.M. on the clock than whether it is 9:00 A.M. or 9:17 A.M. The night belongs mainly to another mode of consciousness, the mode of the dreamer, in which linearity and sequence are more fluid, as they are reported to be in the world of the Hopi.[3]

The story that begins this chapter contrasts the two major dimensions of temporal experience. One polarity is the analytic mode typified by the scholar, similar to the pedagogue of the last chapter, who seeks a linear explanation for events (such as, "he did this because . . . "). The other pole is represented in this story and in others by our friend Mulla Nasrudin: a holistic perception of events as intertwined entities, each reciprocally influencing the other. The chaos of events can be selected and analyzed into a linear sequence, and valid inferences can well be made from this particular selection and construction—this is the way in which we usually operate, especially in science. But the events can also be viewed and construed simultaneously as a "patterned whole," as the drawing at the beginning of this chapter so clearly indicates, with all action seen at once, and here drawn in one single, connected stroke. This unified perception is a useful graphic portrayal of the mode of consciousness of the *night* in our metaphor, of the *left* in symbol and myth, the cultural mode of the people of the Trobriand Islands. It does not postulate duration, a future or a past, a cause or an effect, but a patterned "timeless" whole.

In reviewing the differences between the modes of operation of the two cerebral hemispheres of the brain, Joseph Bogen observed that one of the most important differences between them is "the extent to which a linear concept of time participates in the ordering of thought."[4] As he and other neuropsychologists have pointed out, our two cerebral hemispheres seem neurologically specialized to process information in two different, complementary modes, the left hemisphere working more linearly than the right. The left hemisphere of the cortex, which subtends language and mathematics, seems to process information primarily in a sequential manner, appropriate to its specialties. The right side of the cortex processes its input more as a "patterned whole," that is, in a more simultaneous manner than does the left. This simultaneous processing is advantageous for "spatial literacy," the integration of diffuse inputs—such as orientation in space, and movement such as dance—when motor, kinesthetic, and visual input must be quickly integrated. This mode of information-processing, too, would seem to underlie an immediate "intuitive," rather than a mediated "intellectual," integration of complex entities.

TIME IN PSYCHOLOGY

In considering time, most psychologists have unfortunately taken for granted that a "real" time, external to our personal and social construction, does exist and that this time is linear. If this were the case, we would possess a physical "sense" of time just as we have a visual "sense." The implicit idea of many of these researchers has been that we therefore perceive an external and real time (identified with the clock) with a special organ of perception.

Even a little reflection will reveal, however, that the clock is not a time "receiver" but a special time *definer*. Nevertheless, linear clock time is so ingrained in our own personal constructions of reality that it has even influenced scientific research paradigms and has thus led to much confusion in psychology. In 1891, Henry Nichols wrote modern psychology's first review of the research performed on time experience, sounding a theme that was to become the *leitmotif* of many later reviews of such work.

Casting an eye backward we can but be struck by the wide variety of explanations offered for the time-mystery. Time has been called an act of mind, or reason, of perception, of intuition, of sense, or memory, of will, of all possible compounds and compositions to be made up of them. It has been deemed a General Sense accompanying all mental content in a manner similar to that conceived of pain and pleasure. It has been assigned a separate, special, disparate sense, to nigh a dozen kinds of "feeling," some familiar, some strangely invented for the difficulty. It has been explained by "relations," by "earmarks," by "signs," by "remnants," by "struggles," and by "strifes," by "luminous trains," by "blocks of specious-present," by "apperception." It has been declared *a priori* innate, intuitive, empirical, mechanical. It has been deduced from within and without, from heaven and from earth, and from several things difficult to imagine as of either.[5]

With a tributary of research ideas so broad, yet so shallow, it was hardly surprising that the mainstream of psychological thought drew less and less from time as a dimension of consciousness. With John Watson's purging of "mentalism" from psychology in the early 1900s, time's tributary almost dried up. The flow of research on consciousness as a whole began to slacken, the work on time even more so.

The reasons why time research has been and remains so scattered and so offensive to an "objectively" minded psychology can be clearly seen. To perform an analysis of the experience of time, one can point neither to an *organ* of consciousness, such as the eye, nor to a physical continuum, such as the wavelength of light, for study by objective methods. There is no immediate physical or physiological point of departure for a scientific analysis of time experience. There is no process in the external world that directly gives rise to time experience, nor is there anything immediately discernible outside ourselves that can apprehend any special "time stimuli." It is therefore not too surprising that psychological research on time as a dimension of consciousness has been so diverse, so incoherent, and so easily forgotten.

Yet some researchers continue to overlook the lack of a time organ, and attempt to approach temporal experience as if it really were a sensory process, as if we had a special time "sense." In ordinary speech we often use the phrase "a good sense of time" to refer to someone who is consistent with respect to the clock, to someone who is "on time." This may be a useful everyday idea, but as a scientific concept it has seriously impeded an understanding of temporal experience.

Even within ordinary experience, time has too many referents to be considered a unitary sense. The novelist Lawrence Durrell cites a few of the many times of experience: "One lies here with time passing and wonders about it. Every sort of time trickling through the hourglass, time immemorial, and for the time being, and time out of mind. The time of the poet, the philosopher, the pregnant woman, the calendar."[6]

The simple confusion of one construction of time with another has caused great difficulties for professional researchers in many disciplines, among them philosophy, biology, psychology, and physics. This confusion stems from the underlying, implicit belief that a "real" linear time exists somewhere outside of man. To take one example, in *The Problem of Time*, Gunn points out that one stumbling block in physics has been the confusion of different time concepts, of physical time with either mathematical or clock time.[7] This mirrors the case within the psychology of consciousness, where the confusion has been between the time of experience and either biological time or the linear time of the clock.

Many psychological experiments have been performed to find out how "accurately" such "real" time is perceived. "Real time" is, of course, identified with the clock. To call the clock "real time" is somewhat like calling American money "real money": it is parochial at best. A useful psychological analysis should be concerned with time as a dimension of consciousness, as it exists in itself, not with how it relates to hours, days, burning rope, a sundial, or some other mode of defining time. It should answer the question, How is linear time constructed?

In considering time as a dimension of consciousness, we must distinguish between the different modes of temporal experience to ensure that we not confuse one mode with another. First, we will briefly consider the general dimensions of linear time: the present, duration, simultaneity, the concept of causality. Then we will undertake a closer analysis of duration, the mode we usually experience, and consider one approach to understanding how this continuing experience is constructed. Finally, after a brief recounting of drug experiences, we will consider other aspects of time experience, especially the nonlinear mode, in which all action is experienced as a "patterned whole."

THE DIMENSIONS OF LINEAR TIME EXPERIENCE

The Present

We continually experience the immediate present passing by, the time that is always *now*. This is the time of our immediate contact with the world, very short, continuously changing, fading away, forever being replaced by a new *now*. William James quotes an anonymous poet: "the moment of which I speak is already far away." In the linear mode, time is directional, a duration carrying us from the past into the future; the present is always fleeting away behind us, as the poet laments. In the nonlinear mode, however, the present exists and is all that exists.

In modern psychological research, the idea of a fleeting, immediate present seems to have held up under some rigorous experimental analyses. Peterson and Peterson, among others, have demonstrated the existence of an immediate memory process, fleeting and decaying quickly, that is distinct from the more permanent memory. George Miller and others have shown that the information-processing capacity of this immediate memory is fixed at a very low amount and is difficult to modify by training.[8]

Duration

The other continuous mode in which we experience linear time is that of duration. This constitutes our normal experience of time passage, of hours lengthening and shortening, of a recent event seeming "a long time ago," of one interval passing more quickly for one person than another or more quickly for the same person at one time than at another. Duration is the continuing, persevering, normal time of our lives. The short, decaying present is continuing but always fading from consciousness. The experience of duration is malleable. One "hour" seems quite long, another brief. Our experience of duration seems to be constructed on the remembrance of things past—retrospection.

It therefore may be that our linear experiences of time are divided along the lines of memory: the present (within these terms) constructed from short-term storage, the past or duration from the contents of long-term memory. There will obviously be a high correlation between these experiences, but since not all experience enters our permanent store, the correlation will not be perfect.

Simultaneity

A less immediate dimension of our consciousness of time is its cultural definition. Our culture is largely linear, scientific, clock oriented. We "break" time into small units, and "time" events precisely. But other cultures do not share this orientation. Some "break" the flow of events into larger chunks of simultaneity, and some dispense with the linear, sequential mode entirely.

When do we experience events as occurring "at the same time"? What is "at the same time"? Henri Bergson pointed out that this experience depends on one's frame of reference, on how finely the "grain" of time experience is divided.[9] The experience depends on the mode of consciousness employed as well. If we take one second as the basic unit, we must construct an experience of what occurred "at the same time" that is quite different from what we would construct if we considered all events within the time needed to boil rice as being "at the same time."

Causality

Causality can be inferred only within a linear mode of temporal consciousness. The information-processing of this mode divides the flow of events into serial lists that can be sequentially analyzed, studied, and manipulated. Succession and duration are the under-pinnings of causality, for without a concept of past and future, of discrete events that follow temporally, it would be impossible to perform scientifically meaningful analyses. In combination with language and mathematics, this linear construction of temporal ex-perience constitutes the essence of the active mode of consciousness.

THE CONSTRUCTION OF DURATION

It is duration, more than any other continuing experience, that un-derlies our lives. We continually experience the passage of time: We move out of the past into the future; we experience one hour passing quickly, another dragging on and on and on and on. Sometimes an entire year will pass with almost no notice, especially as we age; yet some years are so event filled they seem to last forever.

Albert Einstein once jokingly explained, "When you sit with a nice girl for two hours, it seems like two minutes; when you sit on a hot stove for two minutes, it seems like two hours. That's relativity." Many psychologists, ignoring that ordinary temporal experience is personally and relativistically constructed, have searched for an internal organ of duration rooted in one biological process or another. This postulated "organ" has been termed a *biological clock.* Again, this search follows from the "sensory-process" paradigm of how we experience time, used primarily by those who would try to determine the "accuracy" of our time experience in relation to the ordinary clock. Such thinking confuses, once again, a convenient construction with reality. A similar confusion was once displayed by a group of farmers in the Midwest, who opposed the introduction of daylight saving time on the grounds that the extra hour of sunlight would burn the grass.

Much difficulty results from trying to postulate an internal biological clock as the basis of ordinary temporal experience. A multiplicity of physiological processes, such as heart rate and basal metabolism, have been suggested as *the* clock, but many experiments have shown that these processes each seem to move at different rates. No single internal process that could be the biological clock has been found. There are, of course, many internal rhythmic processes that are quite important for consciousness, but these do not necessarily relate to time as it is experienced.

We seem to *construct* our experience of duration from the filtered contents of normal consciousness. When these contents are artificially restricted, as in sensory deprivation, our experience of duration shortens. Conversely, multidimensional, complex experience causes duration experience to lengthen.

That our experience varies is not, of course, a new observation. It has strong antecedents in the work of the relativity-oriented time analysts, in Einstein's little joke, and in the work of the French philosopher Henri Bergson. Bergson noticed that duration is experienced differently by different people and that it might even lengthen or shorten for one person relative to other experiences. The idea of a "sense" of time may be useful in ordinary discussion, when we might wish to compare experience to the clock, to discuss someone who is habitually not "on time," for instance, but as a scientific metaphor it has led to a search for a nonexistent organ of time experience and to an implicit acceptance of a linear real time as existing independently of our consciousness.

We can replace the "time sense" metaphor with a "construction of time" similar to our understanding of how the rest of normal consciousness is constructed. Temporal experience can then be studied without necessarily being tied to any process external to consciousness, be it a biological, chemical, or ordinary mechanical clock.

The Storage-Size Metaphor

To begin thinking about physical memories, consider the computer. If we put information into a computer and instruct it to store that information in a certain way, we can count the number of spaces in its memory that it uses to store that information. We can then relate our constructed experience of the duration of a given interval to the amount of information we remember about that interval. If more events, or more complex events, occur in that interval, the experience of duration should lengthen.[10]

The more we experience and remember about a given situation, the longer our construction of its duration will be. Look at A in Figure 5–1 for thirty seconds, then look at B for the same time. Chances are that your experience of duration was longer for the latter figure, even though you "knew" that the experiences were equal in clock seconds. A piece of music that contains 40 events per minute is experienced as shorter than one with 80 events per minute; the latter is experienced as shorter than one with 120 events per minute. If increasingly complex figures are displayed, such as A and B in Figure 5–1, the experience of duration lengthens, as it will for tapes that contain increasingly complex sequences of sounds. But ultimately it is memory on which we construct linear time. Suppose you go on an interesting vacation. Just before you return home, the period of vacation seems quite long. After you return and become immersed once again in your daily life, the duration of the vacation suddenly seems to collapse. When away, the memory of your experiences is complex: "We went to Waikiki beach, ate in that famous restaurant, listened to Dorman's orchestra, then traveled to another island, stayed here,"

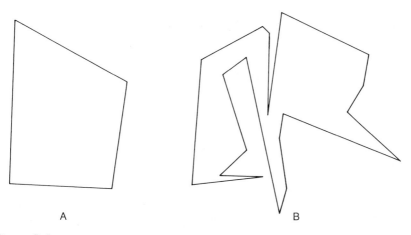

A   B

Figure 5–1

and so on. When you are home again, this complexity collapses; you might code the experience as "I was in Hawaii for two weeks."

The psychologist J. J. Harton studied a similar phenomenon. He found that intervals containing successful events were estimated as shorter than those containing failures. He postulated that a successful experience becomes more organized in memory than a failure.[11] With increasing organization, the storage size of the interval is smaller (as when the code is known) and the duration experience lessens. In one of my own time experiments, the more organized the memory of the shape of a line figure was, the shorter the experience of duration was.

Duration experience, then, is malleable, a personal construction formed from the stored portion of normal experience. If we can understand that "duration" is only one possible way to construct a dimension of ordinary consciousness, not a sensory process reflecting a "real" time existing independently of ourselves, we can make some sense of the vast confusion in psychological research on time and at least open up to consideration other possible ways in which our experience of time might be constructed.

DRUG EXPERIENCES AND TIME: A TRANSITION BETWEEN THE TWO MODES

Certain drugs, such as marijuana, psilocybin, LSD, and the amphetamines, including MDA, may radically alter the "reducing valve" of the normal sensory systems. If the dosage is relatively mild, the great increase in the contents of consciousness may produce an effect similar to increasing the amount of information reaching the person. Smokers of marijuana, for instance, typically report that their experience of duration lengthens during the period of intoxication and also report that they experience "more" during that interval.

But with stronger doses the effect sometimes overwhelms the linear mode of consciousness entirely, and induces a nonlinear mode of experience. Very often this experience cannot be placed in linear coordinates, for it is outside this mode of operation, outside words, outside normal time. The best the verbal-logical mode can do to account for these experiences is to term them *timeless*. These experiences, for many, represent the first significant break from a normal linear consciousness, normal reality, and normal time. For some, the break into a new area of experience is unsupported by the remainder of their lives and their training, and they may not be able to return to normal consciousness. The very discontinuity of these experiences is difficult for many to deal with.[12]

NONLINEAR TIME EXPERIENCE

During each complete day, personal consciousness flows in and out of linearity. Each night we dream and enter a world in which a linear sequence of time has less meaning. Events in the dream space seem fluid. When we recall dreams and try to place them in a linear mode, we often cannot decide whether one event preceded or followed another. At other times, almost randomly, moments that are out of time come to each of us. They are moments in which there is no future, no past, merely an immediate present. Our linear, analytic world is for the moment destructured. These moments naturally do not lend themselves to analysis, for analysis and language itself is based on linearity. Often a word spoken during such a moment will be enough to return the experience to linearity, back into time as we ordinarily know it.

That we now lack a psychological framework for these nonlinear time experiences means not that they should be ignored entirely but that we must develop a suitable structure if we are to incorporate them into contemporary science. One tentative step in that direction might be to regard these "present-centered" moments as shifts toward a right-hemisphere predominance. One approach to this problem could be in the study of the time experience of brain-damaged patients or split-brain people. It has been found, for instance, that left-hemisphere damage interferes with the perception of sequence, while right hemisphere damage does not.[13]

These "timeless" experiences are often produced by psychoactive drugs, which overwhelm the linear construction and allow "an infinite present" to exist. The receptivity and present-centeredness of these experiences are sought in meditation, which also attempts to undo deliberately the "normal" process of constructing consciousness. It is to poets that we must look for any verbal celebration of this mode of time experience. One of the most successful attempts to discuss the indescribable mode of time is found in Burnt Norton, by T.S. Eliot:

Words move, music moves
Only in time; but that which is only living
Can only die. Words, after speech, reach
Into the silence. Only by the form, the pattern,
Can words or music reach
The stillness, as a Chinese jar still
Moves perpetually in its stillness.
Not the stillness of the violin, while the note lasts,
Not that only, but the coexistence,
Or say that the end precedes the beginning,
And the end and the beginning were always there
Before the beginning and after the end.
And all is always now. Words strain,
Crack and sometimes break, under the burden,
Under the tension, slip, slide, perish,
Decay with imprecision, will not stay in place,
Will not stay still. Shrieking voices
Scolding, mocking, or merely chattering,
Always assail them. The Word in the desert
Is most attacked by voices of temptation,
The crying shadow in the funeral dance,
The loud lament of the disconsolate chimera.

The detail of the pattern is movement,
As in the figure of the ten stairs.
Desire itself is movement
Not in itself desirable;
Love is itself unmoving,
Only the cause and the end of movement,
Timeless, and undesiring
Except in the aspect of time
Caught in the form of limitation
Between unbeing and being.
Sudden in a shaft of sunlight
Even while the dust moves
There rises the hidden laughter
Of children in the foliage
Quick now, here, now, always—
Ridiculous the waste sad time
Stretching before and after.[14]

The distinction between these two modes of consciousness is
well-represented in the drawing for "Moment in Time," at the
beginning of this chapter. It depicts a situation that would be a linear
sequence in "normal" consciousness as a unified "patterned whole."

The distinction between the two modes of time is also made in the Zen tradition. We ordinarily view events as sequence. We see a piece of burning wood *become* ashes. But, to the present-centered consciousness:

When firewood becomes ashes it never returns to being firewood.
But we should not take the view that what is latterly ashes was formerly firewood.
What we should understand is that . . . firewood stays at the position of firewood.
There are former and later stages. We do not consider that Winter *becomes* Spring or that Spring *becomes* Summer.[15]

In this mode, all action occurs in an infinite present. There is no attribution of causality or construction of sequence. All events occur simultaneously. Although linear, analytic thought forms the basis for a complex, technological society, other societies have developed around the present-centered mode. It is the conflict between these two modes of consciousness that has caused much cultural and personal misunderstanding. A Westerner may wonder what the Zen monk is talking about when he speaks of "no time" existing. We wonder why a person from India cannot seem to build a bridge on time. Yet this question is relevant only within our particular construction of reality, not in the nonlinear mode, although the ability to switch and to employ each mode in appropriate situations is quite important.

Recall the Trobrianders, a culture that Dorothy Lee reports as based on nonlinearity and on present-centeredness.[16] To take an example similar to that of firewood and ashes: when we ordinarily view the process of the maturation of a plant (for example, a yam), we see a sequence. We experience the *same* yam turning from ripeness to overripeness in sequential time. The Zen monk does not share our view, nor does the Trobriander. The ripe yam (which in the language of the Trobriander is called *taytu*) *remains* a ripe yam. When an overripe yam appears, it is a different entity, not causally or sequentially connected with the ripe yam. It is another entity entirely and is even given another name, *yowana*. There is no temporal connection between events in the world of the Trobriander, in Lee's words, "no tenses, no distinction between past and present." "What we consider a causal relationship in a sequence of connected events is to the Trobriander an ingredient in a patterned whole."

The two modes are personified by the scholar and by Nasrudin in the story: analysis in time is essential to the dominant mode in which consciousness is constructed in modern cultures; a "patterned whole" (or gestalt) and a total present-centeredness is likewise essential to the way in which the Sufi or, in classic practice, the Zen monk constructs his consciousness and seems to be a dominant mode of the people of the Trobriand Islands and of the Hopi Indians of the Southwest.

The temporal dimension is one key in a more complete science of consciousness. The recognition that the linear mode of time is but *one* possible construction brings to consideration other modes of temporal experience, those associated with phenomena outside the range of the normal. For us, an event is considered "paranormal" if it does not fit within the coordinates of ordinary linear time. But if linear time is but one possibility, these unusual events, unusual communications, may in fact occur, even though they cannot be charted in the coordinates of linearity. The laws that govern such experiences may not be those that govern normal consciousness: the experience of the night is not that of the day.

The nonlinear mode is a daily part of the experience of each person. It is deliberately cultivated in "mystical" traditions as a complement to ordinary consciousness. It is sometimes brought about by the administration of consciousness-altering drugs. It is the dominant cultural mode of the Trobriander and of the Hopi Indian. It is a mode associated with the intuitive, holistic side of ourselves.

FOR FURTHER READING

ROBERT E. ORNSTEIN. *On the Experience of Time.* Baltimore: Penguin Books, 1969.

HENRI BERGSON *Time and Free Will.* New York: Harper & Row, 1960.

J. T. FRASER, ed. *The Voices of Time.* New York: George Braziller, 1966.

T. S. ELIOT. *Four Quartets.* New York: Harcourt Brace Jovanovich, 1943.

CARL G. JUNG. "Synchronicity: An Acausal Connecting Principle." In *The Interpretation of Nature and the Psyche.* Bollingen Series LI. New York: Pantheon Books, 1955.

6 The Traditional Esoteric Psychologies

The Value of the Past

Nasrudin was sent by the King to investigate the lore of various kinds of Eastern mystical teachers. They all recounted to him tales of the miracles and the sayings of the founders and great teachers, all long dead, of their schools.

When he returned home, he submitted his report, which contained the single word "Carrots."

He was called upon to explain himself. Nasrudin told the King: "The best part is buried; few know—except the farmer—by the green that there is orange underground; if you don't work for it, it will deteriorate; there are a great many donkeys associated with it."[1]

In our society, those who are intrigued by such questions as how the mind works or the nature of human consciousness or the rules that govern evolution often become psychologists, philosophers, physicians, or psychiatrists. In the cultures of the Middle and Far East, those similarly intrigued by consciousness and the questions that surround it have generally entered the relevant disciplines of their society, such as Sufism, or in previous eras, Hinduism, Buddhism, yoga, and the Islamic form of Sufi study.

These traditional, "esoteric" psychologies emphasize a personal empirical approach to knowledge and so are different both in format and in technique from the Western scientific attempt to achieve an "objective," impersonal knowledge. Until quite recently, the culture of the West has lacked the basic premises that could allow us to appreciate the intent and application of the esoteric traditions, just as our rug seller lacked the constructs necessary to appreciate numbers higher than 100. An impersonal, objective, scientific approach, with its exclusive emphasis on logic and analysis, makes it difficult for most of us even to conceive of a psychology that could be based on the existence of another intuitive, "gestalt" mode of thought. And, like Nasrudin in our story, we may find on acquaintance with these traditions some phenomena of worth mixed in with less useful ideas.

Our preceding analysis of consciousness within the modern framework does, however, allow us to begin consideration of the esoteric psychologies. From modern psychology we learn that our normal, stable consciousness is a somewhat arbitrary personal construction. Although this construction has been a success, it is not the only way in which an external "reality" can be approached. Consciousness changes through the day, is radically different at night, and can be altered by techniques. Scientific knowledge is perhaps the highest development of the linear mode, but the linear mode is only *one* mode possible for us. We find that another major mode of consciousness manifests itself culturally, personally, and physiologically. It is a mode of consciousness that is arational, predominantly spatial rather than temporal, and receptive as opposed to active. Such a mode is difficult to encompass within the linear, verbal terms so dominant in our culture, but it is this mode of knowledge that is predominantly cultivated within the esoteric traditions.

For the first time in our intellectual history, we are now in a position to begin a serious consideration of a psychology that can encompass a "transcendence" of time as we ordinarily know it; consider arational mentation; use exercises for control of the "autonomic" nervous system; develop techniques for entering a state of "void" or "no mind"; and employ procedures for inducing communication that is "paranormal" to ordinary conceptions of what is possible for man. Within esoteric tradition, these experiences are held to be first signposts of a more comprehensive and intuitive knowledge.

Since these experiences are, by their very mode of operation, not readily accessible to causal explanation or even to linguistic exploration, many psychologists and other students of the mind have been tempted to ignore them or even to deny their existence. These traditional psychologies have been relegated to the "esoteric," or even to the "occult," the realm of the mysterious—the word most often employed is *mysticism*. It is the taboo area of inquiry, often symbolized by darkness, the left side of ourselves, the night.

One meaning of *esoteric* is "deeply hidden, inaccessible, needing special training." There is, of course, much esotericism in modern science as well. In the past century, many academics, scholars, and researchers have become exceedingly specialized, with many devoting their careers to the exploration of "one approach to a part of a part of a problem." Many, if not most, psychologists can no longer be fully conversant with all the research currently in the field, since it includes everything from electrochemical analyses of single cells on the retina to demographic analyses of voting patterns.

Inaccessibility, difficulty, and an elitist "professionalism" are accretions that, unfortunately, form around almost every human endeavor. They have formed around the traditional esoteric psychologies as well as around modern scientific psychology. In each area of inquiry, a certain parochialism has tended to creep in. For . instance, a scientific psychologist may be interested in the relationship of consciousness to the brain and may become an electroencephalographer, one who measures the tiny voltages that appear at the scalp and attempts to relate these signs to states of consciousness. In time, his vision may narrow to the complex problems of analysis of the EEG, and his interest may become focused on technique rather than content. A similar narrowing of vision has occurred in psychology as a discipline since the advent of behaviorism.

In the traditional psychologies, one group may find that a certain technique works well in a given situation, be it relaxation, concentration, or movement. Its members may tend to apply the technique in situations where it is inappropriate or with people for whom it is inappropriate. Because the technique works for them, they come to believe that it *ought* to work for everyone at all times. The technique becomes the end and may become an obsession. Those who are involved in using such a technique—whether it is a particular meditation technique, a certain breathing exercise, or a set of awareness training procedures—can become fixated and restricted to what the technique has to offer. The adherents may set up schools to teach the "sacred" ritual, forgetting that each technique has its relevance only for a certain community at a certain time. *Instead of focusing on knowledge or human development, people often become mere adherents of an organization and do not experience the benefits of the technique.* Just as this can happen with any scientific procedure that is overextended or that persists for too long, the original application and intent of the esoteric technique may become lost, although the surface appearance of the enterprise is well maintained. Religious organizations may construct elaborate cathedrals and design robes, just as scientists may well develop elaborate equipment and professional journals, but all too often the enterprise may become limited to a propagation of the means, with the original end, the desired objective, forgotten.

Within either the scientific or esoteric traditions, this sort of parochialism can lead to a disdain for those who employ another procedure, theory, or technique in an attempt to reach the same end. The very word *academic* has come to mean a distinction that has little real significance. Within the esoteric traditions, religious arguments mirror the process. A small stylistic difference in a "sacred" prayer or a meditation may cause a schism that leads to lasting and sometimes violent disagreements. It has even been the cause of major wars.

The disdain is often greater between members of the modern and the traditional esoteric psychologies. Many Westerners see those of the Orient as following a path of self-indulgence, performing useless and ridiculous rituals and withdrawing from life while many starve around them. From the adherents of a ritual form of mysticism often come hysterical attacks on their idea of "materialism" and on the consciousness of Western man as a total "illusion."

Although the mutual antagonism has, at times, bordered on the fanatic, the disdain does mark a certain imbalance in each of the major approaches when they are taken to extremes. On the one hand, many cultures seem unable to feed, clothe, and house their people adequately. They sometimes lack a full measure of the skills needed to organize and coordinate effort. The underdevelopment and undertraining of a linear causal mode of analysis may in some part contribute to these problems. On the other hand, the development of a hyperanalytic, "rational" science, unbalanced by a holistic perspective born of intuition, can proceed, if unchecked, to a point close to self-destruction. This lack of an overall framework or perspective can lead to a certain sterility and irrelevance in the content of scientific inquiry. At worst, science can become the pursuit of technology for its own sake, the performance of experiments simply because they *can* be performed, or the building of a new highway simply because it *can* be built. In both cases, the imbalance contributes somewhat to major cultural problems.

For Western students of psychology and science, it is time to begin a new synthesis, to absorb and transplant some of the concepts and ideas of the traditional psychologies into modern psychological terms, to regain a lost balance. To do this, we must extend the boundaries of inquiry of modern science, *extend our concept of what is possible for man.*

It is the very esotericism of both systems that is an obstacle to this process. The language and procedures of the traditional esoteric psychologies seem difficult to comprehend, let alone practice. There is, too, our own tendency to want conclusive proof at once in our own verbal, logical, and causal terms. If, for instance, a man reports experiences that we consider "paranormal," we naturally want him to perform them in *our* laboratory under *our* strict conditions in *our* time scale. The potential hazards of such impatience can at least be clarified by considering the following example.

Suppose we tell an illiterate peasant from Afghanistan, "Human beings can construct space vehicles that can take you to the distant planets up there in the sky." He may at first simply dismiss the possibility from his mind, then later, if we say it often or compellingly enough, allow it some credence. He may become excited, since this concept is for him a radical extension of the possibilities open to him in his life. He now believes that human beings are capable of building a "magical spaceship."

But we must inform him that to accomplish the task of planetary travel, he must first learn an entirely new language, such as English, and then a new discipline, that of mathematics. After learning the basics of English grammar he will need advanced training in the language. Only then can he study technical manuals. He will also need the cooperation of many other similarly trained people who have interlocking skills and who wish to assist in such a complex project. There is also the question of money, and countless other considerations.

Our peasant knows nothing of this. He cannot see why, if it is indeed *possible*, as we claim, for man to fly to the planets, he cannot do it *now* in his own terms. If we try to be helpful and give him a first book on English in order to allow him to make the necessary first step, he may be either offended or incredulous. "What do these stupid marks on paper have to do with the grandeur of a flight to the planets?" he may ask. If he does not follow our advice, he may attempt to fly to Venus by prayer, or by wooden wings. He may take along some friends who are similarly excited with the idea. When his group fails, he will likely come to believe that space flight is really an impossibility and that anyone who claims it to be possible is simply gullible, "unscientific," or even a liar.

As Western students of psychology, we may need to overcome similar tendencies in ourselves when investigating an area that is so new, so spectacular, and so unknown to us. And the problem for us is indeed great, for there is no other area of human experience, save perhaps sexuality, about which so much garbage has been written. The Sufi poet Rumi noted this process when he wrote, "Counterfeiters exist only because real gold does exist."

We are not about to write off Western science merely because, in some cases, it has committed excesses; so we should not ignore Eastern science because of its imbalances or because of the misinterpretations heaped around it.

The next two chapters of this book are preliminary attempts to consider some of the ideas and the methodologies of the traditional psychologies within a more conventionally Western framework—in hopes that the pace of necessary synthesis may be quickened. These chapters are a bit longer and more discursive than the others in the book, since they introduce areas of inquiry largely unrepresented in contemporary psychology.

FOR FURTHER READING

PHILIP KAPLEAU. *The Three Pillars of Zen.* Boston: Beacon Press, 1967.

WALPOLA RAHULA. *What the Buddha Taught.* Rev. ed. New York: Grove Press, 1974.

FREDRICK SPIEGELBERG. *Spiritual Practices of India.* New York: Citadel Press, 1962.

ARTHUR DEIKMAN. "Deautomatization and the Mystic Experience." *Psychiatry* 29 (1966): 329–43.

All the preceding have been reprinted, in whole or in part, in Robert Ornstein, ed. *The Nature of Human Consciousness.* San Francisco: W.H. Freeman; New York: Viking Press, 1973.

CLAUDIO NARANJO and ROBERT ORNSTEIN. *On the Psychology of Meditation.* New York: Penguin Books, 1977.

7 The Education of the Intuitive Mode

The Blind Men and the Elephant

Beyond Ghor there was a city. All its inhabitants were blind. A king with his entourage arrived nearby; he brought his army and camped in the desert. He had a mighty elephant, which he used in attack and to increase the people's awe.

The populace became anxious to learn about the elephant, and some sightless from among this blind community ran like fools to find it. Since they did not know even the form or shape of the elephant, they groped sightlessly, gathering information by touching some part of it. Each thought that he knew something, because he could feel a part.

When they returned to their fellow citizens, eager groups clustered around them, anxious, misguidedly, to learn the truth from those who were themselves astray. They asked about the form, the shape, of the elephant, and they listened to all they were told.

The man whose hand had reached an ear said: "It is a large, rough thing, wide and broad, like a rug."

One who had felt the trunk said: "I have the real facts about it. It is like a straight and hollow pipe, awful and destructive."

One who had felt its feet and legs said: "It is mighty and firm, like a pillar."

Each had felt one part out of many. Each had perceived it wrongly. No mind knew all: knowledge is not the companion of the blind. All imagined something, something incorrect. The created is not informed about divinity. There is no Way in this science by means of the ordinary intellect.[1]

The "ordinary intellect" works analytically. It operates separately on individual elements of otherwise organized wholes. If the complementary mode of operation is developed, an individual's consciousness is more complete, according to the traditional esoteric psychologies. The story of the blind men and the elephant is often used to convey the differences in these two modes.

The complementary operation of intellect and intuition is hardly restricted to the procedures of the esoteric traditions, although they are specialists in cultivating such working. The physicist Robert Oppenheimer contrasted the modes:

These two ways of thinking, the way of time and history, and the way of eternity and timelessness, are both part of man's efforts to comprehend the world in which he lives. Neither is comprehended in the other nor reducible to it . . . each supplementing the other—neither telling the whole story.[2]

I have been using the metaphor of the light of daytime and the darkness of night to describe the essential difference between these two types of psychology we are considering. The traditional esoteric psychologists are specialists of the "night," having developed procedures for contacting and mastering subtle phenomena masked by the brilliance of the day. The paradigm of contemporary psychology might well be extended to include a recognition that under certain conditions man is potentially sensitive and permeable to often unnoticed sources of information that exist within himself and on earth. A fuller treatment of this possible shift in emphasis is given in Chapter 10, which treats biofeedback training and "states of consciousness," and in Chapter 11, where biological rhythms, gravity, and "paranormal" communication are discussed.

Sometimes the metaphorical distinction between light and darkness can become quite literal. Carlos Castaneda, an American anthropology student, spent several years living in northern Mexico with an Indian shaman. In several extraordinary books, Casteneda records the conflict he experienced between the major modes of consciousness; because of his own highly verbal and analytical nature he found it very difficult to comprehend a more intuitive mode:

I told Don Juan how much I enjoyed the exquisite sensation of talking in the dark. He said that my statement was consistent with my talkative nature; that it was easy for me to like chatting in the darkness because talking was the only thing I could do at that time, while sitting around. I argued that it was more than the mere act of talking that I enjoyed. I said that I relished the soothing warmth of the darkness around us. He asked me what I did at home when it was dark. I said that invariably I would turn on the lights or I would go out into the lighted streets until it was time to go to sleep.

"Oh!" he said incredulously. "I thought you had learned to use the darkness."

"What can you use it for?" I asked.

He said the darkness—and he called it the "darkness of the day"—was the best time to "see." He stressed the word "see" with a peculiar inflection. I wanted to know what he meant by that, but he said it was too late to go into it then.[3]

Since Western intellectual thought is heavily dominated by verbal analysis, the procedures of the traditional esoteric psychologies may seem a bit strange at first, as their function is to train a complementary mode of knowledge. Such a training is primarily concerned with questions that are usually forgotten or ignored within the Western tradition, questions considered unanswerable within linear and scientific terms. These include such personal and primary questions as, What is the meaning of life? What is man? What is the nature of consciousness? Is consciousness individual or cosmic? Indeed, to the strict logical positivist, these questions would have no possible answer, since they cannot be tested experimentally.

Many questions on the meaning of life and other areas may be posed simply and reasonably. But, say the esoteric psychologists, they unfortunately cannot be *answered* in the same manner. *Thus, the procedures of the esoteric psychologies are "incomprehensible" only when we consider that "comprehension" is restricted to the mode of verbal logic.* These exercises and techniques are, then, attempts to consider many questions excluded from science and logical inquiry, attempts carried out intuitively, personally, rather than in formal, intellectual terms.

This point is made in a story of the Sufi tradition. A group of conventional wisemen came to visit Nasrudin's village, and prepared to address the townspeople. As they arrived on stage, Nasrudin— scruffy as usual—clambered up on stage to join them. "Why are you up on stage, Nasrudin?" they asked, somewhat askance at the inelegant figure. "I am here to answer some of the questions that you cannot. Shall we begin with some which baffle *you*, gentlemen?"

The techniques of the esoteric psychologists are intended to augment our normal mode of knowledge. They attempt to provide a tacit means of understanding of one's own self, of one's place in the world. These psychologies aim beyond technique, beyond "states," toward a personal knowledge, so that each person can experience for himself or herself an "answer" to the most primary questions of psychology and philosophy. The procedures of the traditions do not attempt a change in the *contents* of consciousness, but rather in the mode of consciousness.

THE TRADITIONAL ESOTERIC PSYCHOLOGIES: SOME GENERAL REMARKS

Any written account of these psychologies is limited by its very linearity; yet we *can* learn from such an account while granting that it may not be complete, just as a written description of ski lifts, bindings, equipment, and intermediate ski techniques does not substitute for the experience of skiing down the slope.

One distinguishing feature of the traditional psychologies is their practicality, almost what we would now term "applied psychology." These disciplines cover many aspects of life that our Western educational process often omits—*how* to breathe, *how* to care for the body, *how* to master bodily functions usually considered "involuntary." These esoteric traditions approach psychology as a practical, personal discipline and emphasize techniques that effect alterations in body states and in consciousness for the purpose of gathering knowledge that is other than, but additional to, the intellectual.

In esoteric and religious traditions, human life is considered one part of a larger whole, reciprocally influencing and being influenced by the "environment," as in the story "Moment in Time," which begins Chapter 5. The concept of the environment in these esoteric psychologies is also much more inclusive than the Western one. It includes the importance of subtle geophysical forces, for example, the rhythmic changes that daily occur on earth, the light-dark cycle, internal and external biological rhythms, and the effects of microclimatic conditions, such as the ionization of the air. Until quite recently, these forces have not been included within the Western scientific worldview.

However, lest we become immediately carried away with this new and exciting area of research and personal experience, as might our Afghan peasant friend, we should once again note the very serious difficulties that many of the esoteric psychologies have encountered in their own social and cultural areas. The source of their problems has been quite similar to that of contemporary Western psychology. Each system tends to cling to specific techniques whose original purpose has been forgotten. In the traditional esoteric psychologies, for example, a balanced development of intellectuality and intuition is usually sought. Since many who become interested in these traditions are well developed intellectually, the exercises usually stress the development of the receptive, holistic mode. The specific techniques employed for this purpose sometimes come to be considered all-important. Then the intellect may become devalued, cast aside, ignored, in an overreaction against it. This may happen with an individual and even within an entire discipline, leading to an "official" devaluation of the intellect and the preaching of an incomprehensible doctrine. A similar process, although entirely reversed in content, has occurred within contemporary science and has led to an unbalanced development of an "objective" approach. The original aim may become forgotten, but techniques persist.

Let us consider an example of this tendency in esoteric traditions. In some esoteric practices, it has been found useful for *certain people* of a culture different from our own at *certain periods* of their study to renounce sexual practice, largely to remove the biasing effects of their expectations on consciousness. But such "renunciation" has often been extended far beyond these bounds, leading in the Hindu tradition, for instance, to people who withdraw entirely from sexuality and who consequently distort those of the opposite sex as "temptation."

A comic instance of such distortion occurred recently, when a Hindu holy man visited San Francisco. Upon his arrival at the airport, he had to be shielded by his aides, for even seeing a woman was forbidden by his religious practices; he had remained shielded from women for his entire life in India. The television news showed various women's liberation demonstrators attempting to crash through the barricade and stand in front of this exponent of "higher consciousness." Even when the rejection of normal sexuality is not so extreme, many lesser distortions filter through as a result of such an attempt to withdraw from life.

Similarly, the achievement of a transitory state of receptivity and quiescence through meditation may lure the practitioner into withdrawing completely from continuing cultural life, leading him or her to ignore serious personal and social problems, considering them "illusory." Although the corrective to such a withdrawal is often applied within these traditions, it is not often heard. Ustad Hilmi writes: "Traditions about monasticism and isolation are reflections of short-term processes of training or development, monstrously misunderstood and grotesquely elaborated by those who want to stay asleep."[4]

Many other difficulties exist. For example, the virtue of humility is often taken as the "end point" in the esoteric traditions and may even become a moral imperative, but this personal characteristic is to be taken not as an end in itself, but as a *technique*. "It enables a person to function in a certain manner." Similarly, specific diets developed for a certain community at one stage may be promulgated across cultures and epochs—the style may remain but the original context is lost, and the diet remains as an empty ritual.* Dress and other exercises such as dance can also follow this process.

If we can keep a wary eye on the excesses of both types of psychology, we may be able to rid each of their accumulated imbalance and achieve a synthesis of the highest elements in both types, rather than of their accretions. Two main sections follow in this chapter. The first presents for consideration several areas of interest not well represented in Western thought, such as the nature of subtle body energies, the concept of nonattachment, and death as it relates to psychology. The second section is an attempt to present many of the esoteric rituals in terms of training of intuition. The following chapter treats meditation exercises. In both chapters, the stress is on the communality within diversity.

ESOTERIC TRADITION: SOME AREAS OF INTEREST

Physiological Self-Mastery

For many years reports have come from India that yoga adepts can control "involuntary" functions of the body. Since our dominant Western paradigm had, until recently, ruled out the possibility that we can contact these faint internal signals, we have tended to ignore

---

* Not eating meat, or eating only a certain type of meat or vegetable, are examples.

these reports. As we begin to credit, even as a working hypothesis, that such things may be possible, we can examine the evidence more dispassionately. A new branch of research has appeared, which uses contemporary psychophysiological methods in the study of yogic self-regulation.

In a study conducted at the Menninger Foundation by Elmer Green, a yoga master demonstrated his ability to raise the temperature at one point in his hand while simultaneously lowering it at another point. At the end of the experiment, the two points of the hand were eleven degrees apart in temperature. Other recent reports document that yogis can control their blood flow and blood pressure, and can lower their basal metabolic rate by more than 15 percent for hours on end. One yogic exercise, the *shavasana* ("dead man's pose") has been shown to be effective in lowering blood pressure; obviously, this exercise might be very useful in treating hypertension.[5] These experiments, together with the new technology of biofeedback training, indicate that our Western scientific tradition may have grossly underestimated our own capabilities for self-regulation. "Self-knowledge," according to many teachers, is the aim of the esoteric traditions, but in yoga it takes on a most intimate, physiological meaning. The instances cited here hardly begin to indicate the potential of self-regulation for the control of internal states, both psychological and physiological.

The Influence of Body States on Consciousness

Many of the esoteric traditions emphasize the practice of cultivating certain body postures and exercises. Within these traditions more consideration is given to the interrelatedness of consciousness and "the body" than is usual in Western psychology. In yoga, a series of postures (*asanas*) is often included as part of the practice. Breathing exercises are performed in many of the traditions. Fasting is a technique often used to so upset the balance of ordinary awareness that another mode can develop. Ritual movements and dances are performed, such as *tai-chi ch'uan* and the dance of the dervishes.

The Esoteric Concept of Subtle Body Energies

In a realm even further from the usual Western scientific thought is the esoteric concept of subtle "body energies." Most of these esoteric concepts may be merely convenient fictions, metaphors once found to be useful images, which unfortunately have become hardened and concrete with time and translation. However, similar concepts were common in Western science until about the turn of this century. They included the *vital principle* of Hans Driesch and the *élan vital* of Henri Bergson. These ideas, such as *vitalism* in biology, did not prove very useful and were discarded. In everyday discourse, we use these concepts quite loosely. One might say, "I don't have much *energy* today," in the sense of vitality or "life force." The esoteric traditions as they are primarily practical psychologies, have developed this everyday concept and in some cases have refined and perfected the use of these "energies." Consider the following example from the contemporary Japanese discipline of aikido.

Ask a friend to lift you three times. Do not do anything out of the ordinary the first time. On the second lift, think "up," but do not tell your friend that you are doing so. Imagine your "energy" focused just above your head. Actively imagine it flowing upward through your head. On the third lift, think "down." Visualize your legs as part of the earth, and imagine your "energy" flowing downward through the soles of your feet. Do *not* tense your muscles or make any other attempt to help or hinder the lift. Then reverse roles. Lift your friend, but ask him or her to change the order of the three procedures (and not to inform you, of course). You will both easily be able to feel the results of each other's "convenient visualization."

This is a very simple demonstration; no one has yet tried to determine whether any measurable process has actually been altered at a biological level, but something has been changed, even if it is only conceptual, beyond our usual concepts of how our "energy" can operate.

In aikido, this "energy form" is named *ki;* in Chinese it is called *chi.* It forms the basis of the *tai-chi ch'uan* exercise, a rhythmic series of movements intended to balance the "flow of *chi* energy" throughout the body. A similar attempt at "energy direction" underlies the oriental martial arts, the Japanese karate and judo, and the Chinese kung fu.

The concept of *chi energy* also partially underlies the Chinese technique of acupuncture. The practitioner of this discipline is taught to recognize the points in the body through which the *chi* energy flows. In some cases, needles are inserted in these strategic centers to balance this energy flow. Even if the metaphor of the "energy form" proves to be incorrect, the phenomenon may remain of interest, if only as a cultural vehicle for suggestion: witness the recent experience of travelers and physicians in Chinese hospitals. Now that China is beginning to become more accessible to Western scientific observers, perhaps these techniques can be more fully explored.

The very diverse and sometimes abstruse Indian traditions postulate several types of body energies. *Prana* is closest to the ordinary concept of energy. It is held to be the "life force," the living element in all organic existence. Many of the special yogic breathing exercises (*pranayama*) are said to accumulate it.

A much more extraordinary form of energy in the yogic tradition is named *kundalini*. This form of yoga postulates seven centers (*chakras*) in the body, distributed from the root of the spine to the top of the head. In *kundalini* yoga, the aspirant attempts to concentrate on these centers and to raise the "kundalini energy" through them. This is considered an exceedingly powerful and potentially destructive experience, and many have afterward found it almost impossible to regain normal consciousness. The Arabic fairy tales of a powerful genie locked in a bottle are warnings within these esoteric traditions about an unprepared opening up of energy or capacity.[6]

These *chakras,* or centers in the body, may actually be constructive visualizations or metaphors that have been taken too literally by some adherents. Considering them to be physical centers may be an instance of intuitive knowledge unchecked by intellect. On the other side of the coin, an attempt to identify the *chakras* with physical points of the body's anatomy, such as the endocrine system or autonomic ganglia, may be a very unfortunate confusion of metaphor with physical fact. A similar situation once existed in psychoanalysis, when some actually searched brain structures for the site of the id, ego, and superego. Idries Shah thus writes on the *lataif,* the Sufic system of body centers.

The activation of the special Organs of Perception (lataif) is part of Sufi methodology analogous to, and often confused with, the chakra system of the Yogis. There are important differences. In Yoga the chakras or padmas are conceived as physically located centers in the body, linked by invisible nerves or channels. Yogis generally do not know that these centers are merely concentration points, convenient formulations whose activation is part of a theoretical working hypothesis.[7]

Baraka is the name given to a special energy form within Sufism. The word is sometimes translated as "blessing" or "impalpable grace." The Jewish tradition involves a very similar concept, that of *baruch*, "blessing." The Sufi conception is more developed than many others. The *baraka* is held to be transmitted from individual to individual or from places to individuals—often from teacher to student, if the student is sufficiently advanced in his practice to receive it. This concept is the basis of the medieval tradition, still current in the Middle East, of the master and his apprentices, who learn in the ordinary way and also pick up "something else" from the master's presence.

To the Western sensibility, these ideas on "subtle body energies" seem to border on the archaic or absurd. We relegate such ideas to the realm of magic and superstition, where the vast majority of them may well belong, given the continual tendency toward misinformation and degeneration in esoteric tradition. But that such concepts may *almost* always be safely considered unsophisticated and naive does not necessarily mean that *all* of them can be. Here, one of the teachers of Gurdjieff, a well-known "mystic" of the early twentieth century, discourses on breathing exercises to a Western student.

"I taught Gurdjieff to breathe. I say this and you burst into a flood of hows, whys, and ifs and buts and can I teach you? The answer is 'I can but I will not.'"

"May I ask, Sheikh, why only breathing?"

"Only! Only! Stupid question! More stupid than to have asked why or how. Do you think that to learn to breathe correctly is easy? Does your shallow panting do more than supply your blood with the minimum amount of oxygen needed to keep that portion of your brain that you use alive? One of the functions of correct breathing is to carry the baraka to the farthest recesses of the deep consciousness. Undeveloped men try to use thought or random action to affect the consciousness. Neither of these works, as the dose and the direction and the intensity are not known to them. Only to breathe! Do you know how long it takes before you can be trained to take your first Real breath? Months, even years, and then only when you know what you are aiming for."

"Gurdjieff came to me with a capacity to breathe, and I taught him how to do it and how to breathe with his system, his consciousness, and his entire being. You breathe to sustain your level of existence. Higher man breathes to maintain the breakthrough that he has made into a superior realm of being. Your ignorance, while not surprising, terrifies me. Gurdjieff stayed with me for twenty years. Yes, twenty years! Five months in Erzurum and the remainder of the time in rapport with me wherever he was learning to use his breath. Do you know what can be carried into your consciousness by your breath? Do you know why a Sheikh will breathe on a disciple? Do you know why a Sheikh breathes into the ear of a newly born child? Of course you do not! You put it down to magic, primitive symbols representing life, but the practical reasons, the deadly serious business of nourishing the inner consciousness, passes you by."[8]

And, although this is frankly quite a conceptual leap, we should at least begin to consider the possibility that Western psychological science has overlooked a subtle idea of internal body energies, as the stars may be missed in the brilliance of the daylight. Our current knowledge of these "energies" may be similar to that of physics just before electricity was discovered, explained, and harnessed. At the very least, esoteric traditions offer a set of useful conceptual metaphors for the body that may enable us to function in a more integrated manner and may perhaps introduce new areas of research. These new approaches might allow an extended manner of considering the body in physiology and in medicine. Idries Shah has given this subject some thought. Concerning Indian magicians, he writes

In common with several Western investigators, I have been forced to the conclusion that we must conceive of the existence of some principle, whose harnessing becomes a possibility through the disciplines of the Indian priest-magicians. Occult it may be—since anything which is not understood may be termed occult: it is much more likely that there are forces—perhaps akin to magnetism or electricity, or forms of these—whose functions we do not as yet understand. After all, we know very little of the Nature of electricity or magnetism, even today. We know how to use these forces, and we know what they can do. Yet they were known for centuries before they were harnessed. What places this "occult force" in a slightly different category is the apparent fact of its use through mind control.

On the other hand, it may well be that one day machines will be developed which can control this strange force or power. From personal observation of the trance-like condition of the practitioners, my own feeling is that the greatest barrier preventing the objective study of this power is the lack of scientists prepared to undergo the rigorous training necessary to become adepts.[9]

The Ignoring of Thought

In many writings, traditional psychologists stress that thoughts, the "mind" in the restricted "left-hemisphere" sense, are primarily barriers to entering the other mode of consciousness. Patanjali, the author of the *Yoga Sutras*, defined his discipline: "Yoga is the inhibition of the modifications of the mind." In Zen the intent is to "stop conceptualizing while remaining fully awake." Thoughts and expectations construct and maintain personal consciousness. To alter this construction, say the esoteric psychologists, ordinary thoughts must be placed in abeyance for a while. Thus a function of concentrative meditation is to "turn off" that active verbal mode and, especially, to avoid thinking. Some monks even take "vows" of silence, to further restrict the province of verbal intellect. Certain highly developed and seemingly bizarre exercises are performed to rid the practitioner of a strict reliance on verbal intellectuality. These often involve questions that have no rational solution: the koan exercises of the Zen tradition is one example. In one exercise, the Zen master brandishes a stick over the pupil's head and says fiercely, "If you say this stick is not real, I will strike you with it. If you say this stick is real, I will strike you with it. If you don't say anything, I will strike you with it." What can you *say?*

The anthropologist Castaneda complains to his teacher, Don Juan:

"For years I have truly tried to live in accordance with your teachings," I said. "Obviously I have not done well. How can I do better now?"

"You think and talk too much. You must stop talking to yourself."

"What do you mean?"

"You talk to yourself too much. You're not unique at that. Everyone of us does that. We carry on an internal talk. Think about it. Whenever you are alone, what do you do?"

"I talk to myself."

"What do you talk to yourself about?"

"I don't know; anything, I suppose."

"I'll tell you what we talk to ourselves about. We talk about our world. In fact we maintain our world with our internal talk."

"How do we do that?"

"Whenever we finish talking to ourselves the world is always as it should be. We renew it, we kindle it with life, we uphold it with our paths as we talk to ourselves. Thus we repeat the same choices over and over until the day we die, because we keep on repeating the same internal talk over and over until the day we die.

"A warrior is aware of this and strives to stop his talking. This is the last point you have to know if you want to live like a warrior."

"How can I stop talking to myself?"

"First of all you must use your ears to take some of the burden from your eyes. We have been using our eyes to judge the world since the time we were born. We talk to others and to ourselves mainly about what we see. A warrior is aware of that and listens to the world; he listens to the sounds of the world."[10]

Nonattachment

We create our personal world by thought and expectation, and it is desire, the esoteric psychologists hold, that gives rise to much of thought. As some students in these traditions work on the suspension of thought by meditation, others work on the suspension of desire.

Needs, hopes, and wants are strong biasing factors in personal consciousness. When hungry, we are likely to search out food or even to create food images and smells. Since we continuously "tune out" aspects of the environment that do not suit our needs, we ignore much when in severe need. If hungry, we might not notice the river flowing by, people speaking, or what we are reading. At these moments, we are almost totally concerned with food and construct our world around food.

An attempt at nonattachment to objects and to sensory pleasures is another exercise designed to destructure normal consciousness. There are several different types of such practices, involving either prohibitions on behavior or the cultivation of a psychological state that combines renunciation and nonattachment. In the Judeo-Christian tradition, these practices usually involve behavioral restrictions. Some religious believers are required to abstain from eating meat during Lent. The usual result of this kind of practice is that awareness is focused on the forbidden object. Most people find themselves craving meat, thinking about it, devising substitutes (vegetarian imitations of meat, for instance), looking forward to the end of the period of prohibition.

But according to esoteric traditions, the practice of renunciation is intended to create a psychological state of *cessation*, not enhancement, of desire, and this cessation is not necessarily tied to any change in external behavior. These traditions emphasize that merely abstaining in practice, but still desiring, fantasizing about, or planning to consume the object is worthless—perhaps worse than not giving it up at all.

Renunciation is the process, it is said, of conquering desire, of not requiring or needing anything. The Hindu practices emphasize the cultivation of a psychological state of nonattachment, as well as prohibitions on actual behavior. Many yogis are vegetarian and chaste, and live in poverty. Often yogis withdraw from society and its "temptations" into an *ashram*, in which they live as monks on a simple diet. Christian monasteries often emphasize psychological nonattachment and actual cessation of certain "impure" behaviors—vows of poverty, chastity, solitude—a separation from the culture in order to "purify" oneself.

Classically in the Japanese Zen and currently in the Sufi tradition, both in the East and the West, the emphasis is solely on the psychological state of nonattachment and not on prohibitions in actual practice. Both Zen and Sufism emphasize, as they do in the exercise of self-awareness, that one does as one wishes as long as one is not attached to it.

The difference between this aspect of Sufism and Zen, on the one hand, and much of the yogic and Christian tradition, on the other, is illustrated in advice given to Rafael Lefort, who traveled to the Middle East in search of spiritual teachings:

"Are you prepared to leave the world as you know it and live in a mountain retreat on a very basic diet?" I signified that I was.

"You see," he nodded his head regretfully, "you still feel that to find knowledge you must seek a solitary life away from impure things. This is a primitive attitude and one satisfactory for savages. . . . Can you comprehend the uselessness of abandoning the world for the sake of your selfish development?

"You may need a course," he went on, "at a Sarmoun Center, but that will not mean total abandonment of your mundane worldly activity provided you do not allow it, nay invite it, to corrupt you. If you have enough skill you can actually harness the negative forces to serve you . . . but you must have enough skill."[11]

Zen masters also point out that "worldly" activity can be a perfect vehicle for development, as long as one is free from attachment. Pleasures are legitimate in Zen, provided that one does not "cling." The Sufi admonition is, similarly, "Be *in* the world, but not *of* the world." The attempt here is to dissociate the important aspect of renunciation, the psychological state of nonattachment, from external behavior. This is illustrated by the experience of a student who felt unduly bound to her habit of cigarette smoking. Gurdjieff, who stressed that people are often the "slaves" of their habits, instructed her to give up smoking. On returning to him a year later, she told him triumphantly that she had given up smoking and was no longer a "slave" to her cigarette habit. Gurdjieff smiled and offered her a very expensive Turkish cigarette, indicating it was not the specific behavior but the fact that she had been subject to her habit that was important. Only when she no longer needed to smoke was it permissible to smoke again. Gurdjieff himself kept a quite well known larder stocked with delicacies from all parts of the world.[12]

Yet, why is nonattachment to "worldly" pleasures a major part of the meditative disciplines? One answer can be given in terms of our analysis of ordinary consciousness. Recall that normal consciousness is constructed in light of past experience, expectations, and needs. The esoteric traditions consider that a major barrier to the development of an extended consciousness is that we continuously tune out those aspects of the external environment that do not suit our needs at the moment. A Sufi tale illustrates this general point:

"Two men were sitting in a cafe, and a camel walked past.
"What does that make you think of?" said one.
"Food," said the other.
"Since when are camels used for food?" said the first.
"No, you see, *everything* makes me think of food."[13]

The practice of nonattachment can be considered an additional way to remove the normal restrictions on awareness. If there are no desires, there is less bias at any one moment toward specific "tuning" of perception. Our awareness of the external environment becomes less restricted, less of an interaction, less a function of desire of the moment, and more like a mirror.

There is another function of nonattachment. If, for instance, one *needs* nothing from another person or from the external environment—prestige, attention, food, love—one can exist "for them" as a mirror, like Omar Khayyám, Suzuki Roshi, or Christ. We sometimes reach this state when our needs are satisfied. Many of us observe that the world appears different when we are in love or are a success. It is also commonplace to observe, however, that the sensualist is often the one who becomes the renunciant, a "worldly" man who gives up all for his religion—a Thomas à Becket.

But nonattachment is not a *detachment* from life, as many have assumed. That some have withdrawn from life does not imply that such was the original purpose of this exercise. The process of non-attachment is, rather, an attempt at present-centeredness, an acceptance of sensual pleasure as it comes, without clinging to it. A dervish saying echoes: "When it is time for stillness, stillness; in time of companionship, companionship; at the place of effort, effort. In the time and place of anything, anything."[14]

Death

Many persons deliberately confront death. They may drive a car quickly, race on skis, or climb mountains, all with the purpose of returning full awareness to the immediate moment, in which a false move might well kill. This is another means by which we often attempt to destructure the usual mode of consciousness. There is no time for our incessant internal talk or for any fantasies about the future or regrets about the past when in danger.

Since death is inevitable for everyone, it forms a part of the traditional psychologies. The awareness of one's own death is employed in these traditions in a manner like that of the motorcyclist or the driver of a racing car. This awareness can remove some of the transitory bias from normal consciousness. Many actions, disagreements, petty jealousies, begin to seem trivial and hardly worth pursuing in the face of a personal death. Our own death is something that we usually ignore and are trained to ignore; yet, the writers of the traditional psychologies suggest, its lesson can be taken while we are still alive. Uwais, a contemporary of Mohammed, was asked,

"How do you feel?"
He said, "Like one who has risen in the morning and does not know whether he will be dead in the evening."
The other man said, "But this is the situation of all men."
Uwais said, "Yes, but how many of them *feel* it?"[15]

Within these traditions, the death of an individual is regarded as much less final than is usual within Western society. Here is the poet Rumi:

What Shall I Be?

Again and again I have grown like grass;
I have experienced seven hundred seventy molds.

I died from minerality and became vegetable.
I died from vegetableness and became animal.
I died from animality and became man.
Then why fear disappearance through death?
Next time I shall die
Bringing forth wings and feathers like angels:
After soaring higher than angels—
What you can not imagine. I shall be that.[16]

THE EDUCATION OF INTUITION

Western educational systems concentrate largely on verbal and intellectual training. We do not possess a large-scale training system for the other side, but it is just this training that is the specialty of the esoteric psychologies. They form a complement to most of modern Western education. If we examine some of the techniques and exercises of the esoteric traditions, we find that they generally seem to work in the tacit language of the receptive mode.

In the Chinese *I Ching*, this mode is named *K'un*—"the receptive." In Sufism it is variously called *deep understanding, intuition,* or *direct perception.* In Zen, the word *kensho,* a word for the enlightenment experience, also means "to enter inside," a meaning similar to intuition; *Satori* in Zen is often pictured as a flash of intuition illuminating a dark area.

There are, then, two major ways in which people have approached knowledge about themselves and the nature of life. One, the scientific and logical, employs the steady introduction and accumulation of information; the other, the intuitive, attempts the development of another "organ of perception," as the Sufis term it.

Given even all we have considered here, these practices may still be difficult to fully grasp. Perhaps an analogy can help. Suppose we say to a group of pretechnological people: "There is information available 'in the air,' so to speak, which you normally cannot receive. It is present in this room, on the floor, in the walls, above the ceiling. It exists where you walk, where you sleep, it literally permeates every cell of your body; but you do not yet possess the receptive capabilities to make use of it. If you work with us, you may be able to construct a piece of specially tuned apparatus, and you may then be able to receive these ever-present, subtle, ordinarily unseen signals.

Among other things, there is music, special instruction, and diversion available to you on this new avenue of sensation. You will be able to perceive events in the past and events taking place at this moment at great distance. You can receive this information almost whenever you wish, if you possess the proper sort of receptive capabilities."

Now this sounds like obvious nonsense to most of these people, but to us it is simply a description of television. The TV signals are carried by high frequency electromagnetic radiation; at all moments such radiation is present, in the room in which you read, outside "in the air." Without a proper receiver *it might as well not be present,* for our normal sensory systems cannot receive high-frequency electromagnetic energy directly. But if the proper technology exists, we can tap into a dimension of knowledge almost always available and *already developed.*

We can then begin to comprehend the statement of the traditional psychologists that their teaching is "not for the intellect" and "not for the rational mind." This training is for our tacit, "intuitive" side. The techniques of the traditions work in the tacit language of that mode, including body movement, music, spatial forms, sounds, crafts, dreams, and stories that function as word pictures.

Geometric Forms

The employment of spatial form, the special province of the right hemisphere, plays a large role in esoteric psychology. Often a room or an entire structure will be built in order to affect that mode of consciousness directly in a certain manner. One surviving example is the Alhambra, the Moorish palace in Spain. It is intended to have an effect that is spatial, experiential, and difficult to encompass linearly. More familiarly, we can note the perceptual effects of Gothic cathedrals and churches, and of certain rooms whose structural pattern produces an effect on us.

The student of esoteric psychology is often invited to contemplate specially constructed, two-dimensional geometric patterns, in the Middle Eastern "magic carpets" or in yogic *mandala.* They may serve as the focus of concentrative meditation. Often an apparently simple form will contain many different levels of organization within it. The student may also attempt to see many of these levels of organization at once, as well as the "gestalt" of the figure. One from the Sufi tradition is reproduced in Figure 7-1.

Figure 7-1 A Sufi contemplation object

Crafts

Our usual Western concept of "metaphysical" or "spiritual" training involves abstruse ideas and ritual, including secret initiatory rites and occult symbols. In fact, however, the education of these adepts has been far more concerned with such things as movement in space, visualization, and especially crafts—all in the province of the right hemisphere of the brain.

A student of George Gurdjieff traveled to the Middle East to study the same methods by which Gurdjieff was trained. He found that Gurdjieff studied "mundane" activities, crafts for the most part, in addition to his breathing exercises and reading. He was taught to weave carpets, to do calligraphy, to hammer copper—all activities that we would not normally associate with "mysticism," until we consider that these activities each call on the tacit, spatial, intuitive mode.[17]

Dreams

The way of the esoteric traditions involves mastery over the "involuntary" physiology, as well as over the "unconscious." Each night we dream, but we dream unaware. If we do become aware of a dream, it may be only in passive observation of events. Rarely do we discuss remembered versions of a dream with a friend or with a therapist. We do not usually consider the third of life spent asleep as an opportunity for self-discovery. If we do return from our dreams with an image or a thought, it is personal, shared only infrequently with others. We have no psychological or cultural mechanism for allowing dream consciousness to enrich the remainder of life.

In other cultures, however, techniques have been developed for actively entering the world of the dream. The Senoi of the Malay Peninsula are reported to work with dream consciousness, taming and interweaving it with the fabric of their social life. The interpretation of dreams is a feature of Senoi child education and is part of the shared knowledge of the tribe. It is practiced by ordinary citizens as a feature of their daily lives. The breakfast in the Senoi house is similar to a dream clinic, in the words of Kilton Stewart, "the elder males hearing and analyzing the dreams of their children."[18]

The most intriguing aspect of the Senoi dream work is a technique for actively entering and reshaping the dream while it is still in progress. This technique is taught at the group meetings. If a child dreams of falling, for instance, and is terrorized, the elder may answer with enthusiasm, "This is wonderful. It is one of the best kinds of dreams. Now, where did you fall and what did you discover?" The child may respond that it did not seem so wonderful to him, that he was frightened. The adult informs him that every aspect of the dream world has a purpose beyond his understanding while he is asleep. The child is taught to relax and enjoy himself while dreaming, and to remember that the dream is "the quickest way to get in contact with the powers of the spirit world." A frightful falling dream, then, can be transformed into a flying dream, for instance. The flying is encouraged until the dreamer can return with something of value to the society.

Kilton Stewart reports that the Senoi believe and teach that the dreamer is always in control of the dream and that he should always advance and attack when in danger. The student is taught that the dream is his own property, that he creates his own images. "Bad" or "evil" characters in the dream are considered negative only if one is afraid and retreats from them. They continue to seem fearful as long as the dreamer refuses to come to grips with them. A tiger is often a frightening image to these jungle children, but the authorities tell them, "That tiger is *your* tiger; you can make friends with him in the dream. He can teach you his dances or his games. Play with him until you learn something."

Our information on this technique is currently limited to Stewart's account. He is extremely enthusiastic about the effects of the self-mastery of dreams in the Senoi culture, and perhaps overly optimistic. The technique may never serve the same function in our culture that it does for the Senoi. Even so, the cultivation and mastery of dream consciousness is a possibility that has yet to be fully explored in contemporary psychology. Stewart concludes that some difficulties in modern civilization may have arisen because people in our culture have failed to develop "half their power to think. *Perhaps their most important half* [italics mine]." He reports that the Senoi seem to suffer little in an intellectual comparison with Westerners, although how he determined this is not clear. However, our capacity to solve problems in dreams is certainly undeveloped compared to theirs.

Music and "Magic" Words

Western music is primarily melodic, consisting of temporal patterns of tonal organization. Many Westerners find Indian and Arabic music to be boring, full of monotony. But according to the traditional psychologists, music can be used for special purposes, to communicate in an unusual manner. The contemporary Indian musician Ali Akbar Kahn says, "Real music is not for the mind or for the body, but for the spirit which exists independently of each."

In the music of the Middle and Far East, melody plays a small role. Rather, it is the very *sound* of the music itself, the tonal quality, that is important. (It is this component of music that is associated with the right hemisphere of the brain.)[19] In these esoteric traditions, tones of certain frequencies are held to stimulate parts of the mind that normally go untouched. The *mantra* of yoga and the dervish call, are considered "magic" words. It is often thought that the "special" properties of these words lie in their *meaning*. Actually, the "magic" lies in the *sound* of the words, which are designed to have certain effects on consciousness. Idries Shah comments on the derivation of the very word Sufi:

But acquaintance with Sufis, let alone almost any degree of access to their practices and moral traditions, could easily have resolved any seeming contradiction between the existence of a word and its having no ready etymological derivation. The answer is that the Sufis regard *sounds* of the letters S, U, F (in Arabic, the signs for *soad, wao, fa*), as significant in the same order of use in their effect on human mentation.[20]

Benjamin Lee Whorf, one of the most thoughtful analysts of language, considers the use of the *mantra* in Yoga:

Speech is the best show man puts on. It is his own "act" on the stage of evolution, in which he comes before the cosmic backdrop and really "does his stuff." But we suspect the watching Gods perceive that the order in which his amazing set of tricks build up to a great climax has been stolen—from the Universe!

The idea, entirely unfamiliar to the modern world, that nature and language are inwardly akin, was for ages well-known to various high cultures whose historical continuity on the earth has been enormously longer than that of Western European culture. In India, one aspect of it has been the idea of the *mantram* and of a *mantric art*. On the simplest cultural level, a mantram is merely an incantation of primitive magic, such as the crudest cultures have. In the high culture it may have a different, a very intellectual meaning, dealing with the inner affinity of language and the cosmic order. At a still higher level, it becomes "Mantra Yoga." Therein the mantram becomes a manifold of conscious patterns, contrived to assist the consciousness into the noumenal-pattern world—whereupon it is "in the driver's seat." It can then set the human organism to transmit, control and amplify a thousandfold forces which that organism normally transmits only at unobservably low intensities.

Somewhat analogously, the mathematical formula that enables a physicist to adjust some coils of wire, tinfoil plates, diaphragms, and other quite inert and innocent gadgets into a configuration in which they can project music to a far country puts the physicist's consciousness on a level strange to the untrained man, and makes feasible an adjustment of matter to a very strategic configuration, one which makes possible an unusual manifestation of force. Other formulas make possible the strategic arrangement of magnets and wires in the powerhouse so that, when the magnets (or rather the field of subtle forces, in and around the magnets) are set in motion, force is manifested in the way we call an electric current. We do not think of the designing of a radio station or a power plant as a linguistic process, but it is one nonetheless. The necessary mathematics is a linguistic apparatus, and, without its correct specification of essential patterning, the assembled gadgets would be out of proportion and adjustment, and would remain inert. But the mathematics used in such a case is a specialized formula-language, contrived for making available a specialized type of force manifestation through metallic bodies only, namely, electricity as we today define what we call by that name. The mantric formula-language is specialized in a different way, in order to make available a different type of force manifestation, by repatterning states in the nervous system and glands—or again rather in the subtle "electronic" or "etheric" forces in and around those physical bodies. Those parts of the organism, until such strategic patterning has been effected, are merely "innocent gadgets," as incapable of dynamic power as loose magnets and loose wires, *but in the proper pattern* they are something else again—not to be understood from the properties of the unpatterned parts, and able to amplify and activate latent forces.[21]

Language

The functions of a language in esoteric disciplines are many. First, paradoxically, books are written that announce that this type of teaching is "not to be found completely in books," which either allows our verbal intellect to relax a bit or completely puts off a person who is unwilling even to consider that a consciousness other than the linear and rational could exist. Second, language describes conditions under which certain experiences can take place. In reading a book on sailing, for example, one might obtain a clear idea of the effects of wind currents and angles on hull speed and perhaps where dangerous parts of the coastline are hidden from view, but no one would claim to be an expert sailor who had never been out on the water.

In some very special instances, *language itself* can be the vehicle. Just as the very sound of language can be a primary aspect of communication in *mantra* and in the dervish call, so specially designed situations can contain elements useful for the silent side, encoded in language. Atula Qarmani comments:

How were the texts studied?

By constant reading so that the different levels of meaning should be absorbed gradually. They were not read to be "understood" as you understand the term, but to be absorbed into the very texture of your conscious being and your inner self. In the West the intellectual teaches that you must understand a thing to profit from it. Sufi lore places no reliance upon such a clumsy thing as your superficial ability. The baraka seeps in, often despite you, rather than being forced to wait upon the doorstep until your "intellect" permits it to filter through in an attenuated form.[22]

Oral Literature

In some cultures, especially those of the Middle East, stories or "fairy tales" have several functions. They can both entertain and give pleasure to young children. Often they may contain a useful "moralistic" parable and help to form a common cultural heritage—a shared universe of discourse. They also provide the basis for more advanced instruction later in life.

The logic of these stories is not ordinary: it is more like that of a dream. In the stories, linear time, for instance, has little value. In fairy tales, events occur in, around, before, during, and after each other. Indeed, "magic carpets" which transcend time, exist here. Many symbols in fairy tales, if looked at in terms of the psychology of consciousness, may take on a new meaning. Reflect for a moment on these: a genie locked up in a bottle, whose release may mean destruction; a beautiful and almost unattainable princess imprisoned in a tower; a dragon guarding a precious jewel.

Many books of quite innocent-appearing stories were written to provide a vehicle for the traditional esoteric psychology. Often they have been mistaken for either literal history or trivia. They include *Aesop's Fables*, Greek myths, *The Arabian Nights, Don Quixote*, among very many others.

These stories have recently been given the name *teaching stories,* since their effect is not only to provide pleasure or a useful parable, but also to connect "with a part of the individual which cannot be reached by any other convention," and establish "in him or in her, a means of communication with a nonverbalized truth beyond the customary limitations of our familiar dimensions."[23]

How can these stories work on consciousness and communicate this way? Why are they to be read and reread constantly? To look at it loosely, first consider that we recognize only the familiar. We can hear our name quickly, at lower intensity than most other words. We can recognize an English word more quickly than a random sequence of letters. We see red sixes of hearts much more quickly than red sixes of spades.

The aim, of course, in esoteric tradition is first to sensitize oneself to ideas and information that may be unfamiliar. Teaching stories purposely contain certain specially chosen patterns of events. The repeated reading of the story allows these patterns to become strengthened in the mind of the person reading them. The stories take the mind along unfamiliar and nonlinear paths. Thus it is not necessary to "understand" the stories in the usual intellectual and rational mode. The constant rereading induces consciousness into operating in an unusual manner; it creates patterns of activation or categories that are available in the mind when external events dictate. This practice may allow a person to perceive aspects of reality that are so uncommon and unusual that he or she would not otherwise possess the needed constructs, or "receptive organ." T.S. Eliot wrote, "Only by the form, the pattern, can words or music reach the stillness." It is the genius of this form of literature that intellectual analysis still has a function, although such analysis does not exhaust the story. This literature works on both modes.

These stories are conveyed primarily by oral tradition. It is quite rare at this moment in our culture for one to sit down and listen to stories. Reflect on the obvious differences between reading a piece of literature in the usual way and listening to it. Reading aloud takes longer and allows the events more importance. Listening takes the burden off our eyes and our visual system, and returns balance to the ears, as Don Juan put it. It allows us to "picture" the events in space as they occur. Some of these stories, especially the fairy tales, are illustrated for this very purpose, as are many tales in this book. Finally, listening involves the *sound* of the language, which can communicate to the tonally sensitive areas of the brain through the inflections and higher harmonics of the voice.[24]

The storyteller himself is one of the most important elements in these traditions, using language to make an "end run around the verbal intellect," to affect a mode of consciousness not reached by the normal verbal intellectual apparatus.

These special stories exist in every culture, but like many other esoteric psychological techniques, without some supervision they become altered and degenerate. Sometimes people come to believe that the stories relate literal history; so they must be reformulated for each cultural age by a person or a school sensitive to the many functions that a story can perform. It is currently the work of Idries Shah to reintroduce this material to contemporary Western culture. Shah traveled for many years on several continents, collecting and comparing traditional teaching stories and determining their relevance to Western thinkers.

These stories can be employed in many ways. For instance, they can serve as reflection points, both in terms of "to think about" and "to mirror." Often an action caught in a story forms a pattern that is also present on another level of consciousness, as when an electron-microscope photograph contains the pattern that can be seen in a photograph of a river taken from an airplane or in a picture of the earth seen from a satellite. This is a meaning of the esoteric saying, "As above, so below."

Some stories serve as templates for consciousness, patterns frozen so that we can observe ourselves. In one, Nasrudin is interested in learning to play the lute. He searches out the lute master and asks, "How much do you charge for lessons?" The lute master replies, "Ten gold pieces for the first month, one gold piece for the succeeding months." "Excellent," says Nasrudin. "I shall begin with the second month."[25]

Some quite brief and improbable situations can be simultaneously considered in different ways. Nasrudin was walking on the main street of a town, throwing out bread crumbs. His neighbors asked, "What are you doing, Nasrudin?" "Keeping the tigers away." "There have not been tigers in these parts for hundreds of years." "Exactly, effective, isn't it?"[26] Here Nasrudin is at the same time the fool who performs a superstitious and useless action and a man of traditional psychology whose actions may be incomprehensible to the ordinary.*

In another story, Nasrudin is made a magistrate. During his first case the plaintiff argues so persuasively that he exclaims, "I believe you are right." The clerk of the court begs him to restrain himself, for the defendant had not yet been heard. Nasrudin is so carried away by the eloquence of the defendant that he cries out as soon as the man has finished his evidence, "I believe you are right." The clerk of the court cannot allow this. "Your honor, they cannot both be right." "I believe you are right," says Nasrudin.[27]

This story, like all the other Nasrudin tales, can be considered from several simultaneous viewpoints. First, Nasrudin can represent the aspect of each of us that latches on to any new idea or technique, becomes excited, and maintains its worth to the exclusion of others. When we discover a new person in our lives, a new writer or a new movie star, it seems they can do no wrong. Our older friends and interests are forgotten. In school we may study Greek civilization and decide that the Greeks achieved the ideal way of life; then we study the Romans and feel that *they* achieved the pinnacle of human development, and so on. This same tendency may exist in an entire discipline, for example, in psychology, where an idea, such as be-

---

* There *are* no tigers.

haviorism, may come along, offering a new and useful technique, and we become totally focused on and committed to it, forgetting earlier commitments, interests, and values.

Second, note that Nasrudin is a judge in this story. When we ourselves judge others, we usually are saying in one form or another, "I believe that you are *wrong*." This is evident in close personal relationships, as well as in scientific arguments. Two academics who may have extremely similar educations, ideas, and competences may spend years arguing over a small technical point and miss their numerous essential agreements. Two different churches may exhibit the same tendency. Our education, too, is geared toward finding *differences* between things and trains us to analyze and separate different events as much as possible: "Compare and contrast . . . ." Here Nasrudin is opening up the alternative: emphasize agreement *first*, then perhaps, consider the points of disagreement.

Third, and this recalls the story of the elephant, both the prosecution and the defense may be right *at the same time*, just as the man who says "It is cylindrical and solid" and the man who says "It is long and flexible and emits air" are both correct when one looks at the entire elephant. *From such a more developed perspective, many views that might otherwise seem opposite can be seen as complementary.* In psychology such views might be "consciousness is individual," "consciousness is cosmic," and "we understand immediately, through language," "we understand immediately, through intuition." As scientific and personal knowledge develop, we may gain a measure of perspective and ability to reconcile viewpoints that had once seemed to be opposites.

A very famous Nasrudin story (which we will use again later) opens with a man looking at Nasrudin searching on the ground. "What have you lost, Mulla?" the man asks. "My key," says the Mulla. So they both go down on their knees and look for it. After a time the man asks, "Where exactly did you drop it?" "In my own house." "Then why are you looking here?" "There is more light here than inside my own house."[28] Although this story is intended to be amusing (it has been performed on stage as such), it strikes an obvious superficial moral.

But we can remain with the story a bit and consider some other aspects. Spend a little time with the story yourself, reading it over a few times. Then, close your eyes and imagine yourself frantically searching for something. What are you looking for? Where are you looking? Is there a "lot of light" there? After you have done that, close your eyes once again and contemplate a key. What is your key? Once you have spent some time on the key, say to yourself, "I have lost my key," and see where this takes you. Then spend some time on "My key is in my own house." Note your thoughts.

In addition to the personal associations called up by the story, I offer another, more directly related to the concerns of this book. Two areas of the mind are opposed—the light, or "day," and the dark, or "night." The key is inside the house, in the dark, unexplored area of the house, of the mind, of science. We are normally attracted and a bit dazzled by the light of the day, since it is generally easier to find objects in daylight. *But what we are looking for may simply not be there,* and often we may have to grope around somewhat inelegantly in the dark areas to find it. Once we find what we are looking for in the dark, we can then bring it into the light and create a synthesis of both areas of the mind.

Not all the Sufi stories concern Nasrudin. This is "The Ants and the Pen."

An ant one day strayed across a piece of paper and saw a pen writing in fine, black strokes.

"How wonderful this is," said the ant. "This remarkable thing, with a life of its own, makes squiggles on this beautiful surface, to such an extent and with such energy that it is equal to the efforts of all the ants in the world. And the squiggles which it makes! These resemble ants; not one, but millions, all run together."

He repeated his ideas to another ant, who was equally interested. He praised the powers of observation and reflection of the first ant.

But another ant said: "Profiting, it must be admitted by your efforts, I have observed this strange object. But I have determined that it is not the master of this work. You failed to notice that this pen is attached to certain other objects, which surround it and drive it on its way. These should be considered as the moving factor, and given the credit." Thus were fingers discovered by the ants.

But another ant, after a long time, climbed over the fingers and realized that they made up a hand, which he thoroughly explored, after the manner of ants, by scrambling all over it.

He returned to his fellows: "Ants!" he cried, "I have news of importance for you. Those smaller objects are part of a large one. It is this which gives motion to them."

But then it was discovered that the hand was attached to an arm, and the arm to a body, and that there were feet which did no writing.

The investigations continue. Of the mechanics of the writing, the ants have a fair idea. Of the meaning and intention of the writing, and how it is ultimately controlled, they will not find out by their customary method of investigation. Because they are "literate." [29]

Here the linear, cumulative mode of gathering knowledge is again contrasted with a holistic and tacit mode that can appear only when consciousness is organized differently. This story emphasizes the strengths and limitations of the ordinary mode, and the necessity to operate in a mode appropriate to the kind of knowledge one is seeking. The ants, believing themselves already literate, effectively block themselves from any possible understanding of the meaning of the writing.

To relate this to scientific inquiry, we could attempt to determine, say, a person's voting patterns by examining each cell in his or her body and totaling these chemical and electrophysiological observations in a strictly additive, cumulative manner. This would not only be tedious and expensive but would almost surely not yield an appropriate answer—certainly not before the next election. A more appropriate level of analysis for this situation would be the sociological, rather than the biological. We would then attempt to consider the whole person as he or she exists within the social context, and we would conveniently ignore, for the purposes of this analysis, that he or she is composed of billions of discrete individual cells.

In this higher level of analysis, we would consider factors that are more relevant to the question at hand, such as the income or family status of the person. We would never think of asking, "What is the income of this cell?" In order for the ants in the preceding story to fully understand the nature and meaning of the writing, their *level of analysis itself would have to be expanded*. But, just as the biological and sociological levels of analysis can coexist, so can the personal, individual consciousness coexist with another that is often called *objective* or *cosmic consciousness*. The esoteric practices attempt to suppress temporarily the individual, analytic consciousness (here represented as looking at each cell separately) and to allow the consciousness of the "whole organism" to emerge.

Many have become confused at this point, believing this to be an either-or question—that of the unique existence of one mode or the other. However, the existence of an individual and separate consciousness does not rule out the possibility of the coexistence of another level of organization. Just as the existence of society does not deny the existence of the individual, so the existence in the body of billions of individual cells as separate, discrete, analyzable units does not rule out the existence of an emergent whole person with properties not traceable to a linear combination of cells.

This "higher" level of consciousness is often referred to as the mystic experience—the perception of unity, of "We are all one." This does not mean that we are all *the same thing* and exactly alike, as it is often interpreted. Rather, it means that people are all individual components in an emergent level of organization and that this level of organization may become perceptible in the same way that the cells in a body are individual yet the sum of the cells make up one person.

The shift from the individual, analytic consciousness to a holistic mode, brought about by training our intuitive side, is often referred to by a term that is sometimes translated as "ego death" in esoteric tradition. This shift consists in a breaking down of the constructs that maintain personal consciousness and a transition from this analytic mode to the emergent "gestalt" mode of consciousness.

CONCLUSION

The traditional esoteric psychologies are, in their essence, neither deliberately exotic and incomprehensible nor irrelevant to our concerns. They constitute important new ideas for modern scientific psychology about an area of inquiry and an area of the mind that has largely been ignored and forgotten in contemporary culture and psychology.

Both types of psychology begin from common ground and develop in complementary directions. Both characterize normal consciousness as selective and restrictive, as a personal construction. Modern psychology then proceeds to analyze the accomplishment of this construction. It considers, for instance, the physiology of the eye and the characteristics of transmission of the central nervous system; psychologists perform experiments that demonstrate the effect of biases and conceptions on the contents of personal consciousness.

The traditional esoteric psychologists proceed in another direction, to practical techniques, such as meditation, for circumventing the "reducing value" of normal consciousness, techniques for suspending the normal, analytic, linear mode. More advanced techniques then tune the intuitive mode by working in its own tacit language.

Further development of a modern psychology of consciousness may in large part rest on the integration of these two views—the extended perspective and practical exercises of the traditional psychologies with the technology of the modern—making contemporary psychology more complete once again.

FOR FURTHER READING

RAFAEL LEFORT. *The Teachers of Gurdjieff.* London: Gollancz, 1968.

CARLOS CASTANEDA. *Journey to Ixtlan.* New York: Simon & Schuster, 1973.

CARLOS CASTANEDA. *Tales of Power.* New York: Simon & Schuster, 1974.

The preceding books represent personal encounters of Western students with teachers of the esoteric traditions.

SHUNRYU SUZUKI. *Zen Mind, Beginner's Mind.* New York: John Weatherhill, 1970.

PAUL REPS. *Zen Flesh, Zen Bones.* New York: Doubleday, 1968.

IDRIES SHAH. *The Sufis.* New York: Doubleday, 1971.

IDRIES SHAH. *Tales of the Dervishes.* New York: E.P. Dutton, 1970.

IDRIES SHAH. *The Pleasantries of the Incredible Mulla Nasrudin.* New York: E.P. Dutton, 1971.

IDRIES SHAH. "Contemporary Sufism." In *The Nature of Human Consciousness,* edited by Robert Ornstein. San Francisco: W.H. Freeman; New York: Viking Press, 1973.

L. F. RUSHBROOK WILLIAMS, ed. *Sufi Studies: East and West.* New York: E.P. Dutton, 1973.

KILTON STEWART. "Dream Theory in Malaya." In *Altered States of Consciousness,* edited by Charles T. Tart. New York: Doubleday, 1972.

8 Meditation Exercises

The Man Who Walked on Water

A conventionally minded dervish, from an austerely pious school, was walking one day along a river bank. He was absorbed in concentration on moralistic and scholastic problems, for this was the form which Sufi teaching had taken in the community to which he belonged. He equated emotional religion with the search for ultimate Truth.

Suddenly his thoughts were interrupted by a loud shout: someone was repeating the dervish call. "There is no point in that," he said to himself, "because the man is mispronouncing the syllables. Instead of intoning YA HU, he is saying U YA HU."

Then he realized that he had a duty, as a more careful student, to correct this unfortunate person, who might have no opportunity to be rightly guided, and was therefore probably only doing his best to attune himself to the idea behind the sounds.

So he hired a boat, and made his way to the island in midstream from which the sound appeared to come. There he found a man sitting in a reed hut, dressed in a dervish robe, moving in time to his own repetition of the initiatory phrase. "My friend," said the first dervish, "you are mispronouncing the phrase. It is incumbent on me to tell you this, because there is merit for him who gives and for him who takes advice. This is the way in which you speak it," and he told him.

"Thank you," said the other dervish humbly.

The first dervish entered his boat again, full of satisfaction at having done a good deed. After all, it was said that a man who could repeat the sacred formula correctly could even walk on the waves: something that he had never seen, but had always hoped—for some reason—to be able to achieve.

Now he could hear nothing from the reed hut, but he was sure that his lesson had been well taken. Then he heard a faltering U YA as the second dervish started to repeat the phrase in his old way.

While the first dervish was thinking about this, reflecting on the perversity of humanity and its persistence in error, he suddenly saw a strange sight. From the island, the other dervish was coming toward him, walking on the surface of the water.

Amazed, he stopped rowing. The second dervish walked up to him, and said, "Brother, I am sorry to trouble you, but I have come out to ask you again the standard method of making the repetition you were telling me, because I find it difficult to remember it."[1]

We have considered many questions that arise when one tries to consider the esoteric traditions. In this chapter we focus on meditation. In attempting to understand meditation, the interested student immediately discovers a bizarre and seemingly unconnected variety of techniques. Turkish dervishes spin in a circle. Buddhists concentrate on their breathing. Yogis may gaze at a mandala or at a vase. A person may be asked to contemplate a meaningless phrase, such as "Show me your face before your father and mother met." What do these diverse exercises have in common in terms of their manner of operation and in terms of the experiences that they make possible?

Several aspects of meditation are even more confusing to the interested psychologist. What could be a state of "no mind" or of "mysterious darkness"? People meditate to change consciousness, to bring about what is often called a mystic experience. But how do people describe this experience, and how do the meditation techniques bring it about? Is there any way that these techniques and these experiences can be integrated with a contemporary knowledge of the psychology of consciousness? What relevance do the techniques and the experiences have to contemporary psychology and to individuals? It is these concerns we touch on in this chapter.

Meditation is among the most common and the most highly perfected of the techniques of the traditional psychologies. Such techniques have been employed in almost every culture, from that of ancient Egypt to that of the contemporary Eskimo.

Since they have recently gained some currency within our culture, meditation exercises (and their accompanying psychologies) have aroused much confused repulsion and attraction. In considering meditation, some scholars devalue the entire process as one alien to the Western sensibility, while others are superficially attracted to the trivial and exotic aspects of the technique.

Some of this results from simple misinterpretation. Meditation is often considered to be a form of directed thinking, as when we say "I'll meditate on that," meaning, "I'll think about it, consider it, and come to a conclusion." If meditation is considered an exercise in reason or problem solving, then some of the statements and claims of its Indian and Japanese practitioners seem incomprehensible. When they speak of "thinking of nothing," or of entering a "void" or "nirvana," or of achieving a state of "no mind," the techniques may only call forth disdain in the Western thinker, for how could reason lead to nothingness?[2]

The negative aspects of meditation can become overimportant. For instance, an obsessive overindulgence in these exercises may lead to permanent withdrawal from life, a regression from, and a devaluation of, intellectuality. It is certainly true that, devoid of a proper context, meditation can and has become an empty technique, food for the literal-minded who insist on the "proper" procedure but have forgotten its purpose. And yet it is the attitude and *attention* of the meditator that is important, rather than the specific form of the practice, as is emphasized in the story that begins this chapter.

But the exercises of meditation do not involve reason, and they cannot be understood by means of ordinary logic alone. They are, rather, techniques designed to cultivate a certain mode of operation of the nervous system, at a certain time, within a certain context. *This* is the use of "thinking of nothing."

The other side of our response to the esoteric psychologies is an attraction to the exotic for its own sake. Words like *koan, mantra,* and *karma* spice many conversations these days. The style of dress of the "Indian holy man" is now often adopted by the college student. A diet may be followed out of context, be it kosher or macrobiotic. To this type of mind, the more esoteric and weird the technique, the better.

Some friends of mine recently made a hopeful journey to India. Attracted by the repute of a certain famous guru, they hitchhiked across the United States, found a very inexpensive trans-Atlantic flight, and then traveled overland with great difficulty all the way to the Himalayas in the Indian subcontinent.

Finally, after walking for days and days, they reached the *ashram* (a sort of religious living association) of the guru. After allowing them some time to calm down, the guru saw them. Their hopes were high: perhaps they would receive a mysterious "secret initiation" or maybe even a genuine "magic word." When they had outlined their trek, their difficulties, their expectations, and their hopes, the guru instructed them: "Sit facing the wall, and count your breaths. This is all."

My friends were crestfallen. To have come so far, to have undergone so much, to learn a technique so ordinary! One said later that they "could have learned it at home." But few of them realized that this was the point of the demonstration.

An analysis of any experiential phenomenon in terms of science, here in terms of psychology and physiology, is naturally more limited, more restricted, and drier than the actual experience. When we try to bring any experience within the frame of reference of science, a great deal of its richness and complexity is unfortunately lost in our attempt to gain a measure of precision.

A story in Philip Kapleau's *The Three Pillars of Zen* provides us with a useful point at which to begin a psychological consideration of the practices of meditation.

> The importance of single-mindedness, of bare attention, is illustrated in the following anecdote:
> One day a man of the people said to the Zen master Ikkyu: "Master, will you please write for me some maxims of the highest wisdom?"
> Ikkyu immediately took his brush and wrote the word "Attention."
> "Is that all?" asked the man. "Will you not add something more?"
> Ikkyu then wrote twice running: "Attention. Attention."
> "Well," remarked the man rather irritably, "I really don't see much depth or subtlety in what you have just written."
> Then Ikkyu wrote the same word three times running: "Attention. Attention. Attention."
> Half angered, the man demanded: "What does that word Attention mean anyway?"
> And Ikkyu answered, gently: "Attention means attention."[3]

The concept *meditation* refers to a set of techniques that are the product of a type of psychology that aims at personal rather than intellectual knowledge. As such, the exercises are designed to produce an alteration in consciousness—a shift away from the active, outward-oriented, linear mode and toward the receptive and quiescent mode, and often, a shift from an external focus of attention to an internal one. If this alteration is isolated from the context needed to support it (as when Westerners try meditating), it can be meaningless, or even disruptive. But as a first step in many of the traditional psychologies, meditation is regarded as an extremely important preparation for a more comprehensive personal knowledge. For many, it may also demonstrate experientially that ordinary consciousness is a personal construction and that it can be extended to a new mode of operation.

In terms of one of the continuing metaphors in this book, meditation is a technique for turning down the brilliance of the day, so that ever-present and subtle sources of energy can be perceived within. It constitutes a deliberate attempt to separate oneself for a short period from the flow of daily life and to "turn off" the active mode of normal consciousness in order to enter the complementary mode of "darkness" and receptivity. It is an attempt to inhibit the usual mode of consciousness and to cultivate a second mode that is available to man.

Since reliable information about the various forms of meditation has so far been rather hard to come by in the Western world, we should perhaps first set the background and review some of the general similarities of meditation exercises. Most involve separating the practitioner from daily, ongoing activities. He or she usually sits alone or with a small group in a special place (perhaps constructed) in a naturally isolated area, sometimes near a waterfall. Generally, the meditator attempts to keep all external sources of stimulation to a minimum to avoid being distracted from the object of meditation. This isolation is felt to be especially necessary in modern cities, where the many random sounds, noises, and human voices can be very distracting. In most forms of yoga and Zen, there is emphasis on maintaining a specific posture, the lotus position, in order to keep body movements to a minimum and therefore out of awareness during the meditation period. Traditionally, the straight back is said to lessen the possibility of drowsiness in the reduced-stimulation setting.

General instructions for most beginning meditation exercises are similar: pay attention closely and continuously to the meditation object (say, a vase). This exercise is more difficult than it sounds; most beginners lose awareness of the meditation object quite often. Each time one notices that awareness has shifted away from the object of meditation, one must return the attention to it. In many of the esoteric traditions, each session of meditation lasts about half an hour. In most, although not all, meditation may be practiced twice a day, often in the morning before the day's major work and again in the evening. Beginners usually practice for less time and work up to about half an hour a day. As progress is made, more and more complicated exercises are usually given.

In terms of the psychology of consciousness, there are two general varieties of meditation: those exercises that involve restriction of awareness, focusing of attention on the object of meditation or on the repetition of a word (which Claudio Naranjo terms *concentrative meditation*)[4] and those that involve a deliberate attempt to "open up" awareness of the external environment. In the next section we will consider concentrative meditation; in the section that follows, we will deal with the "opening-up" form.

CONCENTRATIVE MEDITATION

If we review the extraordinary diversity of the techniques of concentrative meditation in different cultures at different times, one general similarity seems to appear: no matter the form or technique, the essence of meditation seems to consist of an attempt to restrict awareness to a single, unchanging source of stimulation for a definite period of time. In many traditions, the successful achievement of this is termed *one-pointedness of mind.*

If the exercise involves vision, the meditator gazes at the object of meditation continuously. If the meditation is auditory, the sound, chant, or prayer is repeated either aloud or silently. If the meditation consists in physical movement, the movement is continuously repeated. In all cases, awareness is focused on the movement or the visual object or the sound.

Classical Buddhist Meditation

In Zen, as a first exercise the student is instructed to count his breaths from one to ten and repeat. When the count is lost, as it will be by beginners, the instructions are that the count should be returned to one and begun again. After he is able to concentrate completely on his breaths, the student then begins a more advanced exercise and focuses attention on the *process* of breathing itself. He thinks about nothing but the movement of the air within himself, the air reaching his nose, going down into the lungs, remaining in the lungs, and finally going out again. This is a convenient way to begin meditating, since breathing is a repetitious, rhythmic, activity that continues whether we will it or not.

In *What the Buddha Taught,* Walpola Rahula gives these instructions:

You breathe in and out all day and night, but you are never mindful of it, you never for a second concentrate your mind on it. Now you are going to do just this. Breathe in and out as usual, without any effort or strain. Now, bring your mind to concentrate on your breathing-in and breathing-out, let your mind watch and observe your breathing in and out; let your mind be aware and vigilant of your breathing in and out. When you breathe, you sometimes take deep breaths, sometimes not. This does not matter at all. Breathe normally and naturally. The only thing is that when you take deep breaths you should be aware of its movements and changes. Forget all other things, your surroundings, your environment; do not raise your eyes and look at anything. Try to do this for five or ten minutes.

At the beginning, you will find it extremely difficult to bring your mind to concentrate on your breathing. You will be astonished how your mind runs away. It does not stay. You begin to think of various things. You hear sounds outside. Your mind is disturbed and distracted. You may be dismayed and disappointed. But if you continue to practice this exercise twice a day, morning and evening, for about five or ten minutes at a time, you will gradually, by and by, begin to concentrate your mind on your breathing. After a certain period you will experience just that split second when your mind is fully concentrated on your breathing, when you will not hear even sounds nearby, when no external world exists for you.[5]

As the student of Rinzai Zen progresses, he or she learns to remain motionless and to sit in the lotus position. As one learns to maintain awareness of the breath successfully, one is given a more advanced meditation exercise: a riddle or a paradox, called a *koan,* to meditate on. To many commentators, at least to those who try to fit it into a linear framework, the koan has been the subject of much misunderstanding and confusion. The question-and-answer routine has seemed to be one for the Marx Brothers. The "question" may be, "Show me your face before your mother and father met." The "answer" may be the student's slapping the questioner in the face. The master "asks" the student, "Move that boat on the lake right now with your mind"; the student stands up, runs over and hits his head against the gong, turns a somersault, and lands in front of the master, "fully enlightened." Since the student "answered" successfully, it is quite clear that the "answers" to the koan are not to be considered logically—as set answers to a rational problem that can be solved by the usual manner of thinking through various rational alternatives and choosing one. In fact, the lack of a rational solution is intended to demonstrate to the practitioner that the solutions in this new mode of experience are not those of the intellect. There is no text in which the meaning of life is to be found.

We might instead consider the koan exercise in the terms of the psychology of consciousness. In these terms, the koan is an extreme and compelling method of forcing intense concentration on one single thought. This is an early koan exercise:

In all seriousness, a monk asked Joshu, "Has the dog Buddha nature or not?" Joshu retorted, "Mu!"

This koan is to be taken not verbally and logically, not as something to be worked through like a problem, but as an extreme exercise in concentration. This is confirmed in instructions given in the lectures of a contemporary Zen master, Yasutani Roshi:

You must concentrate day and night, questioning yourself about Mu through every one of your 360 bones and 84,000 pores . . . what this refers to is your entire being. Let all of you become one mass of doubt and questioning. Concentrate on and penetrate fully into Mu. To penetrate into Mu means to achieve absolute unity with it. How can you achieve this unity? By holding to Mu tenaciously day and night! Do not separate yourself from it under any circumstances! Focus your mind on it constantly. Do not construe Mu as nothingness and do not conceive it in terms of existence or nonexistence. You must not, in other words, think of Mu as a problem involving the existence or nonexistence of Buddha-nature. Then what do you do? You stop speculating and concentrate wholly on Mu—just Mu![6]

Later koan exercises involve other unanswerable questions, such as What is the sound of one hand clapping? and What is the size of the real you? A contemporary Los Angeles Zen master gives, How can I attain enlightenment by driving on the freeway? Because no verbal-logical answer to the question can be found, the koan becomes a useful and demanding focus of attention over a very long period of time. The koan becomes a meditation object, day and night, a constant and compelling focusing of awareness on a single source. The lack of a rational, logical solution forces the student to go through and to discard all verbal associations, all thoughts, all solutions—the left-hemisphere activity usually evoked by a question. He is then forced by the nature of the question itself to approach the condition known as *one-pointedness*—concentrating solely on one thing: the unanswerable koan. It is an attempt actively to destructure the ordinary lineal mode of consciousness.

Focusing attention is helped by the social demands put on the student, by the pressures he imposes on himself to achieve a breakthrough (to solve the koan), by the attitude of his fellow students, and by his interviews (*dokusan*) with the Zen master. In the interviews, the Zen student is often asked to demonstrate his level of understanding by giving an "answer" to the koan. Obviously, the desired answer is not verbal or logical; ideally, it should be nonverbal, nonlineal communication of a more comprehensive understanding and awareness brought about by the *process* of concentrating on the koan. The "correct" answer, which may be only one of many possible ones, seems strange only in terms of logic; it is intended to communicate to the "other" side.

The use of the koan is strongest in the Rinzai school of Zen, which emphasizes sudden alteration of awareness (*satori*) brought about by this extreme concentration on one point over a long period of time while under stress.

Yoga

The practices of yoga are much more varied than those of Zen. Concentrative meditation in yoga is only one part of a totality of activity, each part of which contributes to alterations of consciousness. Many yoga practitioners devote their effort to attempts to regulate consciously many basic "involuntary" physiological processes—blood flow, heart rate, digestive and muscular activity, breathing, and so on. There are many popular and semiscientific reports of yoga masters being buried alive for long periods of time, stopping their blood flow, walking barefoot on hot coals. In an early laboratory study, Anand and his associates found that some yogis could reduce oxygen consumption to levels far below normal.[7]

A common form of yogic meditation practice involves the use of *mantra*. Mantra are often words of significance, such as names of the deity, but for the psychology of consciousness the important element is that the technique uses a word as the focus of awareness, just as the first Zen exercises make use of breathing. The instructions are to repeat the mantram over and over again, either aloud or silently. The mantram is to be kept in awareness to the exclusion of all else; just as in the Zen breathing exercise, when awareness lapses from the object of meditation, in this case the mantram, the attention is to be returned to it. Mantra are sonorous, flowing words, which repeat easily. An example is *Om*. This mantram is chanted aloud in groups or used individually in silent or voiced meditation. Another mantram is *Om mani padme hum*, a smooth, mellifluous chant. Similar mantra have analogous sounds such as *Ayn* or *Hum*, somewhat similar in sound to *Mu* in the first Zen koan.

Quite recently, a form of mantram yoga, transcendental meditation, has become fairly well known in the West, especially in the United States. In this form of meditation, too, the practitioner is given a specific mantram and is instructed to repeat it silently over and over for about half an hour twice a day, in the morning and again in the evening. No special posture is required for the exercise; rather, one is instructed to assume a comfortable posture, such as sitting erect in a chair. The thoughts that arise during the meditation are considered to be of no significance, and as soon as one is aware that one is no longer focused on the mantram, attention is to be returned to it.

The specific mantra used in transcendental meditation are not given publicly, since the devotees of this technique claim that there are special effects of each word, in addition to the general effects of the concentration. But it can be noted here that these mantra are also mellifluous and smooth, including many *m*'s, *y*'s, and vowels, similar to *Om* or the Zen sound *Mu*. The devotees of transcendental meditation also claim that this technique presents the essence of meditation in a form suitable for Westerners.[8]

There is no doubt that mantram yoga, including transcendental meditation, is a very convenient form of a concentrative meditation; it is quite easy to produce and attend to a silent word, anywhere, at any time. Since no special posture is required, the arduous training for sitting in a lotus position is unnecessary. If the essential component of meditation involves concentration on an unchanging stimulus, then transcendental meditation, as well as other forms of mantram yoga, can be said to possess this essence.

Other forms of yoga practice make use of visual meditation techniques. The yogi generally sits in a lotus position and views a specially constructed visual image, a *mandala*. Mandalas take many forms: they may be very simple, like a circle, or extremely complicated, like the yantra of Tantric practice.[9]

Mandalas are used much like mantra. The practitioner focuses his gaze on the mandala and restricts his awareness to the visual input. Any stray thought, association, or feeling that arises is ignored; attention is withheld from the stray thought or association and returned to the mandala. Simple mandalas often employ a circular motif in which awareness is drawn to the center as one continues to contemplate, fixing the gaze more and more closely on the center.

Another visual meditation technique in yoga involves a "steady gaze" (*tratakam*) on external objects. External objects are used in meditation as a focus for a fixed point of concentration, rather than for their physical characteristics; so one can use a stone, a vase, a light, a candle, and so on.[10]

The repetitive processes of the body, such as breathing and the beating of the heart, can serve as similar focuses for concentration in yoga. These techniques are described in Mishra's manual and in many others. Internally generated sounds (*nadam*) can also be focuses for meditation. The sounds used in meditation can be internal, imaginary, or natural. Often the yogi sits near a source of repetitive sound, such as a waterfall, wind source, or beehive and simply listens and concentrates. When these repetitious, monotonous sounds are imagined, the technique becomes quite similar to the silent repetition of a mantram.

The creation of a meditation image can extend to visual meditation as well. Frederic Spiegelberg, in *Spiritual Practices of India*, describes the *Dharana*, or fixation of consciousness procedures, in the *Kasina* exercises:

The point of primary importance is that one should really create such a meditation image to accompany him continuously; only as a secondary consideration does it matter what this particular image may be, that is, through which one of the Kasina exercises it has been produced. Instead of contemplating a disc of earth, for example, one can meditate on an evenly ploughed field seen from a distance.

In the Water Kasina, the yogi concentrates either on the circular surface of water in a jar, or on a lake seen from a mountain. So, too, the fire on the hearth, the flame of a candle, the wind that sways the crests of the trees may also be used as Kasina. The exercise of Color Kasina makes use of round colored discs, and even of bright-colored flags and flowers. In Space Kasina one meditates on a circular window opening, the attention in this case being directed primarily to the dimensional proportions of the opening.

Every image that remains permanently in one's consciousness and every enduring mood can be a help to this fixation of one's consciousness. As a matter of fact, every hallucination, every unappeasable hatred, every amorous attachment provides a certain power of concentration to him who cherishes it, and helps him direct the forces of his being towards a single goal. This is of course more the case with the man who has achieved self-control and freedom from his passions, and who after having mastered his sense impulses succeeds in giving to his consciousness a definite turn of his own choosing. . . . Every activity is of equal value as a basis for a Dharana exercise.[11]

Mudra, another variety of yogic meditation practice, consists of repetitive physical movements, usually of the arms, legs, or fingers. In these exercises, the specified movement of the limbs is repeated over and over in the same way as a mantram. Awareness is continually directed toward the process of making the movements. Mudras vary in complexity; a simple one may involve touching the thumb to the other four fingers in order and repeating this procedure. The mudra may be combined with the mantram. For instance, this fourfold repetitive mudra is often combined with the mantram *Om mani padme hum*, each word corresponding to the thumb's movement to a finger.

The Sufis

Manuals for Sufic practice are not readily available, whereas ones are for yoga and Zen. The Sufis hold that any specific techniques must be administered with the time, place, and state of the student taken into account and that publication of the details of their practices may lead to faulty application of the exercises. They say, for instance, that a technique such as meditation is useful at a specific stage of development and persistence in any technique after the appropriate period would be a waste of time or might even be harmful.

There are, however, fragmentary reports of some Sufic meditation exercises that can be summarized here even though these particular practices were primarily intended to be used in a Moslem culture. Of all the Sufi sects, the Maulavi (whirling) dervishes are perhaps the most familiar to the West. They perform a dance involving spinning and repetition of phrases. George Gurdjieff, who was trained by dervishes, explains the dance of the dervishes as an exercise for the brain based on repetition. Idries Shah writes of these orders: "The so-called dancing dervishes accomplish trance and ecstatic phenomena through monotonous, repetitious circumambulations, and this is marked in the Maulavi order, most popular in Turkey."[12]

The dance of the dervishes involves the repetition of physical movements and, concurrently, sounds. One of the few available first-person descriptions of this dance is found in Roy Weaver Davidson's valuable symposium, *Documents on Contemporary Dervish Communities*. It is an account by Omar Michael Berg, who traveled to a dervish assembly in Tunisia and participated in a dervish dance.

Explanation of the Zikr (repetition). The Dhikr, it was explained to me, is a dance; or, more properly, a performance of a series of exercises in unison. The objective is to produce a state of ritual ecstasy and to accelerate the contact of the Sufi's mind with the world mind, of which he considers himself to be a part. . . . The dance is defined by them as bodily movements linked to a thought and a sound or a series of sounds. The movements develop the body; the thought focuses the mind and the sound fuses the two and orientates them toward a consciousness of divine contact, which is called Hal, meaning "state" or "condition."

Description of the Zikr at Nefta. A double circle is formed in the center of the hall. Dervishes stand while the Sheik intones the opening part of this and every similar ceremony—the calling down of the blessing of the congregation upon the Masters, "past, present and future." Outside the circle stand the Sheik, drummer, and flute player, together with two "callers," men who call the rhythm of the dance. The drum begins to beat, the caller begins to call a high-pitched flamenco-type air, and slowly the concentric circles begin to revolve in opposite directions. Then the sheik calls out, "Ya Haadi!" (O Guide!) and the participants start to repeat this word. They concentrate on it, saying it at first slowly, then faster and faster. Their movements match the repetitions.

I noticed that the eyes of some of the dervishes took on a far-away look, and they started to move jerkily as if they were puppets. The circles moved faster and faster until I (moving in the outer circle) saw only a whirl of robes and lost count of time. Now and then with a grunt or sharp cry, one of the dervishes would drop out of the circle and would be led away by an assistant, to lie on the ground in what seemed to be a hypnotic state. I began to be affected and found that, although I was not dizzy, my mind was functioning in a very strange and unfamiliar way. The sensation is difficult to describe and is probably a complex one. One feeling was that of a lightening; as if I had no anxieties, no problems. Another was that I was a part of this moving circle and that my individuality was gone; I was delightfully merged in something larger.

[He leaves the dance, and later] I went out into the courtyard to assess my feelings; something had happened. In the first place, the moon seemed immensely bright, and the little glowing lamps seemed surrounded by a whole spectrum of colors.[13]

In many cultures the Sufis have employed other forms of concentrative meditation, some of which appear rather similar to those of Zen and yoga. The first line of the Koran is quite often used for verbal repetition.

Having prepared a room which is empty, dark and clean, in which he will, for preference, burn some sweet-scented incense, let him sit there, cross-legged, facing the qibla (direction of Mecca). Laying his hands on his thighs, let him stir up his heart to wakefulness, keeping a guard on his eyes. Then with profound veneration he should say aloud: "La illaha illa'llah." The "La illaha" should be fetched from the roots of the navel, and the "illa'llah" drawn into the heart, so that the powerful effects of the Zikr (dhikr) may make themselves felt in all the limbs and organs. But let him not raise his voice too loud. He should strive, as far as possible, to damp and lower it according to the words "Invoke they Lord in thyself humbly and with compunction, without publicity of speech." . . .

After this fashion, then, he will utter the Zikr frequently and intently, thinking in his heart on the meaning of it and banishing every distraction. When he thinks of "La illaha," he should tell himself: I want nothing, seek nothing, love nothing "illa'llah"—but God. Thus, with "La ilaha" he denies and excludes all competing objects, and with "illa'llah" he affirms and posits the divine Majesty as his sole object loved, sought and aimed at.

In each Zikr his heart should be aware and present (hazir) from start to finish, with denial and affirmation. If he finds in his heart something to which he is attached, let him not regard it but give his attention to the divine Majesty, seeking the grace of help from the holy patronage of his spiritual Father. With the negation "La illaha" let him wipe out that attachment, uprooting the love of that thing from his heart, and with "illa'llah" let him set up in its place the love of Truth (God).[14]

There exist fragmentary descriptions of other exercises used by the Sufis and some of their followers. A student of George Gurdjieff writes of meditating on a series of dots on a piece of paper. The dervishes repeat the phrase "Ya hu" like a yoga mantra or the Zen koan *Mu* and also repeat stories over and over in their minds, as Zen Buddhists do with the koan.

Sufism, however, is not a static or monolithic enterprise. The descriptions of technique are of historical and perhaps psychological interest, but they do not describe a systematic pattern that any contemporary person interested in Sufism will encounter. It should be noted that all Sufis (like all people) are not identical, and a technique offered for one community (such as Turkey in the thirteenth century) may have little or no relevance to another community. This lack of a "fixed system," such as one method of meditation to be applied to everyone, is one reason that Sufi activities are less well understood by scholars and scientists than less sophisticated groupings.

Western Meditation

Similar forms of meditative practices exist in the familiar Western religions as well as in groupings less known than yoga, Zen, and Sufism. In Christianity, for example, the exercise of contemplation performed a function similar to that of meditation in Zen, yoga, and Sufism. Jakob Bohme, the Christian mystic, practiced fixing his gaze on a spot of sunlight on his cobbler's crystal as his object of contemplation throughout the entire day. He then carried this image with him all the time, in the same way, perhaps, that the yogi can construct a yantra at will and observe it. Deikman comments that the Christian mystics Walter Hilton and St. John of the Cross gave instructions for contemplation exercises that were strikingly similar to those of Patanjali, the author of the yoga sutras.

In Hilton one reads, "Therefore if you desire to discover your soul, withdraw your thoughts from outward and material things, forgetting, if possible, your own body and its five senses." St. John calls for the explicit banishment of memory. "Of all these forms and manners of knowledge the soul must strip and void itself and it must strive to lose the imaginary apprehension of them, so that there may be left in it no kind of impression of knowledge, nor trace of thought whatsoever, but rather the soul must remain barren and bare, as if these forms had never passed through it, and in total oblivion and suspension. This cannot happen unless the memory can be annihilated of all its forms, if it is to be united with God. . . ." Patanjali comments, "Binding the mindstuff to a place is fixed attention, focusing the presented idea on that place is contemplation."[15]

Some current practices in the Christian church and in Judaism have some similarities to, and even perhaps their origins in, the practices of meditation. Prayer, in general, is a practice most similar to concentrative meditation. St. John Climacius said: "If many words are used in prayer, all sorts of distracting pictures hover in the mind but worship is lost. If little is said or only a single word pronounced, the mind remains concentrated." The "Russian Pilgrim" said, "If thou wilt that thy prayer be pure, made up of good and lovely things, thou must choose a short one consisting of a few powerful words and repeat it many times."

Many prayers are monotonous, repetitive chants. Judaism makes use of ritual nodding movements and intoned prayers. Hasidism and the Cabalistic tradition contain many elements similar to Sufism, Zen, and yoga, and similarly, the cross and the Star of David appear as contemplation objects in traditions other than the Jewish and Christian; some of the yantras in *Tantra Art*, for instance, contain many six-pointed stars.

Perhaps one reason for today's decline of interest in these more-organized religions is that their original emphasis on direct experiential knowledge has largely been muted. Although certain of the techniques for developing personal consciousness remain, they have often become "automatic," part of a set ritual; they have become something that lacks its original purpose and is sometimes applied to the wrong groups. The Prayer of the Heart in the Greek Orthodox tradition, however, is much less removed from the meditative traditions:

The mind should be in the heart—a distinctive feature of the method of prayer. It should guard the heart while it prays, revolve, remaining always within, and thence, from the depths of the heart, offer up prayers to God (Everything is in this; work in this way until you are given to taste the Lord). . . .

As to other results which usually come from this work, with God's help, you will learn them from your own experience, by keeping your mind attentive and in your heart to holding Jesus, that is, His prayer—Lord Jesus Christ, have mercy upon me! One of the holy fathers said: "Sit in your cell and this prayer will teach you everything."

A Christian breathing exercise is also described.

You know, brother, how do we breathe: we breathe the air in and out. On this is based the life of the body, and on this depends its warmth. So, sitting down in your cell, collect your mind, lead it into the path of the breath, along which the air enters in, constrain it to enter the heart together with the inhaled air, and keep it there. Keep it here, but do not leave it silent and idle;

instead give it the following prayer: "Lord Jesus Christ, Son of God, have mercy upon me." Let this be its constant occupation, never to be abandoned. For this work, by keeping the mind free from dreaming, renders it unassailable to suggestions of the enemy and leads it to Divine desire and love.[16]

A similar focusing of awareness is also part of Taoist meditation. Instructions are given to sit quietly and focus awareness on the center of the body, on one point on the abdomen. The medieval alchemists described long and repetitive exercises—the continual redistillation of water, the prolonged grinding exercises—which were written down allegedly for the "distillation" of base metal in order to transmute it into gold but which can also be considered symbolically as descriptions of attempts to alter man's awareness from his ordinary "base" level to a higher one, symbolized by gold.

Peter Freuchen, in his *Book of the Eskimos*, describes a technique for meditation in which the Eskimo sits facing a soft stone; he takes a small hard stone and begins to carve a circle in the larger one by moving the small stone continuously around and around the larger surface. This practice, similar to the creation of a mandala, often lasts for several days at a time and is designed to produce a trance state.[17] Many primitive peoples, such as the bushmen of the Kalahari Desert, dance in a circle facing a fire, staring at the fire, repetitiously chanting. Some gaze continuously at the full moon, the sun, or at a candle.

This has been a fairly quick, selective review of some of the major forms of concentrative meditation. Each of the major Eastern traditions uses exercises involving different sensory modalities. A chant is repeated in the various traditions: a focusing on the breath, on the heartbeat, on a short prayer, on a longer prayer, on a story, or on natural sounds, such as a waterfall or the humming of bees or vibration. Symbols or pictures of gurus are gazed at steadily, and images are created in the mind's eye of the practitioner. Turkish dervishes may dance in a repetitive whirl; Indian yogis make continuous movements with their limbs; Taoists concentrate on their abdomen. The early Christian Fathers contemplated an object or the cross. These are all externally different forms of the same type of meditation.

The common element in these diverse practices seems to be the active restriction of awareness to a single, unchanging process and the withdrawal of attention from ordinary thought. It does not seem to matter which actual physical practice is followed; whether one symbol or another is employed; whether the visual system is used or body movements repeated; whether awareness is focused on a limb or on a sound or on a word or on a prayer. This process might be considered an attempt to cycle the same subroutine in the nervous system. The instructions for meditation are consistent with this surmise: one is instructed always to rid awareness of any thought save the object of meditation, to shut oneself off from the main flow of ongoing external activity, and to pay attention only to the object or process of meditation. Almost any process or object seems usable and has probably been used. The Sufi story that begins this chapter indicates that the specific focus of meditation is much less important than the maintaining of the object as the single focus of awareness during a long period of time and the character and sincerity of the practitioner. It seems that the sensory mode of meditation, too, matters little. The intended effect is the state of the central nervous system evoked by the process of repetition.

In terms of consciousness, the effect of concentrative meditation is a "one-pointedness" or a "clear" state. The state is generally described as "dark"—in Indian terminology, "the void." It is a withdrawal of the senses, a "turning off" of perception of the external world in order to enter the receptive, "night" consciousness, *the darkness*. In yogic practice this withdrawal is most explicitly sought. In Buddhism, recall that Rahula says, in describing the breathing meditation, that "after a certain period you will have experienced just that split second when your mind is fully concentrated on your breathing, when you will not even hear sounds nearby, when no external world exists for you." Augustine Poulain describes it as "a mysterious darkness wherein is contained the limitless Good, a void, other than solitude."

These techniques have persisted for centuries. Many sensory modalities have been employed, and many different symbols or objects within any one sensory modality have been used. This may indicate that one primary effect of the concentrative meditation exercises is the state of emptiness, the nonresponsiveness to the external world evoked in the central nervous system by the continuous subroutine called up by the exercise, regardless of what the specific input is or what sensory modality is employed. Since we, the bushmen, the Eskimos, the monks of Tibet, the Zen masters, the yoga adepts, and the dervishes all evolved with the same nervous system, it is not so surprising that general similarities in techniques should have evolved.

Some Psychological Research Related to Concentrative Meditation

There is research that casts some light on *how* the meditation exercises affect consciousness: a body of work on the psychological and physiological effects of restricting awareness to an unchanging stimulus. We can examine meditation techniques in these psychological terms. One variety of concentrative meditation, for instance, employs a "steady gaze" on either a natural object or a specially constructed one, a mandala. A very similar situation would arise if input to the eye were always the same, no matter how one moved one's eyes.

Normally, as we look at the world, our eyes move around and fixate at various points in large movements that are called *saccades*. We hardly ever gaze steadily at any one object for a prolonged period of time. Even when we try to fix vision on a single object, very small involuntary movements of the eye occur, called *optical nystagmus*. The image on the retina is kept in constant motion by both types of eye movements, and different cells are stimulated from moment to moment.

A group of physiological psychologists have succeeded in devising a system that will keep a visual image perfectly stable on the retina, even though the eyes are in constant motion. One apparatus for producing this "stabilized" image consists of an extremely small projector mounted on a contact lens worn by the subject. The contact lens moves with every movement of the eyeball, and so does the projector. No matter how the eye is moved, the same image is always projected onto the retina (see Figure 8–1).[18]

This study of stabilized images was undertaken in psychology primarily to investigate Donald Hebb's theory that continuous change in stimulus input is needed to maintain normal awareness. It was felt that "stabilizing" the image would eliminate these continous changes in input that normally occur as we move our eyes. The subjects looking at the stabilized images reported that the images disappeared.

Lehmann, Beeler, and Fender attempted to investigate the brain state evoked by the stabilized image.[19] The electroencephalogram (EEG), recorded at the scalp, consists of the tiny electrical potentials

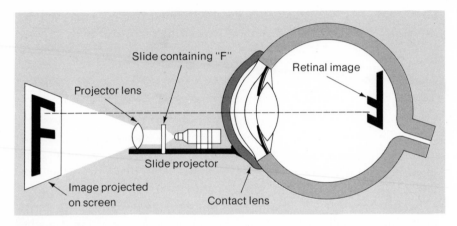

Figure 8-1 In this apparatus, each movement of the eyeball causes the lens and projector to move; thus the image projected stimulates the same area of the retina.

that emanate from the brain. These potentials, which are about 5 to 50 millionths of a volt when recorded at the scalp, are amplified and written out on paper by the electroencephalograph. The first brain rhythm was discovered by Hans Berger in 1924 and was termed the *alpha rhythm*; it consists of rhythmic activity between 8 and 12 Hertz (cycles per second). Since Berger, other rhythms have been classified: *beta*, defined as 12 cycles and above; *theta*, 4–7 Hertz; and *delta*, 1–4 Hertz. The alpha rhythm in the occipital cortex is usually thought to represent a state of decreased visual attention to the external environment. It almost always increases when the eyes are closed or when the eyes are rolled up into the head, cutting off vision.

These investigators recorded the EEG from the occipital cortex of the brain while their subject was viewing the stabilized image. They asked the subject to press a button when the stabilized image disappeared, and they attempted to correlate the subjective experience of the disappearance of the image with the concurrent brain state. They found that the alpha rhythm was likely to appear at the time when the subject reported the disappearance of the image.

Another way to supply the subject with uniform visual input is to present a patternless visual field, termed a *ganzfeld*. A whitewashed surface can serve as a ganzfeld, as can halved ping-pong balls placed over the eyes.[20]

In viewing the ganzfeld, some subjects report an absence of any visual experience—which has been termed *blank-out*. This was not merely the experience of seeing nothing but one of *not seeing*, a complete disappearance of the sense of vision for short periods of time, as Cohen put it. The experience of not seeing usually occurred after about twenty minutes of exposure to the ganzfeld. During blank-out the subjects did not know, for instance, whether their eyes were open. In addition, they could not control their eye movements. Cohen's suggestion was that this continuous uniform stimulation resulted in the failure of any image to be produced in consciousness. He also found that the periods of blank-out were associated with bursts of alpha rhythm. He suggested that the appearance of alpha during these continuous stimulation periods indicated a functional similarity between continuous stimulation and no stimulation at all. He also found that individuals with high-alpha EEG's were more susceptible to the blank-out phenomenon.

Tepas performed a study on the ganzfeld similar to that of Lehmann, Beeler, and Fender on the stabilized image. His subjects watched the ganzfeld for five-minute periods while EEGs were recorded. When the subject experienced the blank-out, he was asked to press a microswitch that marked the EEG record. Tepas found that the alpha activity of the brain increased during the period of blank-out.[21]

Both the situation and the effects of the stabilized image and the ganzfeld are similar to those of concentrative meditation. Consider the activity of the subject in meditation and in the two precisely regulated input situations: in both, an attempt is made to provide unchanging input. The subjective experience is analogous in these situations: a loss of contact with the external world. In both situations, EEG monitoring of the brain's activity reveals an increase in alpha rhythm. The electrophysiological studies of meditation by Bagchi and Wagner; those by Anand and others in India on yoga meditation; those by Kasamatsu and Hirai and by Akishige, in Japan on Zen meditation; and those by Wallace in the United States on transcendental meditation indicate that meditation also is a high-alpha state.[22] The more precisely controlled situations seem to produce, both psychologically and and physiologically, effects similar to those of concentrative meditation.

One consequence of the way our central nervous system is structured seems to be that if awareness is restricted to one unchanging source of stimulation, a "turning off" of consciousness of the external world follows. The common instructions for concentrative meditation underscore this: one is advised to be constantly aware of the object of meditation and nothing else, to continuously cycle the same input. Stabilizing a visual image or homogenizing visual input results in the same experience. A set of instructions from the English mystical tradition presented by Knowles indicates that this blanking-out is a desired function of meditation that can be produced by restriction of awareness.

Forget all creatures that God ever made, and the works of them so that thy thought or thy desire not be directed or stretched to any of them, neither in general nor in special. . . . At the first time when thou dost it, thou findest but a darkness and as it were a kind of unknowing, thou knowest not what, saying that thou feelest in thy will a naked intent unto God.[23]

The interpretations of this experience of a "darkness," of blank-out, of the "void," of the disappearance of any image of the external world would greatly differ with the context: the subject of a physiological experiment would have extremely different expectations and interpretations of his experience than would a person who has sought to reach such experience by involvement in an esoteric discipline. But the experiences themselves have essential similarities and are produced through quite similar procedures.

THE "OPENING-UP" MEDITATION EXERCISES

The second form of meditation exercise is much more closely related to daily activity. These exercises do not attempt to isolate the practitioner from ordinary life processes; rather, they attempt to involve these processes in the training of consciousness. An example is found in the Zen tradition. In the more advanced forms of Zen (in the Soto sect), once the concentrative exercise of counting breaths is mastered, the second form of meditation exercises, shikan-taza is practiced—"just sitting." The Zen master Yasutani Roshi describes this exercise as follows:

Shikan means "nothing but" or "just," while ta means "to hit" and za "to sit." Hence shikan-taza is a practice in which the mind is intensely involved in just sitting. In this type of Za-Zen it is all too easy for the mind, which is not supported by such aids as counting the breath or by a koan, to become distracted. The correct temper of mind therefore becomes doubly important. Now, in shikan-taza the mind must be unhurried yet at the same time firmly planted or massively alert, stretched, like a taut bowstring. So shikan-taza is a heightened state of concentrated awareness wherein one is neither tense nor hurried, and certainly never slack. It is the mind of somebody facing death. Let us imagine that you are engaged in a duel of swordsmanship of the kind that used to take place in ancient Japan. As you face your opponent, you are unceasingly watchful, set, ready. Were you to relax your vigilance even momentarily, you would be cut down instantly. A crowd gathers to see the fight. Since you are not blind you see them from the corner of your eye and since you are not deaf you hear them. But not for an instant is your mind captured by these sense impressions.

This state cannot be maintained for long—in fact, you ought not to do shikan-taza for more than half an hour at a sitting.[24]

We can, then, consider two basic types of meditation exercises—both concerned with a common effect—those that "turn off" input processing for a period of time to achieve an aftereffect of "opening up" of awareness and those that consist in the active practice of "opening up" during the period of the exercise.

Active practice in opening up awareness is practiced generally in the esoteric traditions, but in Zen it is a specific meditation exercise. A less obviously arduous Buddhist practice stems from one component of the Buddha's Eightfold Path and is usually termed "right-mindedness." It requires that one be "conscious" of each action, develop a present-centered consciousness, "open up" awareness of daily activities *while* engaged in them. Rahula says

Another very important, practical, and useful form of "meditation" (mental development) is to be aware and mindful of whatever you do, physically or verbally, during the daily routine of work in your life, private, public, or professional. Whether you walk, stand, sit, lie down, or sleep, whether you stretch or bend your limbs, whether you look around, whether you put on your clothes, whether you talk or keep silent, whether you eat or drink— even whether you answer the calls of nature—in these and other activities you should be fully aware and mindful of the act performed at the moment. That is to say, that you should live in the present moment, in the present action. This does not mean that you should not think of them in relation to the present moment, to the present action, when and where this is relevant.

People do not generally live in their actions in the present moment. They live in the past or in the future. Though they seem to be doing something now here, they live somewhere else in their thoughts, in their problems and worries, usually in the memories of the past or in desires and speculations about the future. Therefore, they do not live in nor do they enjoy what they do at the moment; so they are unhappy and discontented with the present moment with the work at hand. Naturally, they cannot give themselves fully to what they appear to be doing.[25]

In yoga, a form of self-observation is called *the Witness*. Here the attempt is to observe oneself as if one were another person. One tries to notice exactly what one is doing—to invest ordinary activity with attention. The Witness does not judge action nor does it initiate action. The Witness simply observes.

This practice is highly developed in Zen. Right-mindedness, or attention to what one is doing, can be a part of any activity that one performs, no matter how base. There is no action that cannot be used to develop one's consciousness. One simply need be "mindful" of present actions. One can be performing actions that are quite degrading to a Buddhist, such as butchering an animal, but simply by paying close attention to what one is doing, one's awareness can be developed.

A similar exercise attributed to George Gurdjieff consists simply in maintaining continuous awareness of a part of one's body—an elbow, a hand, a leg. Another exercise of this "system" is to perform ordinary, habitual actions slightly differently, such as putting shoes on in the opposite order, shaving the other side of the face first, eating with the left hand (if one is right-handed). These exercises can be seen as attempts to return habitual, "automatic" actions to full awareness.

Recall the phenomenon of habituation. A slight change in input is enough to "dishabituate" and to return the stimulus to awareness. Similarly, slightly altering our usual "automatic" behavior, such as tying shoes, driving cars, shaving, can return the process to awareness.

Similarly, in what is called *karma yoga*, the intent is to treat everyday activities as a "sacrament"—to give them full attention. This exercise performs a function similar to "right-mindedness" and "self-remembering" and is a less extreme version of *shikan-taza*.

Many schools within these traditions combine the two major types of awareness exercises, devoting half an hour or so twice a day to the "shutting-down" form of meditation and as much as possible of the remainder of the day to a form of self-observation.

DISHABITUATION RESEARCH

There have been a few psychological and physiological studies of the state of awareness of practitioners in and after meditation. These studies have used the EEG to measure the brain responses of meditators to external stimulation.

When we enter a room and hear a clock ticking, we ordinarily learn to tune it out fairly quickly. Physiologically, the normal "orienting response" to new stimulation begins to disappear after a few moments and does not reappear. On the psychological level, this pattern could be described as the construction of an internal model of the clock which then allows us to ignore it. But if consciousness were like a mirror, each time the clock ticked it would be "reflected."

The Indian psychologists' studies on yoga meditation showed this result. By recording the yogi's EEG while introducing external stimuli, they confirmed this analysis of the effects and aftereffects of meditation. During the meditation and during the withdrawal, there was no interruption in the alpha rhythm of the yogi's brain because of the external stimuli. However, when the yogi was not meditating, repetition of an external stimulus showed none of the habituation that presumably would have occurred in other subjects.[26]

The Japanese neuropsychiatrists Kasamatsu and Hirai studied the habituation of the orienting response to a repeated click, both in ordinary people and in Zen masters. The subjects in this experiment sat in a soundproof room and listened to a click repeated every fifteen seconds while an EEG was being taken. The normal subjects showed the customary phenomenon of habituation. The response of the brain's electrical activity to the clicks began to decrease after the third or fourth click. After habituation, each time the click occurred there was no response in the brain of the subject: the click had been tuned out of awareness. When the Zen masters were meditating and were exposed to this same repetitive click over a period of five minutes, they did not show the customary habituation; they responded to the last click just as strongly as they did to the first. They did not seem to make a "model" of the repetitive stimulation and so tune it out.[27]

It seems, therefore, that there is dishabituation *during* the advanced form of Zen meditation—that is, a consistent response to a continuing stimulus. There is a "shutting down" of awareness of external stimuli during yoga meditation, but when the yogi is not in meditation, we might expect no habituation to a repetitive stimulus (if he or she is advanced enough in his practice).

A CAUTION ON THE COMMERCIALIZATION OF MEDITATION

If this survey allows some more clarity regarding the practices of meditation, it does remain, before we conclude, to consider several current points of misconception:

First, simply understanding the mechanism of an esoteric practice does not necessarily imply that the practice is useful. The archeological aspects of a psychology of consciousness should be distinguished from the practical and contemporary. Meditations are a set of techniques that have been poorly understood and denigrated in the West. With a current renewed interest in and analysis of their *potential*, we run the risk of "romantic" mystics informing us that these techniques are of immediate use and should be adopted by all.

One sect that has pressed this has been the devotees of transcendental meditation, which has presented and commercially publicized its own research, intending to indicate that meditation has many beneficial physiological effects. The claim is made in their literature that such practice is "the answer to all your problems." The student should note, here, that such a publicity campaign is mainly advertising and not necessarily science. Many of the "scientific validations" are preliminary, uncontrolled pilot studies often marked "submitted for publication," and much of the data are presented in a manner intended only to impress the uninitiated, not necessarily to inform. Caveat meditator.

THE PROCESS OF DEAUTOMATIZATION

In general, the esoteric traditions characterize consciousness in terms similar to those of modern psychology. The Sufis' conceptions are clear complements of those of modern psychology. Sufi teaching stories frequently focus on people who are too preoccupied to hear what is being said, or who misinterpret instructions because of their expectations, or who do not see what is in front of them because of the limitations of their constructs. Their literature emphasizes the constantly changing biases that constitute our normal awareness and how our needs sometimes block us from a more comprehensive perception. "What a piece of bread looks like depends on whether you are hungry." The Sufis quite explicitly consider the effects of our limited category system on consciousness. Many of these descriptions of consciousness could have been a statement of Bruner's about category systems or a summary by Lettvin of his research on the frog: "Offer a donkey a salad, and he will ask what kind of thistle it is." They emphasize that we, like the rugseller, can only be aware of what our conceptions will allow and of what our senses will transmit to us.

The Sufi and other traditions contend that our selective and restricted ordinary consciousness is to be overcome by the process of meditation, among many other possible exercises and techniques. One specific aim in these traditions is to dismantle the automaticity and selectivity of ordinary awareness. The Sufis characterize ordinary consciousness as a state of "deep sleep" or "blindness"—a preoccupation with the irrelevant dimensions of the world. Gurdjieff's image is that man places shock absorbers between himself and the world. "We must destroy our buffers; children have none; therefore we must become like little children." While this may be a fallacious and romantic notion of childhood, the comment on adult perception is valid. In Indian thought, personal consciousness is compared to a "drunken monkey" living solely in his constructs—the world of "illusion." This same thought is a metaphorical meaning of the "fall" of man in the Christian tradition. These metaphors, without their derogatory connotations, can be understood in terms of modern psychology as depicting our selective, constructed awareness, our model building, automaticity, and limited category systems.

One aim of the esoteric disciplines is to remove "blindness," or the "illusion," to "awaken" a fresh perception. *Enlightenment* and *illumination* are words often used for progress in these disciplines, for a breakthrough in the level of awareness—flooding a dark spot with light. In Indian traditions it is described as perceiving more and from a new vantage point. *Satori*, in Zen, is considered an intuitive "awakening." The Sufis speak of the development of a "new organ" of perception.

Reports of the experiences of those who practice the meditative disciplines indicate that a primary *aftereffect* of the concentrative-meditation exercises is an opening up of awareness, a *deautomatization*, as Deikman calls it, which might be a reduction of the normal selectivity of input. After gazing at a blue vase for half an hour at a time for several sessions, Deikman's subjects in experimental meditation reported that the vase appeared "more vivid" and "more luminous."[28] Deikman cites Augustine Poulain, who emphasized that concentrative meditation is a temporary process of withdrawal, similar to the blank-out of consciousness but with an intent to become deautomatized.

It is the mysterious darkness wherein is contained the limitless Good. To such an extent are we admitted and absorbed into something that is one, simple, divine, and illuminable that we seem no longer distinguishable from it. . . . In this unity the feeling of multiplicity disappears. When afterwards these persons come to themselves again, they find themselves possessed of a more distinct knowledge of things, some luminous and more perfect than that of others.[29]

Some speak of seeing things "freshly" or as if for the first time. To Blake, it is a "cleansing of the doors of perception." Others, like Gurdjieff, compare their experiences to those of a child, who presumably has not yet developed many automatic ways of tuning out the world. In Zen, one speaks similarly of seeing something the five-hundredth time in the same way that one saw it the first time.

These descriptions are understandable in contemporary psychological terms—as a process of building a model of the environment, and testing and selecting input against the model. When we see something for the five-hundredth time, we have developed a model for it and can tune it out.

These characterizations of consciousness represent a meeting point between scientific psychological research and the metaphors of the esoteric psychologists. Contemporary psychologists speak of the brain's controlling input, building models, responding "automatically" to the external environment. The esoteric traditions refer to this process as man's lacking full awareness and consider this "blindness" a barrier to his development. The practice of meditation, then, can be considered as one attempt to turn off linear, verbal activity temporarily, and to shut off all input processing for a period of time.

A result of this "turning off" of the input selection systems seems to be that when the same sensory input is later introduced, we see it differently, "anew." When we leave our normal surroundings and go on vacation, we usually return to find ourselves much more "aware" of the immediate environment. We play many of our old records, which we haven't "heard" in a while. We look anew at the plants in our garden, the paintings on our walls, our friends. Getting away and returning seem to have the same effect on awareness as presenting new stimuli.*

We can consider the process of concentrative meditation as similar to that of taking a vacation—leaving the situation, "turning off" our routine way of dealing with the external world for a period, later returning to find it "fresh," "new," and "different," our awareness deautomatized. The direct effects and the aftereffects of these techniques need be separated.

We easily adapt to almost any item or idea. A new technology, a new person, a change in our immediate environment, quickly become an integral part of our lives, part of our personally constructed "model" of the external world. This model-building process is specifically dismantled by the practice of meditation. In Zen, one is invited to stop conceptualizing while remaining fully awake. In yoga, the aim is to leave the "illusion"—to cease identifying the external world with our constructed models of it. The esoteric traditions thus speak of developing a consciousness devoid of normal input selection, model-building, and category systems—one that allows every stimulus to enter into consciousness.[30]

A mirror metaphor is used in many traditions to describe the desired mode of consciousness. The Sufi poet Omar Khayyam wrote, "I am a mirror, and who looks at me, whatever good or bad he speaks, he speaks of himself." The contemporary Zen master Suzuki Roshi says, "The perfect man employs his mind as a mirror, it grasps nothing, it refuses nothing, it receives but does not keep." Christ said in prayer, "A mirror I am to thee that perceivest me." The metaphor of consciousness as a mirror fits well with some of the psychologists' own metaphors. A mirror allows everything to enter equally, reflects each equally, and cannot be tuned to receive a special kind of information. It does not add anything to the input and does not turn off repetitive stimuli; it does not focus on any particular aspect of the world but continuously admits everything equally.

---

*Compare the phenomenon of "spontaneous recovery" in habituation.

"Direct" Perception

The metaphor of the mirror leads to another consideration. Many of the traditions claim to allow people to experience the world *directly*. The Sufis speak of attaining an "objective consciousness," others of "cosmic consciousness." The statement is often made that one can have *direct* perception of reality. Whether one can perceive "reality" directly is not yet a scientific question, but some comment can be made. The ability to "mirror," to be free of the normal restrictions— the tuning, biasing, and filtering processes of consciousness—may be a part of what is meant by "direct" perception.

This state can perhaps be considered as a diminution of the interactive nature of awareness: we do not select or "bet" on the nature of the world, or sort into restrictive categories; rather, we hold all possible categories at once. It has also been described as living totally in the present, of not thinking about the future or the past—a state in which "everything" in the present moment enters into awareness. This does not mean though that one is thus unable to consider the past or the future, or has lost any of the other faculties of planning or competence in ordinary affairs.

MEDITATION, DEAUTOMATIZATION, AND THE "MYSTIC EXPERIENCE"

In classic practice, the two major forms of meditation exercises, the concentrative and the "opening-up" forms, are intended to cause a shift in the mode of consciousness of the practitioner. The concentrative form suspends the normal mode of operation and allows a sensitivity to subtle stimuli that often go unnoticed in the normal mode, as the stars remain unseen in the light of the day. It also produces an aftereffect of "fresh" perception when the practitioner returns to his usual surroundings, in the same way a vacation allows us to "see" our environment anew.

Concentrative meditation, coupled with dishabituation exercises, undoes the normal construction of consciousness. When the normal mode is temporarily dismantled, the other major mode can emerge—that of the "night," the "receptive," the often misunderstood and devalued mode of intuition.

In many traditions, a full emergence of this mode has become known as a "mystic" experience. The word *mystic* may be unfortunate, since many confuse it with *mystical* and with occultism and mystery. The word initially derives from an association with mysteries of life, the ultimate questions—such as, what is the meaning of life—not from muddled thinking or obscurantism. We should not be surprised that the very name given to this experience implies incomprehensibility, since the experience is not within the province of the linear, verbal mode of consciousness. One portion of our mind may simply be incapable of fully understanding the experience of the other part and may give it a name that reflects this lack of comprehension.

This *mode* of knowledge and consciousness, however, is to some degree a part of the daily experience of each of us, although its full development can result from a life crisis, by accident, deliberately, or sometimes "spontaneously." It may be occasioned by many methods other than meditation—by fasting, by ritual dance, by the ingestion of certain psychoactive drugs, all of which upset the normal linear construction of consciousness, and by much more ordinary methods in everyday life. The esoteric psychologies work toward extending normal linear consciousness to include such experience.

The "mystic" consciousness is described by many, in almost every tradition—from the ancient Hindu to the contemporary European. It is described in the Bible, in the Koran, in Whitman, in James's *The Varieties of Religious Experience.* It is the "mysterious darkness" of Augustine Poulain, a mode in which ordinary consciousness of a "multiplicity" of people and objects disappears, to be replaced by the awareness of "unity."

The consciousness of "unity," or "oneness," as it is sometimes called, is perhaps the most fully developed form of this mode of experience. As represented in the story of the blind men and the elephant, the mystic experience involves a shift in consciousness from the analytic, individual, piecemeal approach to knowledge, to a more receptive, holistic mode—one that can encompass the entire elephant as a whole. It is comprehensive rather than fragmented, and thus many objects, associations, and ideas can be linked in a superior manner and are "unified."

A second characteristic of these experiences, as described by William James, is the sense of "realness." They are definite understandings of the relations between things, and they involve reliance on a type of verification that is more intuitive than our usual linear and inferential.[31]

This mode of consciousness is striking in its most-developed form, in which the "vividness" and "richness" of normal consciousness is greatly enhanced, in which linear time, as we know it, has no meaning. Deikman attributes the "vividness" and "richness" to deautomatization. To repeat William Blake: "If the doors of perception were cleansed, man would see everything as it is, infinite."

The contents of this experience are often said to be "ineffable," incapable of being fully communicated by words or by reference to similar experiences in ordinary life. One person echoes this feeling, wishing that he had some competence in the more ordinary aspects of the holistic mode of consciousness, so that he might communicate it more clearly.

What is a "transcendent dimension of being?" Such words on paper are little more than metaphysical poetry. Somehow I feel I could better communicate my experience by composing a symphony or by molding a twisted piece of contemporary sculpture had I the talents required for either form of artistic expression. In no sense have I an urge to formulate philosophical or theological dogmas about my experience. Only my silence can retain its purity and genuineness.[32]

The essence of this mode is simultaneity, and the insights available in it cannot always be translated into sequential terms. As Arthur Deikman wrote, "Ordinary language is structured to follow the logical development of one idea at a time, and it might be quite inadequate to express an experience encompassing a large number of concepts simultaneously."[33]

CONCLUSION: MEDITATION AND THE RELEVANCE OF "CONSCIOUSNESS DEVELOPMENT"

The practices of meditation—whirling, chanting, concentrating on a nonsensical question, thinking or speaking a "sacred" prayer over and over, visualizing a cross, gazing at a vase—are not quite so exotic as those who deliberately seek the esoteric might wish; but neither are they exercises in reason or problem solving. They are exercises in attentional deployment, both those that focus on one stimulus and those that are intended to actively deautomatize ordinary consciousness.

The "mystic" experience brought about by concentrative meditation, deautomatization exercises, and other techniques intended to alter ordinary linear consciousness is, then, a shift from the normal, analytic world containing separate, discrete objects and persons to a second mode, an experience of "unity" and holistic perception. This experience is outside the province of language and rationality, since it is a mode of simultaneity, but it is a complementary dimension of consciousness that adds to and can give comprehension to the ordered sequence of "normal" thought.

But why have people sought to develop this mode, and what value is there in a "mystic" experience? The answers to these questions are not easy. Many of the traditional replies are well known; yet some brief interpretation and comment might be useful.

First, the analytic, linear mode of consciousness cannot encompass many aspects of life that many people want to experience and understand. There is no book or doctrine that can provide self-knowledge, since each person is different. That these phenomena have been "ruled out" of much of Western scientific inquiry does not lessen the need that many now feel to explore these areas personally. Meditation is but one of very many attempts to develop consciousness in such a way that certain relational aspects of reality become accessible to the practitioner.

Second, the analytic mode, in which there is separation of objects, and of the self from others (which the theologian Buber has termed the I–it relationship), has proved useful in individual biological survival; yet concentration on this mode may have evolved to fit the conditions of life many thousands of years ago. The evolution of culture proceeds much more quickly than biological evolution; so the analytic mode may not be as all-important a criterion for our contemporary Western society as it once was, and we may even be said to be biologically obsolete in these terms. The awareness of this separation was a great advantage when survival threatened an individual's existence; for instance, one could locate and isolate an enemy animal and use it for food. This basic need for individual survival is no longer quite so basic for many in the West. Most of us now buy our food; we do not need to hunt for it. Few readers of this book are in any danger of imminent starvation.

The survival problems now facing us are *collective* rather than individual: They are problems of how to prevent a large nuclear war, pollution of the earth, overpopulation; how to relate and understand diverse and divergent ideas, doctrines, and people—all of which have constructed their own "reality." And note well that in these problems, an exclusive focus on individual consciousness and individual survival may work against, not for, a solution. A shift toward a comprehensive consciousness of the interconnectedness of life, toward a relinquishing of the "every man for himself" attitude inherent in our ordinary construction of consciousness, might enable us to take those "selfless" steps that could begin to solve our collective problems. Certainly our culture has too severely emphasized the development of only one way of organizing reality. Perhaps we can now begin to see that the complementary mode has survival value for our culture as a whole. (In a minor way, some recent cultural events can be seen in this light: I refer to the increasing awareness of the earth as one system that is part of the ecology movement and to the increasing development of interdisciplinary training and systems analysis within science.)

Additionally, we should consider that the change in our society to a predominantly technological, scientific one during the last two centuries has caused a radical increase in the environmental stresses placed on each person. Many diseases, such as the increased incidence of hypertension, can in some part be linked to these radical changes in environmental stress. Herbert Benson suggests that the development of increased self-knowledge and quiescence through meditation may be a way in which we can learn to cope with the stress, since the demands placed on us by our society are unlikely to diminish greatly.[34]

These examples are not intended to "reduce" the esoteric psychologies to application to current problems but to emphasize their organic relationship to contemporary life. Most important, it is the shift from an individual and analytic consciousness to the attainment of an overall perspective of "unity," of "Humanity as one organism," that is the primary purpose of the esoteric traditions.

FOR FURTHER READING

PHILIP KAPLEAU. *The Three Pillars of Zen.* Boston: Beacon Press, 1967.

WALPOLA RAHULA. *What the Buddha Taught.* Rev. ed. New York: Grove Press, 1974.

FREDERIC SPIEGELBERG. *Spiritual Practices of India.* New York: Citadel Press, 1962.

ROBERT KEITH WALLACE and HERBERT BENSON. "The Physiology of Meditation." *Scientific American,* February 1972, pp. 84–90.

ARTHUR DEIKMAN. "Deautomatization and the Mystic Experience." *Psychiatry* 29 (1966): 329–43.

All the preceding have been reprinted, in whole or in part, in Robert Ornstein, ed. *The Nature of Human Consciousness.* San Francisco: W.H. Freeman; New York: Viking Press, 1973.

CLAUDIO NARANJO and ROBERT ORNSTEIN. *On the Psychology of Meditation.* New York: Penguin Books, 1977.

CHOGYAM TRUNGPA. *Meditation in Action.* Berkeley, Calif.: Shambala, 1970.

A. KASAMATSU and T. HIRAI. "An Electroencephalographic Study on Zen Meditation (Zazen)." Reprinted in Charles T. Tart, ed. *Altered States of Consciousness.* New York: Doubleday, 1972.

9 A New Synthesis

Why Don't You?

Nasrudin went to the shop of a man who stocked all kinds of bits and pieces.
"Have you got nails?" he asked.
"Yes."
"And leather, good leather?"
"Yes."
"And twine?"
"Yes."
"And dye?"
"Yes."
"Then why, for Heaven's sake, don't you make a pair of boots?"[1]

A BRIEF INTRODUCTION

When a new development or new idea takes root, many of the older ideas can link up and become unified at a more comprehensive level of organization. Sometimes the ideas and possibilities may be waiting for someone like Nasrudin to say "Why don't you. . . ?" And, indeed, the conceptions and techniques of esoteric traditions presage such an extension of the paradigm in modern psychology. When such a change takes place, our conception of what is "normal" and what is "paranormal" may well undergo a redefinition. As with the four-minute mile, once the limits of possibility are transcended, by an action or a new concept, a new realm may open. Beyond practical techniques, the major import of the traditional psychologies is to inform us that we have been too stingy in our estimation of ourselves. We are quite close to the position of the rugseller, having limited ourselves personally, scientifically, and culturally by our conception of the possibilities of the "materials" available. More can be developed within our own bodies and minds than many physicians, psychologists, and philosophers had considered.

Actually, we are a *little* better off than the rugseller or the man whose stock was fragmented and lacked integration. Suppose someone had answered the question, Is there any number higher than 100? with only a Yes, and a scrap of paper with 147, 793, and 960 written on it. We would now have some indication that higher numbers exist, but their relationship with known numbers would be unclear. We might ask, What are the new limits?

Our previous analysis indicated that "normal" consciousness is not complete but is an exquisitely evolved, selective, personal construction with the primary purpose of ensuring individual biological survival. But this mode, although necessary for survival, is not necessarily the only manner in which consciousness can operate. As the material success of organized society eases the task of individual survival, it also does provide a more secure basis for the development of another mode of consciousness. People do not need to spend so much of their effort actively striving for food, shelter, and individual protection. The essence of the active mode of survival is selection and limitation. If we were indiscriminately aware of each quantum of energy reaching us at each moment, we would likely be dead within a day. We must, then, "automatically" limit awareness. Our internal state, too, is automatized. We could not survive if we had to voluntarily beat our hearts seventy times every minute. We screen internal constancies in the external environment. However, although certain internal physiological processes are almost always "automatic," they are not forever beyond volition. For individual biological survival, these processes seem best automatized, but for the further extension of consciousness, it may be necessary to make the effort to deautomatize them.

This is an instance in which the dominant Western paradigm has prevented us from clearly seeing the scientific import of the esoteric traditions. For hundreds of years reports have reached the West of yogis who could stop their hearts and alter their glandular and metabolic activity. But since we considered such control impossible, we have almost completely ignored these fragmentary communications. Esoteric traditions have developed exercises, such as meditation, that deautomatize ordinary, outward-oriented consciousness, as well as techniques for deautomatizing internal states. Physiological studies of yoga masters point to a possibility of self-mastery far beyond what is considered the current limit. The impetus given by this possibility feeds the new research in physiological feedback training, which combines a concept of increased self-mastery with modern technological methods.

The automatization of ordinary consciousness is a tradeoff: for the sake of survival, we lose much of the possible richness of experience. We tune out the constancies of the environment and discard many subtle or slow-changing phenomena. But if a person's consciousness is deautomatized, he may be able to notice factors that are always present but which he has ignored. If the person is a scientist, he or she could then turn the full intellect to the study of sources of influence on human beings too subtle and constant to enter ordinary consciousness. These sources include the rotation of the earth, the impingement of the biosphere, and the gravitational field.

Most modern psychologists might think it quite strange to consider these subtle geophysical forces as part of a psychology of consciousness. It is, however, becoming clear that humans are not so closed a biological system as once thought. Some recent research confirms the esoteric assertion that subtle environmental forces do influence us, although their influence is often obscured by more brilliant phenomena.

A NEW SYNTHESIS

The concepts of deautomatization and potential shifts in mode of consciousness are key elements in a new synthesis: they each enable an awareness of factors that previously escaped attention. It is here that the work of the esoteric traditions is most fruitfully considered as a complement to Western science. Additionally, the writers of these traditions direct attention to areas of consciousness that are ususally not considered in contemporary science.

To point to something at a critical time is often all that is needed. If we merely inform a person that although a six of spades is usually black, it could also on occasion be red, he might be able to see what is in front of him. This is one initial result of the esoteric traditions.

Two modes of consciousness can function complementarily in the study of the psychology of consciousness. Gaining personal knowledge may initiate us in the new area of inquiry, but once there, we can make full use of modern scientific techniques and instruments to explore and map the territory. We can then "translate" some of the ideas and the metaphors of the esoteric traditions into more modern scientific terms *when appropriate* and combine technology with a traditional perspective.

We are just at the first moments of this new synthesis from which an extended concept of man is beginning to emerge. A few of the elements that go into it are noted here.

1. Two major modes of consciousness exist in man and function in a complementary manner. Since the dominant mode in our culture is verbal and rational, recognition of the existence of the second mode may well lead us to a cultivation of the intuitive and holistic aspects of ourselves. The first mode is active, associated with our biological survival—the *day* in our metaphor. The second mode is receptive and constitutes the dark, subtle area of consciousness, metaphorically, the *night.*
2. Personal and scientific attention is shifted inward to the importance of consciousness *itself* as an object of inquiry and to the

self-control of internal states. Physiological feedback research thus involves a fundamental redirection of technology toward the internal rather than the external environment.

3. Human beings are not so closed a biological system as the Western scientific community once thought. We are sensitive and permeable to subtle sources of energy from geophysical and human forces that often lie unnoticed in the brilliance of the day.

4. The concepts of "normal" and "paranormal" are in process of change. It was, for instance, previously considered "paranormal" to claim self-control of the autonomic nervous system or to claim sensitivity to subtle geophysical stimuli.

These "elements" are merely a brief sketch; the synthesis has not even begun to take on any recognizable form. This is not the time to delineate the final form of this new psychology, but rather a time, once again, to extend the boundaries of inquiry of modern psychology and to explore the new field with fresh conceptions. The following chapters, then, are the very beginnings of this exploration.

Chapter 10 deals with self-regulation, which combines the esoteric emphasis on self-mastery with modern technology. Biofeedback is no substitute for the esoteric practices, nor is it a perfect translation of them into modern language. Enlightenment, although rather difficult to define, is certainly not relaxation, serenity, or even mental health. Yet in their own limited ways (compared with the esoteric traditions), biofeedback and self-regulation are significant extensions of contemporary science.

Chapter 11 is much more tentative and speculative. It deals with the beginnings of research on subtle environmental factors, techniques in body therapies, and psychotherapies that respond to this new input. It concludes with a consideration of a contemporary example of esoteric psychology.

10 Techniques of Self-Regulation

There Is More Light Here

A man saw Nasrudin searching for something on the ground, "What have you lost, Mulla?" he asked.

"My key," said the Mulla.

So the man went down on his knees too, and they both looked for it.

After a time, the other man asked: "Where exactly did you drop it?"

"In my own house."

"Then why are you looking here?"

"There is more light here than inside my own house."[1]

Our ordinary consciousness is largely directed toward active manipulation of the external environment. For the most part we remain unaware of internal physiological processes, those phenomena occurring "within our own house," in the dark. We each tune out subtle internal stimuli and direct attention outward, toward the external world, in order to survive. We would not be able to accomplish much if we had to "take time" to digest our food, pump additional blood to an injury, or "consciously" direct the operation of the kidneys. It is almost always more economical to place these processes on "automatic," out of direct awareness.

The split in personal consciousness between outward and inward phenomena has led to a paradigm in science that conceptually divides the nervous system in two. The central nervous system, which includes the brain and the nerves that direct skeletal muscle activity, is concerned with thought, voluntary action, and manipulation of the external environment through the limbs. The autonomic nervous system maintains the internal milieu—it controls the activity of the heart, the stomach, and the glands.

For the most part, this internal function is automatized, out of volitional control. Once again, that a process is almost always in a certain state does not mean it must remain so under all conditions. But the very labels affixed to this portion of ourselves have effectively "legislated" it beyond any possibility of self-regulation—in addition to *autonomic*, it has at times been termed *involuntary*, and even the *vegetative*, nervous system.

This is another example of how a concept of what is possible determines what is considered "normal" and "paranormal." The reports of yogic self-regulation were often ignored as scientific evidence. They did not fit easily with the conventional paradigm of two nervous systems with fundamentally different natures, one "voluntary," one "autonomic."

Normally, we are little aware of the processes within our kidneys or of alterations in our blood-flow pattern, and for the most part we do not need to be more aware. Yet the esoteric traditions note the effect of controlled inner states on consciousness. In some of the exercises of the esoteric traditions, the priorities are reversed: ordinary, outward-directed consciousness is "turned off" by specialized exercises, such as meditation, that produce a shift to an inward, receptive state. In this other mode, ordinary awareness is irrelevant, for its brilliance would overshadow the faint internal signals. And when the proper exercises are performed, these normally invisible signals are brought into consciousness, and what was "autonomic" in ordinary awareness can be changed.

We can thus extend our interpretation of the Nasrudin story to physiological levels. Like many, Nasrudin is accustomed to look for the key outside himself, in the light of the day. But it lies inside, within his own "house," in the darkness.

YOGIC SELF-CONTROL

Of all the esoteric traditions, it is yoga that places the most emphasis on physiological self-regulation. Well-documented reports such as those of Elmer Green are only now becoming readily available. As the psychophysiological study of these adepts progresses, their capacities will be charted with increasing accuracy. Some very preliminary studies report yogis living on diets that seem impossible to Western science. Some have reported that Tibetan adepts can raise their body temperature enough to melt ice on cold nights high up in the mountains.[2] This mastery over the body is considered only a beginning technique in the esoteric traditions—a means by which consciousness can be changed.

And yet, once our concept of human possibility is slightly extended, this "paranormal" self-regulation seems much less spectacular, less unattainable by the rest of us. We may even note that many people possess such capacities in a rudimentary form. One person may be able to relax or to sleep at will, another can slow the heart, another is able to hold his breath for long periods of time, and so on.

Several exceptional individuals have developed these "paranormal" capacities to some extent. In *The Mind of a Mnemonist*, the Russian physiologist Luria describes a man who could perform fantastic memory feats and who could also raise the temperature in one of his hands while simultaneously lowering it in the other, simply by mental imagery.[3]

The famous escape artist Houdini learned some degree of autonomic control in order to perform his "amazing" feats. In one of his tricks, his hands would be fastened in a set of handcuffs, and he would be placed in a locked trunk and thrown under water. Yet he would escape. How? He held no key (he was searched often enough), and the locks were burst-proof. With an ordinary conception of capabilities, most thought the task impossible. If that conception is slightly extended, the "amazing" feat becomes less so. As with Nasrudin, the key was inside. Houdini had swallowed the key (which unlocked both the handcuffs and the trunk) before the demonstration began, and having learned control over his digestive system, he regurgitated the key once inside the box and opened the locks from the inside.

We could collect many other reports of individuals who have more self-mastery than the ordinary. The import of the esoteric traditions, practical psychologies that they are, lies in their development of procedures that allow the student to *train* himself in the deployment of these extraordinary capacities.

More careful scientific study of these adepts may enable us to find out just how much self-mastery and self-knowledge *each person* could achieve, given the development of a more modern method of training, although the applications of this self-control may well be different in the Western context.

Our normal educational process is primarily directed toward the active mode—the verbal, intellectual, and manipulative processes. We learn to write, to play ball, or to play a musical instrument through a process of feedback. When we err in playing a note, or in penmanship, or in mathematics, our teacher corrects us. But we do not have a similar tradition in our culture of learning about the internal environment. We learn little about our emotions, little about what happens in our bodies when we are angry or afraid. We learn little even about the nature, function, and placement of our internal organs. A recent English survey reports that most people do not know where their bladders, kidneys, or intestine are.[4] If our education could be refocused slightly to direct more attention inward, many might learn to control internal organs as they learn to manipulate external forces. The forces involved, however, are subtle and are usually screened out of personal awareness.

RESEARCH ON PHYSIOLOGICAL SELF-CONTROL

There is a body of scientific evidence consistent with the esoteric approach to the nervous system. A series of investigations that K.M. Bykov began in Russia in 1924 demonstrate that the autonomic nervous system is only *relatively* autonomous and is subject to voluntary control. Bykov and his associates used Pavlov's method of the conditioned response. That a bell sounds means nothing in itself to a hungry dog; but if the sound of the bell always precedes feeding, the dog will begin to salivate each time the bell sounds.

Several investigators working in Bykov's laboratory demonstrated that many "involuntary" processes could be conditioned. Experimental animals could learn to increase or decrease their body heat as well as to alter the heat in specific limbs by controlling the blood flow to those limbs. They could control their heart rhythms and remove blocks in the heartbeat introduced by morphine. Pancreatic secretion could be affected, and the urine excretion of the kidneys could be increased or decreased. They could change the volume of blood in the spleen, alter the secretion of bile, and affect many other processes. Previously, these processes had been considered unalterable, part of the "automaton," the body.[5]

The work of the Russians clearly indicates that there is far more modifiability of the heart, liver, spleen, kidneys, blood flow, and so on, than we normally suppose. It also indicates that the division some have made between "mind" and "body"—the mind as a process of reason and will, the body as an automaton, à la Descartes—is unnecessarily limiting. Bykov and Gantt wrote: "The gap between the two disconnected worlds of *psyche* and *soma* is being bridged."

There have been many other sources of evidence on the possibility of internal self-regulation. The original explorations of Sigmund Freud and Josef Breuer on hysteria point in the same direction. One of their early patients was a woman whose hand was paralyzed. Here paralysis took the shape of a glove, which Freud considered "anatomical nonsense," since the muscles that would have been affected by a "real" paralysis did not stop at the line marked by gloves. Freud's brilliant insight was that this paralysis was under the voluntary, although in his terms "unconscious," control of the woman. From this woman's problem and from those of many other of Freud's patients, the concept of psychosomatic medicine was born—the very name of the discipline linking the worlds of the mind and the body. Freud discovered that the woman's paralysis could be cured by bringing this "unconscious control" into her awareness.[6]

The discipline of psychosomatic medicine has so far been limited to removing the misapplications of self-regulation, as in Freud's and

Breuer's work. But there is an important theoretical point for consideration: that one can voluntarily bring about paralysis in the shape of a glove indicates that one can achieve precise control of the blood flow and musculature in quite specific areas of the hand.

As long ago as 1885 Western scientists studied individuals with capacities for unusual self-regulation. Tarchanoff published a paper documenting voluntary acceleration of heart rate in man.[7] In 1939 Ogden and Shock documented voluntary hypercirculation.[8] The esoteric claim to control internal states seems much less fantastic and unusual when this evidence is considered. Since yoga adepts spend many years attending to these processes with the intent to alter them, it seems reasonable, in view of Bykov's work and that of psychosomatic medicine, that these alterations can be accomplished.

Certainly the most sophisticated and the most theoretically relevant research in the voluntary alteration of physiological processes has been that of Neal Miller and his associates, of Rockefeller University. The research has been designed explicitly to investigate the possibility that learning may take place in the autonomic nervous system.[9] Bykov's work had been limited to classical (involuntary) conditioning, which learning theorists have considered inferior to voluntary learning (operant conditioning). Bykov's work, as he himself stated, was intended to show that the activity of the autonomic nervous system could always be modified by the central nervous system.

Miller's work indicates that alterations in blood flow, and in the activity of internal organs and the glands, can be brought about voluntarily by the type of learning that psychologists consider to be "higher." Most important, their research demonstrates that learning can take place within the autonomic nervous system seemingly without the involvement of the voluntary skeletal musculature. When the attempt is to chart the new possibilities of human self-regulation, these "academic" distinctions may not seem very important. Most often it will be of no practical concern whether an action, such as slowing the heart rate, may be accomplished with or without the involvement of the skeletal muscles. However, the distinctions are theoretically of great significance, because they rule out any possible conception of an "autonomic nervous system" existing alone.

Miller and his associates, notably Leo DiCara, studied experimental animals (rats, mostly) with electrodes, thermistors, or photocells implanted at specific sites in the stomach and kidneys, in the cardiovascular system, and in the brain (Figure 10-1). Information about selected activity in these sites (for instance, blood flow) was converted into electrical stimulation to "rewarding" areas of the brain. In order to increase the rate of the electrical brain stimulations, the animals had to alter that specific aspect of their autonomic activity—in this example, blood flow. Miller eliminated the influence of the skeletal muscles in this autonomic learning by administering the drug curare, which selectively paralyzes the skeletal musculature and allows no central nervous system commands to reach the muscles.

With sensors implanted to amplify internal signals and with the information translated into direct brain reward, the animals could quickly learn to alter blood flow, blood pressure, stomach acidity, kidney functioning, and the electrical activity of the brain. Miller required that differential control over each process be demonstrated—for instance, both the raising and the lowering of blood flow, both the increase and the decrease of the kidney functions. Once the information is made directly available to awareness, many involuntary processes seem quite modifiable. The processes controlled can be surprisingly specific. In one experiment, sensors were implanted in both ears of a rat, and reward was given only when there was a difference between the blood flows in the two ears. In this situation, the rat could not produce the desired results by altering a general process, such as an increase in blood flow or an alteration in heart rate. The rat learned to control its blood flow to each ear differentially, raising it first in one and then in the other.

Another result of Miller's studies relates directly to meditation as a process of turning off competing activity, metaphorically, turning off the light of day. When Miller first administered curare to his animals, he feared it might slow their rate of learning to control physiological processes. The reverse turned out to be true. The animals that were paralyzed by curare could learn much more quickly to alter their heart rate, blood flow, kidney functions, and so on. Curare is a drug that halts all ordinary movements and the proprioceptive impulses that would normally enter awareness. It may be, then, that curare in these experimental animals performs a function similar to that of meditation in people. Both are means of reducing irrelevant activity, and both may make the detection of faint internal signals much more possible.

Figure 10-1 The reward for correct visceral responses in Miller's experiments is electrical stimulation of the brain. Here an electrode is implanted in a "pleasure" center of the brain of a rat under anesthesia.

One unfortunate aspect of this quite important work is that it has recently seemed difficult to repeat, especially the studies using curare. Miller and associates have attempted again and again to repeat earlier studies, with little success. Yet the basic phenomena remain unchallanged: autonomic self-regulation and changes in glandular and muscular activities are possible. Fortunately our interest in these new areas does not depend on the work of one laboratory alone, but on work in several laboratories—some begun at the same time as Miller's, some stimulated by his work.[10]

Bernard Engel and his associates at the National Institutes of Health have demonstrated control of both heart rate and heart conduction in a patient population.[11] David Shapiro and co-workers at both Harvard and UCLA (notably Gary Schwartz at Harvard) have pursued a more basic research strategy and have demonstrated differential learning of speeding and slowing the heart, and raising and lowering blood pressure, by ordinary college students, often in a single session of feedback training.[12]

THE PROCESS OF INTERNAL CONTROL

The basic feedback experiment is quite simple in concept, yet it rests on complex technological achievements. In research on brain waves, for instance, electrodes are placed on the scalp at several points. If the experiment is "alpha feedback," the entire EEG is filtered, leaving only the 8 to 12 Hertz (Hz) alpha band. Then the filtered EEG is converted into a tone or a light that signals the presence or absence of alpha to the subject. Ordinarily, we remain unaware of the transitory alterations of our brain and of brain electrical activity, but with sensitive equipment to detect, amplify, and "feed-back" these weak internal signals, we are placed in a new and intimate relationship with ourselves.

As we listen to the tone varying in loudness, we can gradually come to discriminate internal states and eventually to discover which internal manipulations produce the desired changes in the brain. After control is learned, the feedback apparatus may no longer be as necessary, since we may possibly reproduce the desired internal state without the feedback apparatus.[13]

A similar research procedure is usually followed in the experiments on self-control of heart activity and the tension of the muscles. The physiological monitoring machinery may be expensive and complicated, but the entire process is less so. From one viewpoint, this research may be an electronic adjunct to yoga; from another, physiological cybernetics; and from another, purely behaviorism (operant conditioning).

Contrary to what has been claimed in the popular press, however, physiological feedback research is in the earliest of stages. Although some writers have given the impression that instant enlightenment through electric Zen is just around the corner for all, this prophecy will never be fulfilled. Current developments in feedback training are hardly in the same league with the procedures of the esoteric traditions. But although research speculation has often been presented as fact, what *has* already been discovered is enough to change the old concept in the scientific community of our inability to self-regulate the brain, heart, and muscular activity. In the esoteric traditions, this mastery is often only a prelude to further development—in some cases, merely an exercise, in others, one aspect of complex methodology.

Within the framework of modern science and clinical research, this "prelude" may open up new medical and educational possibilities. Self-control of muscle tension and heart activity may well have direct therapeutic applications for ordinary people. The brain-control work has certainly received the most popular attention, since the brain is the most mysterious organ in the body, and anything that relates to the brain takes on a special air. But the precise moment-to-moment workings of the brain are still largely unknown, and the EEG is far from perfect as an instrument for learning about the brain. Furthermore, EEG feedback research is the most difficult to carry out, and of all these experiments, it is by far the furthest away from any true practicality, although it has had the most play in popular media.

RESEARCH

Yet, a research tool, biofeedback holds great promise. Relationships between physiological and mental states have posed some of the most important questions in psychology for many years. Feedback may enable a person to hold a physiological state constant for a long period of time, which may enable the mode of operation of the nervous system to be carefully monitored and correlated with verbal and other measures of consciousness. This type of research might allow us to develop an external index of internal "states of consciousness," so that experimenters may be able to train the occurrence of desired nervous system conditions. A similar development occurred some time ago in dream research, when it was discovered that people moved their eyes rapidly while they were in the process of dreaming. These rapid eye movement (REM) periods then enabled the scientific study of the dream state. For example, researchers could predict the appearance of dreams and wake subjects after REM periods for dream recall.

As it relates to the understanding of consciousness, biofeedback training may allow us to renew the exploration of introspection, which has been dormant since Titchener, since reports of self-observation may now be correlated with an objective physiological index, such as the EEG. A major research problem is that the EEG is a somewhat poor instrument for studying the most complex organ in the world.

At first it was sufficient to monitor alpha from an arbitrarily selected area on the scalp. This approach was given some support by the finding that many subjects seemed to report a common experience during alpha control. They described the high-alpha state as "relaxed," "dark," "back of the head," especially when alpha from the occipital area was being trained. But these commonalities are no longer overwhelmingly impressive. A much more precise and complex configuration of electroencephalographic activity must be specified in order to study the relation of brain events to subjective events.

After all, the areas of the brain are specialized for different sorts of information-processing. Brain injury to one hemisphere or the other produces different effects on the verbal and spatial modes; for instance, damage to the occipital cortex will result in loss of visual experience. The appearance of a certain brain rhythm indicates a different mode of information-processing, *depending on the area from which it is recorded*. To speak, for instance, of a high-alpha state without describing both the area from which it is recorded and the concurrent activity throughout the brain is an incomplete and almost useless statement.

The alpha rhythm does seem, though, to indicate a diminution of information-processing activity in a given area of the brain. For instance, when the eyes are closed, alpha in the occipital (visual) cortex is increased, and as mentioned earlier, during the "turning-off" form of meditation, alpha is generally enhanced.

As noted earlier, David Galin and I have recently compared the EEG activity of the two sides of the brain during the performance of tasks designed to engage predominantly one or the other cerebral hemisphere. An increase in alpha rhythm appears in the hemisphere less involved in the task. There is more alpha in the left hemisphere during spatial information-processing than during verbal thought. This reverses for the right hemisphere: there is more alpha in the right side during verbal information-processing than spatial. The brain seems to "turn off" the area not involved in the situation. This research may lead to a more functionally relevant form of EEG feedback, one which takes the lateral specialization of the brain into account. With the development of this technique, students, for instance, may be able to learn to place themselves in the "correct" brain state for different kinds of information-processing situations, one for making ceramics, the other for reading.[14]

MEDICINE

Our medical endeavor is primarily directed toward the treatment of diseases, not toward individual responsibility for health. We attempt to control bodily problems from the "outside" with drugs, rather than to employ the individual's built-in capacity for self-regulation. The disease of hypertension, for instance, is most often controlled by multiple drugs, some of which must be used to balance the effects of others. As each new drug is developed, as each new surgical procedure is perfected, less and less responsibility for the cure is delegated to the patient himself. Although we have achieved an extraordinary amount of sophistication in drug and surgical therapy in Western medicine, this development has been a bit unbalanced. We have almost forgotten that it is possible for the patients *themselves* to learn directly to lower their blood pressure, to slow or speed their heart, to relax at will.

Perhaps we might begin the long process of returning at least some responsibility to the patient, of allowing much more active roles in self-healing. The current developments in self-regulation research may, in time, enable a physician to prescribe specific kinds of training for certain disorders instead of drugs. Some possible uses of feedback in medicine might include reduction of hypertension, the control of gastrointestinal disorders, the lessening of tension headaches, the regulation of cardiac arrythmia. In a few years, inexpensive trainers might possibly be developed to allow the patient to monitor and to control disorders, and once the control is learned, to aid in preventing the recurrence of the disorder.

Little is known about the eventual applications of feedback training at present. The limits of our voluntary physiological alteration, as well as the aftereffects of such changes, are still items for speculation and for further empirical research. However, it is known that in addition to the brain and heart rhythms, blood flow, the galvanic skin response, the muscular tension of certain muscle groups (the frontalis muscles on the forehead), and skin temperature are alterable in people.

Johann Stoyva and Thomas Budzynski at the University of Colorado Medical Center have been investigating the possibility of "deconditioning" or "desensitizing" by feedback. In behavioral psychotherapy, many psychological problems—such as phobias, headaches, and anxiety—are thought of simply as faulty learning.[15]

According to this view, a neurotic person simply responds in an inappropriate manner and becomes anxious and increases muscle tension in a situation that does not call for it. The therapy consists in training the person to relax, instead of tensing, in response to the "threatening" stimulus. Stoyva and Budzynski have used the electromyogram (EMG), which measures muscular tension, as an indication of relaxation in response to previously threatening stimuli. With a large number of subjects and a follow-up study, they have shown that people trained to decrease muscle tension (from the forehead) in a feedback situation can significantly reduce their tension headaches.[16] In their program at the Menninger Foundation in Kansas, Green and associates are drawing from the "autogenic training" of Luthe. This training consists primarily of a set of phrases to be repeated by the patient (such as, "my limbs are heavy," and so on) for which there is evidence of therapeutic utility. These, combined with more direct feedback on temperature and blood flow, have been useful in treatment of migraine headaches.[17] Their findings indicate that the process of learning to relax in a situation that previously had elicited anxiety can be greatly speeded up by the use of physiological feedback techniques. If a person can "hear" his own muscle tension and brain electrical activity, he can monitor them continuously and keep them more precisely in the desired state. These examples, built around current research, are an exciting and useful development of science's new view of the nervous system, although to the esoteric traditions these are just the beginnings of the possibilities.

EDUCATION

There are two possible uses of self-regulation training in education. First, it might increase the efficiency of ordinary education by training attentional deployment, using physiological indicators so that information can be more efficiently received. Second, feedback may extend our concept of education itself to include teaching students, in the most intimate manner, to contact their own internal states.

The great increase in the number of students has resulted in less and less individual attention for each student. Computer-assisted instruction is often held to be the answer to this problem, but this technique does not consider the individual student, except perhaps in taking his pace and level into account. The application of computing machines to teaching has primarily been directed toward the development of very fast drill and practice machines. This type of instruction has never tried to take the "state" of the learner into account.

While reading, for instance, we all have experienced times when our attention lapsed and we were "looking" at the pages yet nothing registered in our awareness. At other times, we may have been too tense or too preoccupied to "pay attention" to what was presented to us.

Physiological feedback training may be of help here. Suppose that research could delineate certain physiological processes that are associated with, say, efficient verbal information-processing. We would then connect the student's nervous system, as well as his hands and eyes, to the computer teacher, which would present information only if there were an appropriate pattern of physiological activity. In order to see the text, the student would need to produce a physiological state in which he could read efficiently. If his attention lapsed (and if we could find a pattern of physiological activity that correlated with this), the material would disappear from view and the student would be made immediately aware that he needed to change his mode of information-processing.

We do not really know now whether we will actually be able to find patterns of physiological activity that unequivocally indicate efficient attention and memory, but this general aim is certainly worth investigating. We have little firm evidence to go on as yet, save for the one obvious step of working with students who are motivated to learn but who are so tense they cannot. These students might be trained to produce low levels of muscular tension before they can see the information being presented. Allowing a computer-tutor to monitor the physiology of the learner could be one of the possible solutions, and an extremely valuable one to the existing problem of over-crowded schools. It may be possible to train different modes of awareness—verbal, logical, spatial, and so on—based on different patterns of brain activity, taking the brain's lateral specialization of function into account.

However, the larger import of the newer view of our voluntary capabilities is that the definition of education *itself* may be broadened. We distinguish two types of knowing: one concerned with the reception of information, one concerned with direct experience. We shy away from the experiential mode in education, for it is not "objective," not easily monitorable. But if the proper feedback devices are developed, we could include in each person's basic learning experience a training in his or her own capacities of self-regulation. We could teach relaxation to students just as we teach baseball. The concept of "physical education" could be expanded to include the mastery of internal states. We could allow people to be more sensitive to the state of their own bodies, and more in keeping with the intent of the esoteric psychologies, to know themselves in a most intimate way, to know more often and more consistently what they wish.

In the past, these capacities have been trained only by those who could learn the esoteric procedures of the traditional psychologies. With sensitive technological devices to bring the very faint and subtle signals into ordinary consciousness, this general form of self-mastery may be the province of many—in schools, in hospitals, in clinics, in educational resource centers.

A CAUTION

In any new and exciting area of research, the claims sometimes outweigh the usefulness. For instance, there are no developed programs for therapy that is built soley around biofeedback. Most, if not all, of the commercially available machines are either faulty or, if they work, will train something that is hardly useful (EEG alpha) or perhaps harmful (blood pressure changes). The responsibility for this rests largely on the early workers in EEG feedback who allowed many to be misled as to the state of the art of this training. It is an area in which many new possibilities may be available, but few of them have been delivered. It is clear that less promises and more research work and empirical data would be useful.

A CONCLUSION

Physiological feedback represents a high point of synthesis within modern science, yet it too is in its inception. It combines a traditional knowledge of the possibilities of human self-mastery and the most sophisticated tools of modern science and technology. The new synthesis may well extend the personal capacities of many in this culture, and in a readily assimilable way.

This research so far in biofeedback marks the merest beginnings of a new attempt to turn the direction of modern technology itself inward, away from the control and manipulation of the external environment. Just as technology has often limited man's personal capacities, so it can also extend them. Technology *itself* is neutral and can be employed to make man less or more human. In the feedback paradigm, technology has been refocused toward an extension of our own personal capacities rather than a diminution of them. This is a new development, man using his own technology to discover himself, personally, and at the same time to observe himself in an objective, scientific manner. Rarely have the two forms of knowledge been combined in a single situation.

FOR FURTHER READING

LEO V. DICARA. "Learning in the Autonomic Nervous System." *Scientific American*, January 1970, p. 39.

RALPH EZIOS. "Implications of Physiological Feedback Training."

The preceding have been collected in Robert Ornstein, ed. *The Nature of Human Consciousness*. San Francisco: W.H. Freeman; New York: Viking Press, 1973.

THEODORE BARBER et al., eds. *Biofeedback and Self-control Reader.* Chicago: Aldine-Atherton, 1971.

THEODORE BARBER et al., eds. *Biofeedback and Self-control.* 1970–1975. Chicago: Aldine-Atherton, 1971–76.

WOLFGANG LUTHE. "Autogenic Training: Method, Research and Application in Medicine." In *Altered States of Consciousness*, edited by Charles T. Tart. New York: Doubleday, 1972.

LEE BIRK, ed. *Biofeedback: Behavioral Medicine.* New York: Grune & Stratton, 1972.

11 An Extended Concept of Human Consciousness

Fishes and Water

Fishes, asking what water was, went to a wise fish. He told them that it was all around them, yet they still thought that they were thirsty.[1]

Although undeveloped, biofeedback research and the new ideas of the developments of consciousness are examples of a new synthesis, of an extended conception of human capability and of contemporary methodology to carry it out. In terms of scientific knowledge, other aspects of this synthesis and most of the systems and techniques concerned with them have hardly begun to be developed; thus much of this chapter must be theoretical and speculative, and can attempt merely to point to what might be studied rather than to what is known.

But the new synthesis does take into account that human beings are sensitive to the geophysical environment in ways not ordinarily considered in modern science; that body states may link the geophysical surroundings to consciousness; that the intentions of many forms of psychotherapy may have been unduly restricted; that man is potentially sensitive to subtle "paranormal" communications from other people; that a truly contemporary system of the development of consciousness may be possible. These are a very few of the possible new directions of scientific inquiry, as I see them. The chapter ends by pointing to a complementary new synthesis, a fresh attempt at a contemporary projection of the esoteric traditions.

THE GEOPHYSICAL ENVIRONMENT

Like fish, human beings live in an unnoticed ocean, yet ours is one of air, light, and gravity. We inhale and exhale 10,000 liters of air each day. Light energy constantly impinges on us. Gravity is always present, wherever we are on earth. Our sense organs, by their very physiological design, detect only a small fraction of the available energy. Of the energy to which we are sensitive, it is primarily *changes* in the input that are transmitted to the brain. Any process beyond the "ordinary" sense range, as well as any constant process within our normal sense range, usually escapes our consciousness. We are aware of the quickly changing shapes of light images, but the light-dark rhythms of the earth move too slowly for our notice. We are aware of the air only when it is polluted. Gravity has shaped even the most intimate details of our structure, but since it is so constant and so slow to change, like water by the fish, gravity is easy to ignore.

The physiological and psychological effects of these subtle geophysical factors are difficult to conceptualize—like trying to imagine what a fish's physiology would be like without water. The contents of contemporary psychology (among many other academic disciplines) reflect our personal lack of awareness of the geophysical surrounding: psychologists have devoted thousands of experiments, for example, to exploring how lists of nonsense syllables are learned, and yet have performed almost no research on the effects of the air, of light *per se*, or gravity, on man. Not only do individual people tend to screen out the subtle constancies of the environment, the scientific community does the same.

Yet these factors are constant and are important in behavior and psychology. The seasons come and go; the moon rises and sets; the earth turns continuously. But people in our culture now live most of their lives indoors, perceptually isolated from these geophysical changes. The person living in a city, for instance, may miss seeing the moon for months on end. We remain unaware of the shortening and lengthening of the days; our artificial environment dissociates us from the geophysical world. Once again, let us return to the metaphor of stars and daylight: forces subtle and constant are difficult to perceive in the brilliance of daylight. Ordinary personal consciousness usually places these forces "on automatic," as it does the weak internal signals of the "autonomic" nervous system. It is beyond the norm to sense these weak energies, and generally we do not.

And yet, the esoteric psychologies have emphasized that under certain conditions, man can engage in subtle communication with the geophysical surroundings and with other people, communications sometimes considered "paranormal." Biofeedback training is beginning to synthesize the two kinds of psychologies; the current interest in biological rhythms, in the effects of the air, light, and gravity on man, and in "extrasensory" perception may represent some future elements of this new synthesis.

Biological Rhythms

Ordinarily, we consider ourselves stable beings with enduring personal characteristics. This consideration extends to our perception and scientific conception of other people as well. We may categorize one person as "aggressive" or "smart" or "moody" and file our memories of him in this category. The stability of an individual's personality is in large part a construction of ordinary consciousness.

The idea of a person's stability, whether our own or someone else's, seems to be a simplifying assumption that each of us makes to stabilize our personal world, just as our ordinary, immediate assumption of the rectangularity of rooms is a simplifying assumption.

The everyday assumption of stability, whether about personality or about biology, does not seem to withstand a more rigorous empirical analysis. A new field of research challenges this assumption. The earth is constantly moving, constantly changing. The sun rises and sets each day, yet the days slowly, imperceptibly lengthen and wane throughout the cycle of the year. There are well-known seasonal cycles of nesting, growth, migration, and so on—and others that are less clearly demarcated and less well known. There exist cycles in our daily lives as there are cycles in the earth. We are, for example, more sensitive to respiratory diseases at night than during the day.

The light–dark cycle of the earth is perpetually in a process of gradual alteration, and the growing and flowering of plants are in phase with this rhythm. Mating among animals is most prevalent during springtime. From research already done, we know there is a rhythmic structure in our bodies, in our brain waves—all somewhat linked to the cycle of the day. But even these daily changes are so subtle and slow that they are partialed out of personal consciousness and are largely ignored by the scientific community.

Internal biological rhythms are subtle, and most are not marked by an obvious external signal, such as the full moon. One of the few rhythms in humans that does manifest as a readily observable event is woman's menstrual cycle. Premenstrual tension is experienced by many women in the three to four days preceding the onset of the menses. Gay Luce writes, "An estimated 60 percent of women suffer some palpable change at this time, perhaps just mild irritation, depression, headache, or decline in attention or vision." Body temperature undergoes daily rhythmic changes in both men and women. According to Luce, a person whose temperature peaks in the morning usually finds his or her highest periods of intellectual functioning during those morning hours, whereas a temperature peak in the late evening usually signifies a "night person."[2]

The lack of awareness of our rhythmic structure may cause grave mistakes both in psychological research and in our personal assessments of others. To take one example, if a psychotherapist or physician sees a patient only early in the morning, he may be seeing a person whose activity, internal physiology, and mood differ radically during the remainder of the day.

These rhythmic variations in a person's state can sometimes become quite extreme. One salesman was subject to periodic psychoses every four days. If he attempted to work on his bad days, he found himself completely unable to do anything but sit tensely in his car all day. He finally became aware of the rhythmic nature of his illness and remained home each fourth day, so he could work normally during the other three. Most biological rhythms are more subtle than periodic psychoses, but many intellectual and personal capacities may undergo such variations.[3]

People who travel on transcontinental airplanes often report feeling "out of sorts" for a few days after the trip. This feeling is apparently caused by the inability of our internal rhythms to adjust quickly to time changes. The discomfort cannot be attributed to the length of the air ride itself, for travelers on north–south routes of equal length do not experience similar problems in adjustment. Most people are not yet conscious enough of their rhythmic structure to plan around these factors. Nevertheless, some account is beginning to be taken of biological rhythms. For instance, many companies and governments are sending executives to meetings three or four days early so that their efficiency will not be disturbed by the alterations in time zones.

To take another example, the light–dark cycle of the earth varies daily. Our visual system is, of course, responsive to changes in light, but we are rarely aware of how the presence of light energy itself is important in the maintenance of many life processes. Alterations in the light–dark cycle affect the periods of the blossoming of flowers. The biologist Karl Linnaeus once constructed a "flower clock" that "kept time" by the opening and closing of different flowers during the day.

In the spring, the exposure to increasing amounts of light sets off a chain reaction in the brains of many mammals. This reaction involves the pituitary gland and results in an increase in sexual hormones. In experimental tests, optic fibers have been implanted in the pituitary gland, and the artificial introduction of light energy has resulted in a stimulation of sexual activity. The precise function of the pituitary and even the pineal glands in man remains unclear, but Von Bount, Ganong, and their associates have found that light energy does enter the brains of mammals directly, not only through the visual system.[4] The direct presence of light inside the brain may provide a mechanism that can explain sensitivity to factors of which "ordinary consciousness" remains ignorant, for example, alterations in the absolute amount of light present during a season. But how and where this process might occur, if it does occur, is completely unknown. Some preliminary reports indicate that light may possibly regulate the menstrual cycle. A group of women whose menses were irregular were asked to sleep in lighted rooms during the fourteenth, fifteenth, and sixteenth nights of their cycle (that is, the normal ovulation time of regular cycles). Gay Luce reports that for many of them the menses became regular.[5]

In brief, many personal and biological cycles remain unnoticed. Daily as well as monthly cycles are difficult to perceive, unless there is a physical event, such as menses or the new moon, to mark them. A yearly cycle is even more difficult, and one of ten years, still more so. In addition, the scientific study of biological rhythms is extremely laborious and technically arduous. Such a study may require daily or even hourly records to be kept over many years. Then complex computer analysis may be required in order for any subtle rhythms in the data to emerge. This field clearly involves exacting and tedious research, but, in the words of Gay Luce, "Not knowing about our rhythmic structure is like not knowing that one has a heart or lungs."

Air

We are continually in a process of exchange with the air, a fact so obvious that it is largley taken for granted, much as is water by fish. Deprived of air for ten minutes, we would die.

Subtle alterations in the quality of the air do affect us. When we are depressed indoors, we may open the windows to get "fresh" air. With more leisure and means, we might travel to a resort in the high mountains or to one by the sea. In many different cultures, certain "winds of ill-repute," such as the Khamsin, the Mistral, the Santa Ana, and the Foehn, are reported to affect the health and moods of many. In the seasons when these winds blow, admissions to mental hospitals, crimes of violence, and certain illnesses are reported to increase. Similarly, at these times judges are said to exhibit greater leniency than usual.

The traditional esoteric psychologists have noticed the effects of variations in air quality on man. For instance, many teachers of esoteric psychology emphasize that "nutrition" for man exists on several levels. In certain places, the air contains a form of this human "nutrition." In considering the esoteric conception of energy forms, we discussed earlier the yogic concept *Prana.* The yogi Vishnudevananda says of it, "Prana is in the air [but] . . . not in any of its chemical constituents. Animal and plant life breathe this energy."[6] Another book on yoga is more explicit about the mechanism. It suggests, "take every opportunity to spend time in rural surroundings, especially in large open areas, such as deserts, meadows, sea shores, or lakes. Atmospheric ions, which are minute charges in air molecules, are negative in large open spaces of this kind."[7]

The presence of the minutely charged atmospheric ions may constitute a physical analog of the esoteric "energy form" of Prana. In the Hindu tradition, Prana is held to be the "life force," from which health and creativity flow, the force that aids in physical as well as psychological growth. At this point, we cannot measure precisely how much overlap there is between negative air ions and the concept of Prana, but some interesting similarities do exist. The esoteric traditions have long taken advantage of favorable microclimatic conditions for their students. Schools have often been located on mountain tops, near waterfalls, or near the ocean. Some recent biological studies have determined that the ionization of the air in these places is predominantly negative.

Many aspects of the esoteric traditions stress that when breathing exercises are performed, "time and place" must be taken into account. The "time" is the acknowledgment of the rhythmic structure of man. The "place" may refer, in part, to the presence of the favorable microclimate—negative ionization. The relationship between breathing and consciousness has been stressed in esoteric traditions. As it does for "body energies," our colloquial language preserves some of the dimensions of this relationship. To note one instance, *inspiration* refers both to creativity and to the process of breathing.

On somewhat more conventionally empiric grounds, research is just beginning on the effects of atmospheric ionization on human (plant and animal) physiology and consciousness. In one study, the "stuffy" feeling in rooms is reported to disappear when negative ionization is introduced, and the mood of those present is also reported to be altered.[8] The "winds of ill-repute" have been measured and found to carry an unusually high amount of positive ions.[9]

In smog, as well as in certain wind patterns, absence of ions, or preponderance of positive ions, have been linked to health disturbances. Some recent research has suggested that changes in air ions can alter resistance to infectious diseases. An experiment by A.P. Krueger of the University of California at Berkeley indicates that mice who are deliberately exposed to an infectious disease die more quickly in a positively ionized atmosphere than in ordinary room air. For this study, Krueger and his associates observed mice living in chambers in which the air ion content was rigidly controlled. Measured amounts of arithrospores carrying coccidioidomycosis (an infectious lung disease) were introduced into the noses of the mice. By the thirtieth day, 55 percent of the mice that had been breathing positively ionized air were dead, compared with 30 percent of those breathing laboratory air.[10] In other studies, an increase in negative ionization seems to speed up tissue growth.[11] The increase of positive ions is reported to slow down the growth of certain plants.[12]

Some less well controlled research suggests that negative ionization aids in healing, especially in recovery from burns.[13] A Russian report contends that deprived of negative ions in the air animals die within a month.[14] Although not all these reports have been fully confirmed and few deal with research done directly on humans, it is now clear that atmospheric ions, present as subtle quantities in the air, do affect man, other animals, and plants.[15]

Research into the effects of ionization is now in its beginning stages. Many of the important questions have not yet even been asked. For instance, how much ionization is needed to have significant effects on man? Does negatively ionized air alter mood systematically? Could the introduction of negatively ionized air produce results similar to those achieved by difficult and esoteric breath manipulations? Can healing be aided significantly by the introduction of postinjury or postoperative doses of negative ionization? Photochemical smog strips ions from the air, leaving a balance of positively charged ones. Could some of the deleterious effects of polluted air be countered by the artificial generation of negative ions? We need more carefully controlled studies (such as those performed by Krueger) to give us systematic answers to these and other questions, since our ordinary consciousness is inadequate to perceive the subtle effects of the air's ionization.

Gravity and Structural Integration

One of the forces ignored in personal consciousness is gravity, since we have no specific organ, no "eye" that could "see" it. Because gravity is perpetually present and virtually unchanging in its effects, those effects are imperceptible to us. But just as the structure of fishes has evolved to suit the medium of water, so our structure has been shaped by the gravitational field.

One recent approach to the study of man does take the gravitational field into account, the technique of *structural integration*, developed by Ida Rolf.[16] This is a body-centered technique and gives due weight to the esoteric consideration that body states and subtle "body energies" can affect consciousness. The disciplines of aikido, tai-chi ch'uan, kung fu, karate, and hatha yoga, among many others, followed a line of development similar to that of structural integration. The interrelatedness of body states and awareness is part of ordinary experience as well but has not been much explored by contemporary scientific psychology. To take an obvious example, pain is a dimension of consciousness associated with damage to the body, and when we are in pain, our awareness is radically different than in times of well-being.

Many of the contemporary scientific approaches to consciousness are purely mentalistic, as if the brain were really a disembodied computer. It has, however, been noted by many theorists that the primary job of the brain is to control the body, and the body has evolved to function within the gravitational field.

Just as biofeedback training may be a more modern approach to self-regulation than is hatha yoga, and negative ion generators might translate a traditional conception of "energy" into a modern form, so structural integration may constitute a more modern approach to some of the difficult body alignment exercises.

The techniques of structural integration combine the esoteric emphasis on the interrelatedness of body states and consciousness with a much more modern knowledge of anatomy and physiology.

This practice is a craft in which the skilled hands of the practitioner attempt to align the body with the gravitational field. Working on somewhat similar assumptions, the yogic tradition has emphasized that the body is not fixed in structure but is plastic and can be altered through a series of postures (*asanas*).

Structural integration extends the concept of the body's plasticity; the practitioner attempts to quicken this process of alignment by active manipulation. Whereas biofeedback techniques newly link the disconnected worlds of *psyche* and *soma*, structural integration works from the other end, manipulating the body structure to affect consciousness—a *somatopsychic* approach.

But could these bodily changes affect consciousness? Recent research on this point reveals a convergence of structural integration and some aspects of contemporary psychology. We have earlier discussed one major theoretical approach to consciousness in psychology that holds that the contents of ordinary consciousness depend predominantly on the preparation for motor output. This approach begins with the understanding that the major job of the brain is to run the body. The hypothesis implies that ordinary consciousness consists in an implicit preparation to respond to the external environment. This mode is active, obviously concerned with physical manipulation of the environment and the biological survival of the organism. The movements of the limbs and eyes, and the requirements of speech, involve large areas of the cerebral cortex. The most radical statement of this theory is that the "readiness" to issue a motor command that constitutes the brain's preparation for action *is* the contents of ordinary awareness.

In this theory, any alteration in body alignment, limb position, or responsivity to central commands would eventually alter the "readiness" of the brain, and consciousness would be changed. Through experimental tests of structural integration, we might be able to study whether alterations in consciousness can be caused by changes in the patterns of muscle activity.

The technique of structural integration opens up many other possibilities for research, since it is directly manipulative and since the alterations in body structure are held to occur quickly and to be measurable. First, we will need some sound documentation of the actual changes that occur in the body as a result of structural integration. Additionally, we might ask *which* body changes can affect consciousness, whether memories might have some triggers in the body as well as in the brain, whether radical alterations in breathing patterns, for instance, can affect processes of awareness, and even whether orthodox medicine might benefit from a holistic approach to the body. There are only tentative and sketchy research reports at present, which neither confirm nor deny the claims of the technique.

THE SEEDS OF SYNTHESIS: OTHER CONTEMPORARY APPROACHES

Gestalt Therapy

Two new forms of psychotherapy similarly contain the seeds of the new synthesis. The process of Gestalt therapy is an alternate route to the present-centeredness sought in meditation. In concentrative meditation, one is continuously instructed to discard thoughts. In Gestalt therapy, the thinking process is given the pejorative term *computing,* and the participant in this technique is invited to concentrate more on the immediate situation, to "stay in the present continuum of awareness." In addition, this system strongly emphasizes that ordinary consciousness is a personal construction and that each person is capable of and even responsible for, changing the contents of his own consciousness.[17]

Gestalt therapy also recognizes the verbal-intuitive split in consciousness. Often we may utter an innocuous phrase such as, "I am very pleased with this," while our voice and gestures indicate just the opposite. The practitioners of Gestalt therapy invite the participants to become aware of their body language and therefore to bring their *whole** selves into consciousness. This is often done by constantly asking the participant, What is your body telling you? What is your tone of voice saying? What is your hand saying? In essence, these questions are saying, What is happening within your nonverbal, "right-hemisphere" side? Bring it to your consciousness.

Fritz Perls, the originator of the technique, comments on the two modes of consciousness:

*From which comes the word *Gestalt,* not to be confused with the Gestalt psychology of Wolfgang Kohler.

The right hand is usually the motoric, male, aggressive side that wants to control, to determine what is, to decide what is "right." The left side is the female side; it is usually poorly coordinated. *Left* means awkward in many languages: *gauche* in French, *linkisch* in German. When there is a conflict between emotional life and active life, there is neurosis. . . . But when both power and sensitivity are working in coordination there is genius. . . . Ultimate awareness can only take place if the computer is gone, if the intuition, the awareness is so bright that one really comes to his senses. The empty mind in Eastern philosophy is worthy of highest praise. So lose your mind and come to your senses.[18]

Research on "Paranormal" Phenomena

Contemporary science has rediscovered that man does possess many capacities beyond those usually considered normal. A few years ago it would have been considered "paranormal" to claim control over blood pressure, but now a freshman in a psychological experiment can expect to learn some measure of blood-pressure control in half an hour. In most life situations, we are not very aware of the subtle signals of our internal physiology, but under certain conditions we can make contact with these phenomena that are usually obscured by our normal functioning.

To recapitulate briefly: The structure of our nervous system allows us only a limited selection from the available stimulation. Our eyes, ears, and brain each select, and we must then construct a stable personal consciousness from this limited input. Although we are usually insensitive to many aspects of the geophysical environment, we may, during special conditions or after special exercises, become sensitive to them. We do not possess a receptor for gravity; yet we have evolved to take advantage of this force. We are not normally aware of the light that enters our brain directly; yet it is there and may affect the pituitary. Our autonomic nervous system is usually screened from ordinary awareness; yet we may contact it, either by boosting the strength of the signal, as in biofeedback training, or by reducing the competing noise, as in the esoteric traditions.

The ordinary mode of consciousness can be characterized as analytic, sequential, and limited by the characteristics of our sense organs. A second major mode of consciousness is available to us; it may be characterized as receptive and holistic, one in which all action can be perceived simultaneously. For thousands of years the development of this mode has been primarily the province of the esoteric traditions. Within the writings of these traditions, many faculties considered paranormal are described, for example, the symbolic portrayal in "The Man Who Walked on Water," at the beginning of Chapter 8. Meditation is reported to bring about a state of "darkness," a shift in the receptive characteristics of consciousness, so that sensitivity is increased to a new segment of the internal, personal, and geophysical environment.

The linear sequence of events is our own personal, cultural, and scientific construction. It is certainly convenient and is perhaps necessary for biological survival and the development of a complex, technological society, but it is only one of the many possible constructions of consciousness available to man. In the linear mode, we receive and process input primarily in sequence, one event following the other like the hours of a clock. If a second mode exists in which the concept of future and past are irrelevant, then many phenomena within that second mode will seem to "transcend" the ordinary notion of time—but only for those who attempt to account for *all* phenomena within the linear and sequential mode.

Thus a shift to the mode of the "night" may well enable an "extraordinary" communication. This "paranormal" communication can exist between different systems inside one person or between individuals and the geophysical surroundings or between two people.

The problem for a scientific inquiry into these phenomena is, of course, that science is restricted to the linear and analytic. Each investigator would like "proof" of these phenomena within his own terms. However, just as an illiterate peasant must satisfy the requirements of technology in order to construct a spaceship, so Western scientists must be prepared to satisfy the conditions of these subtle phenomena in order to demonstrate their reality.

For instance, when we chart the fluctuations of biological activity over many days, an often-unnoticed rhythm emerges. When we measure the tiny electrical charges in the atmosphere before and during a certain wind, a subtle phenomenon emerges. When we build a machine to amplify the subtle internal signals of which we are usually unaware, they can come to consciousness.

Similarly, even to begin any scientific analysis of paranormal communication, certain relevant questions must be asked. In what mode of consciousness do these communications occur? What is the nature of the information transmitted?

Just as with biofeedback training and biological rhythms, some clues may be found in the writings of the traditional esoteric psychologists, the specialists in the intuitive mode. Their writings often report that at night, during sleep, when the normal, outward-oriented consciousness is turned off, when the "silent" side is dominant, some people can receive this unusual form of communication. The paranormal communications reported in esoteric traditions are often of great importance and of great emotional significance. It might be said that "emotion is the fuel of this manner of communication."[19] In a scientific experiment, then, it might be quite difficult to observe such communication in a "neutral" laboratory, employing information of little import to the receiver. The obtained results may only be of statistical significance. The Hot Line between Washington and Moscow was not instituted to play cards.

If we take the mode and the nature of the communication into account, and the conditions of training, we may be able to study these subtle phenomena in the laboratory. At the dream laboratory of Maimonides Hospital in New York, Montague Ullman and his associates have begun to investigate paranormal communication in this manner.[20] Their study concerns "transmission" during sleep, using information of varying degrees of emotional significance. In these experiments, the "receiver" goes to sleep in a closed room and is monitored by the EEG. The physiological signs of dreaming include a change in the frequency characteristics of the EEG and the appearance of rapid eye movements. The REM periods are used conventionally as an indicator of dreaming in the sleeping subject.

When the EEG of the "receiver" shows that he is dreaming, the "sender," physically isolated from his partner in another room, opens one of twelve envelopes containing a painting. The reproduction might be Salvador Dali's *The Last Supper* or a quiet scene at the beach. The sender concentrates on transmitting the scene to the receiver.

At the end of a dream period, rapid eye movements stop. Using the EEG as an indicator, an experimenter in the control room near the receiver awakens the sleeper at the end of his REM period and tape-records the receiver's remembered contents of the dream. Of course, this experimenter does not know what was in the envelope.

The sender then awaits the onset of the next REM period and re-sumes "transmission"; the receiver is again awakened after the dream. This process continues throughout the night.

Later, the transcripts of the recordings are sent to a panel of judges, who do not know which painting was "sent" during which dream. The judges attempt to match the transcripts of dreams and the set of twelve paintings. Each painting has, then, a chance probability of being judged the stimulus that was "sent." An increase in that probability beyond chance would presumably be due to the similarity of the dream and the painting. The matches for the paintings con-taining highly emotional situations have been found to be quite interesting; the matches have as yet not been repeated, so their significance awaits further evidence.

These experiments are but one series that seem to indicate that emotionality has an effect on this mode of communication, but these reports will need confirmation by other investigators.[21] During nor-mal, waking consciousness, the communication may be obscured by the brilliance of the active mode, and the information may not come to awareness. Some studies of paranormal communication have found, for instance, consistent changes in physiological reactions that the person is not aware of. An intriguing but preliminary study at the Stanford Research Institute considered this approach. A subject was seated in a quiet room, and her EEG was recorded. When a light is flashed, the occipital EEG (recorded over the visual area of the brain) usually shows a diminution in alpha activity. In this experiment the light was flashed, but in a remote room, and the subject's EEG was compared with intervals in which there were no flashes and in which there were 6 or 16 per second. A significant decrease in alpha power was found in the 16 Hz interval, although the subject could not "consciously" identify the intervals of flashes.[22]

Since the internal cues may be present, as in biofeedback training, yet not reach verbal awareness, perhaps people can be trained to be more sensitive to information available to them, either through an analogous feedback system or through simple training of correct and incorrect response in a guessing situation.[23] If the subtle nature of the phenomenon is considered and if the mode of consciousness of the participants is considered, these subtle, paranormal communications might be scientifically studied. But these communications are weak and often go unnoticed in the light of the day; the research done is difficult and often preliminary, uncontrolled, or unsatisfactory, and is often of the propaganda variety.

Contemporary Sufism: The Work of Idries Shah

A new synthesis is in process within modern psychology. This synthesis combines the concerns of the esoteric traditions with the research methods and technology of modern science. In complement to this process, and feeding it, a truly contemporary approach to the problems of consciousness is arising from the esoteric traditions themselves.

When we refer to these traditions, we refer largely to teachers, exercises, and techniques of the past. The Buddha formulated his techniques especially for those in India 2,600 years ago. Mohammed's school and teaching were formulated for the Middle East 1,300 years ago. But although he was speaking primarily to those of his own time and place, Mohammed made many statements that apply to many teachers of these traditions, independent of their situation. One that is relevant to this discussion was "Speak to those in accordance with their understanding."

Sufism has existed in many cultures over a long period. Much of the exotic aspects of the esoteric traditions is due to improper importation of ideas relevant to other areas. To the question, What is Sufism? Idries Shah (currently at the head of the Sufi tradition) recently answered: "Sufism is experience of life through a method of dealing with life and human relations. This method is based on an understanding of man, which places at one's disposal the means to organize one's relationships and one's learning systems. So instead of saying that Sufism is a body of thought in which you believe certain things and don't believe certain things, we say that the Sufi experience has to be provoked in a person. Once provoked, it becomes his own property, rather as a person masters an art."[24]

Our cultures have changed drastically since the time of Mohammed, and any formulation of that tradition must undergo a fresh adaptation. Such a new formulation is currently being presented by Shah. His work employs current technology when appropriate and draws from contemporary research in psychology and philosophy. Sometimes it requires an extension of contemporary technology; for example, it involves the design and construction of a machine to produce negative ionization of the air. This modern technological work is coupled with the special form of literature that he has recently reintroduced to this culture, a contemporary version of an oral tradition, using material freshly translated into modern idiom. We have become familiar with these stories throughout this book, for they introduce the chapters and are discussed in a major section of Chapter 7. These Sufi stories are so useful in their purpose as psychological documents that they also can be used to summarize this book.

Our "ordinary" consciousness is selective and limited. Concepts of what is possible limit personal consciousness, performance, and scientific paradigm—we constantly ask ourselves questions such as, Is there any number higher than 100? There are many ways in which we limit our awareness and our possibilities. Throughout much of each day, we act like the double-seeing son and often confuse our own personal construction with external reality.

There is, however, a second mode of consciousness available to man. It exists on many levels, the cultural, personal, and biological. On the biological level, it has recently been shown that the two cerebral hemispheres of the cortex are specialized for different modes of information-processing. The left hemisphere operates primarily in a verbal-intellectual and sequential mode, the right hemisphere primarily in a spatial and simultaneous mode. This right-hemisphere mode is often devalued by the dominant, verbal intellect. Since you have not learned grammar, "half your life has been wasted," said the pedagogue to the boatman. This second mode often appears inelegant, lacking formal reasoning, linearity, and polish of the intellect. It is more involved in space than in time, more involved in intuition than in logic and language. It is a mode often forgotten and ignored, especially within the scientific community, but one that may prove important for science, and even for our own survival. "Have you ever learned to swim?" asks the boatman of the pedagogue. Since it is nonlinear, this second mode is not involved in the "ordinary" realm of cause and effect that underlies so much of our personal and intellectual life. It is present-centered, a mode in which all occurrences are said to exist as a "patterned whole," as in the drawing that accompanies "Moment in Time."

The two major types of psychology have each predominantly investigated one mode of human consciousness. Modern science is primarily verbal-logical—the mode identified with the day. The esoteric traditions have specialized in the tacit, receptive, holistic mode—the mode identified with the night, one largely inaccessible to language and reason. These two modes are portrayed in the story of the blind men and the elephant. One mode of consciousness approaches the elephant by piecemeal investigation; the other attempts to develop a perspective of the whole organism. The techniques of these esoteric traditions are often thought to involve a deliberately exotic and mysterious training, such as the use of special, mysterious "magic words" in meditation. However, the essence of the often-misunderstood technique of meditation is the focusing of awareness on a single, unchanging source of stimulation. It is the attitude, not the specific form of meditation, that is primary. If the exercise is performed correctly, a new set of capacities may emerge, symbolically portrayed in "The Man Who Walked on Water." The techniques of meditation, the dishabituation exercises, and other special exercises, such as crafts, music and dance, are in their totality designed to cause a shift from the ordinary analytic consciousness to the holistic.

We do not often realize that we may possess the separate pieces of a complete consciousness, until Nasrudin in his role points it out to us. As a guide, he may ask, Why don't you make a pair of boots out of the material at hand? And yet, like Mulla Nasrudin, we have often been looking for the key to understanding ourselves in the brilliance of the day. But it may not be there. It lies within, in our dark side, a side often forgotten because "there is more light here." Once we can locate the key within the dark area, we may be able to bring it out into the light and to achieve a new synthesis of the two modes of investigation, as in the emerging technology of biofeedback training.

When consciousness is changed, many begin to worship experiences or states. Yet these experiences may occur and still be meaningless, as happened to the sultan who was in exile. Since we construct our ordinary world around the limited input from our sensory systems, we remain largely unaware of much of our immediate environment, either because we lack the receptive organs or because the phenomena change slowly. But although fish are unaware of the medium in which they live, we need not remain unaware of our own geophysical ocean. Under certain conditions, this additional comprehensive awareness can be developed. This can lead to a new synthesis within each person, within science, and within the diverse and often antagonistic cultures of the world.

FOR FURTHER READING

LAWRENCE LESHAN. "What is Important About the Paranormal?"

DAVID S. SOBEL. "Gravity and Structural Integration."

A. P. KRUEGER. "Preliminary Consideration of the Biological Significance of Air Ions."

All the preceding have been collected in Robert Ornstein, ed. *The Nature of Human Consciousness*. San Francisco: W.H. Freeman; New York: Viking Press; 1973.

MONTAGUE ULLMAN and STANLEY KRIPPNER. *Dream Telepathy*. New York: Penguin Books, 1974.

GAY LUCE. *Body Time*. New York: Pantheon Books, 1971.

CLAUDIO NARANJO. "Present-Centeredness: Technique, Prescription and Ideal." *Gestalt Therapy Now,* edited by Joen Fagan and Irma Lee Shepherd. New York: Harper & Row, 1971.

IDRIES SHAH. *The Way of the Sufi*. New York: E.P. Dutton, 1970

IDRIES SHAH. *Wisdom of the Idiots*. New York: E.P. Dutton, 1971.

IDRIES SHAH. *The Dermis Probe*. New York: E.P. Dutton, 1971.

IDRIES SHAH. *Thinkers of the East*. Baltimore: Penguin Books, 1972.

Postscript

After all our talk of synthesis, new work, and new understandings, there remains a word of caution, addressed especially to those who work in science. It would be the height of absurdity if we were to settle now for a strictly intellectual understanding of the existence of a second mode of consciousness. The possible danger here is of a new and more elegant reductionism, of a feeling that we have tasted the implications of the esoteric traditions simply by calling them "intuitive education" or another term, reducing them to words and logic once again.

The new possibility can go beyond this—to a confluence of the two streams of knowledge, the esoteric and the modern, in science and in each of us. This confluence cannot affect the contents of science unless enough scientists work in both areas of inquiry, both professionally and personally. We can achieve a more complete science of psychology, but only if enough people make the effort to train those aspects of themselves that are usually uncultivated in Western education. This book only begins to consider some of the very radical possibilities of the esoteric traditions. If it does anything, it will be to further an organic process of synthesis of the two traditions. By its very nature, such a synthesis must draw from the personal experiences, as well as the intellectual investigations, of many. Otherwise, the limits of possibility may close on us once again; then someday someone will need to write a book that begins, "Is there any number higher than *1,000?*"

REFERENCES

CHAPTER 1

1. This story is from a Central Asian oral tradition.

2. Jerome Bruner and Leo Postman, "On the Perception of Incongruity: A Paradigm," *Journal of Personality* 18 (1949): 206–23.

3. The definitive work on paradigms is Thomas S. Kuhn, *The Structure of Scientific Revolutions* (Chicago: University of Chicago Press, 1962).

4. The point is made in Ernest R. Hilgard, "Altered States of Awareness," *The Journal of Nervous and Mental Disease* 149 (1966): 68–79. Reprinted in Theodore, Barber et al., eds., *Biofeedback and Self-Control* (Chicago: Aldine-Atherton, 1971), pp. 763–74.

5. William James, *The Varieties of Religious Experience* (New York: New American Library, 1958).

6. Abraham Maslow, *The Psychology of Science: A Reconnaissance* (Chicago: Henry Regnery, 1969).

7. Jacob Needleman, *The New Religions* (New York: Doubleday, 1970).

8. Thomas R. Blackburn, "Sensuous-Intellectual Complementarity in Science," *Science* 172 (June 4, 1971): 1003–07. Reprinted in Robert Ornstein, ed., *The Nature of Human Consciousness* (San Francisco: W. H. Freeman; New York: Viking Press, 1973).

CHAPTER 2

1. From Idries Shah, *The Exploits of the Incomparable Mulla Nasrudin* (New York: E. P. Dutton, 1972), p. 18.

2. G. William Domhoff, "But Why Did They Sit on the King's Right in the First Place?" *Psychoanalytic Review* 56 (1969–70): 586–96.

3. Jerome Bruner, *On Knowing: Essays for the Left Hand* (Cambridge, Mass.: Harvard University Press, 1962), pp. 2–5.

4. Perhaps the best review of right-hemisphere functions is Joseph E. Bogen, "The Other Side of the Brain, I, II, III," *Bulletin of the Los Angeles Neurological Societies* 34, no. 3 (July 1969). Reprinted in part in Robert Ornstein, ed., *The Nature of Human Consciousness* (San Francisco: W. H. Freeman; New York: Viking Press, 1973).

5. Brenda Milner, "Brain Mechanisms Suggested by Studies of Temporal Lobes," in F. L. Darley and C. H. Millikan, eds., *Brain Mechanisms Underlying Speech and Language* (New York: Grune & Stratton, 1965). Also, Brenda Milner, "Interhemispheric Differences in the Localization of Psychological Processes in Man," *British Medical Bulletin* 27, no. 3 (1971): 272–77.

6. A. R. Luria, *Higher Cortical Functions in Man* (New York: Basic Books, 1966).

7. Roger W. Sperry, "The Great Cerebral Commisure," *Scientific American*, January 1964, pp. 42–52. Offprint no. 174. Michael S. Gazzaniga, "The Split Brain in Man," *Scientific American*, August 1967, pp. 24–29.

8. Bogen, "The Other Side of The Brain."

9. Robert Nebes, "Hemispheric Specialization in Commisurotomized Man," *Psychological Bulletin* 81, no. 1 (January 1974): 1–14.

10. J. Levy, C. B. Trevarthen, and Roger W. Sperry, "Perception of Bilateral Chimeric Figures Following Hemispheric Deconnection," *Brain* 95 (1972): 61–78.

11. Levy, Trevarthen, and Sperry, "Perception of Bilateral Chimeric Figures," pp. 61–78.

12. Roger W. Sperry, "Problems Outstanding in the Evolution of Brain Function," James Arthur Lecture, American Museum of Natural History, New York, 1964.

13. Michael S. Gazzaniga, "The Split Brain in Man," pp. 24–29.

14. Gazzaniga, "The Split Brain in Man," pp. 24–29.

15. R. A. Filbey and Michael S. Gazzaniga, "Splitting the Normal Brain with Reaction Time," *Psychonomic Science* 17 (1969): 335–36.

16. Marcel Kinsbourne, unpublished manuscript (Duke University, 1971). Katherine Kocel, David Galin, Robert Ornstein, and Edward Merrin, "Lateral Eye Movements and Cognitive Mode," *Psychonomic Science* (1972), in press.

17. Marcel Kinsbourne and Jay Cook, "Generalized and Lateralized Effects of Concurrent Verbalization on a Unimanual Skill," *Quarterly Journal of Experimental Psychology* 23 (1971): 341–45.

18. J. Levy-Agresti and Roger W. Sperry, "Differential Perceptual Capacities in Major and Minor Hemispheres," *Proceedings of the National Academy of Sciences* 61 (1968): 1151.

19. Josephine Semmes, "Hemispheric Specialization: A Possible Clue to Mechanism," *Neuropsychologia* 6 (1968): 11–16.

20. Domhoff, "But Why Did They Sit on the King's Right?" pp. 586–96.

21. M. E. Humphrey and O. L. Zangwill, "Cessation of Dreaming after Brain Injury," *Journal of Neurology, Neurosurgery, and Psychiatry* 14 (1951): 322–25. Bogen, "The Other Side of the Brain, II." M. D. Austin, "Dream Recall and the Bias of Intellectual Ability," *Nature* 231 (May 7, 1971): 59.

22. W. I. B. Beveridge, *The Art of Scientific Investigation* (New York: Random House, 1950).

CHAPTER 3

1. This story is from Idries Shah, *Caravan of Dreams* (Baltimore: Penguin, 1972), p. 172.

2. William James, *The Principles of Psychology*, Vol. I (New York: Dover Publications, 1950), pp. 288–89. (Original copyright, 1890).

3. Aldous Huxley, *The Doors of Perception* and *Heaven and Hell* (New York: Harper & Row, 1954), pp. 23–24.

4. J. Y. Lettvin, H. R. Maturana, W. S. McCulloch, and W. H. Pitts, "What the Frog's Eye Tells the Frog's Brain," *Proceedings of the Institute of Radio Engineers* 47 (1959): 140–51. Reprinted in Warren S. McCulloch, *Embodiments of Mind* (Cambridge, Mass.: M.I.T. Press, 1965), pp. 230–55.

5. For an introductory review of this and other related research see Julian Hochberg, *Perception* (Englewood Cliffs, N.J.: Prentice-Hall, 1964).

6. Roger W. Sperry, "The Eye and the Brain," *Scientific American*, May 1956, pp. 48–52.

7. Ivo Kohler, "Experiments with Goggles," *Scientific American*, May 1962, pp. 62–72.

8. Ulric Neisser, "The Process of Vision," *Scientific American*, September 1968, pp. 204–14.

9. Karl H. Pribram, "The Neurophysiology of Remembering," *Scientific American*, January 1969, pp. 73–86.

10. Charles Furst, "Automatizing of Visual Attention," *Perception and Psychophysics* 10, no. 2 (1971): 65–69.

11. Jerome Bruner, "On Perceptual Readiness," *Psychological Review* 64 (1957): 123–52.

12. W. H. Ittelson and F. P. Kilpatrick, "Experiments in Perception," *Scientific American*, August 1951, pp. 50–55. Offprint no. 405. Reprinted in Robert Ornstein, ed., *The Nature of Human Consciousness* (San Francisco: W. H. Freeman; New York: Viking Press, 1973).

13. D. N. Spinelli and Karl H. Pribram, "Changes in Visual Recovery Functions and Unit Activity Produced by Frontal and Temporal Cortex Stimulation," *Electroencephalography and Clinical Neurophysiology* 22 (1967): 143–49.

14. Austin Riesen, "Arrested Vision," *Scientific American*, July 1950, pp. 16–19.

15. Richard Held, "Plasticity in Sensory Motor Systems," *Scientific American*, November 1965, pp. 84–94.

16. Roger W. Sperry, "Neurology and the Mind-Brain Problem," *American Scientist* 40 (1951): 291–312.

17. Leon Festinger, H. Ono, C. A. Burnham, and D. Bamber, "Efference and the Conscious Experience of Perception," *Journal of Experimental Psychology* 74 (1967): 1–36, is clear and contains several interesting experiments.

18. Jerome Bruner and C. C. Goodman, "Value and Need as Organizing Factors in Perception," *Journal of Abnormal and Social Psychology* 42 (1947): 33–44.

19. Albert Hastorf and Hadley Cantril, "They Saw a Game: A Case Study," *Journal of Abnormal and Social Psychology* 49 (1954): 129–34. Reprinted in Ornstein, ed., *The Nature of Human Consciousness*.

20. James, *Principles of Psychology*, Vol. I, p. 239.

21. J. B. Carroll, ed., *Language, Thought and Reality: Selected Writings of Benjamin Lee Whorf* (Cambridge, Mass.: M.I.T. Press, 1951).

22. Dorothy Lee, "Codifications of Reality: Lineal and Nonlineal," *Psychosomatic Medicine* 12, no. 2 (March–April, 1950). Reprinted in Dorothy Lee, *Freedom and Culture* (Englewood Cliffs, N.J.: Prentice-Hall, 1959). Also reprinted in Ornstein, ed., *The Nature of Human Consciousness*.

23. Wilder Penfield and L. Roberts, *Speech and Brain Mechanisms* (Princeton, N.J.: Princeton University Press, 1959).

24. Alfred North Whitehead, quoted in J. De Marquette, *Introduction to Comparative Mysticism* (New York: Philosophical Library, 1949), p. 15.

25. William James, *The Varieties of Religious Experience* (New York: New American Library, 1958), p. 298.

CHAPTER 4

1. The story is from Idries Shah, *Tales of the Dervishes* (New York: E. P. Dutton, 1970), pp. 35–38.

2. Freud's classic work is *The Interpretation of Dreams*, trans. James J. Strachey (New York: Avon Books, 1954). Originally published in 1895.

3. See William Dement, *Some Must Watch While Some Must Sleep* (San Francisco, W. H. Freeman, 1974), for a lucid discussion.

4. The Stanford Hypnotic Susceptibility Scale.

5. Phillip Zimbardo et al., unpublished manuscript (Stanford University, 1972).

6. Ernest R. Hilgard, "A Neo-dissociation Interpretation of Pain Reduction During Hypnosis," *Psychological Review* 80, no. 5 (1973): 396–411.

7. M. T. Orne and K. E. Scheihe, "The Effects of Sensory Deprivation: A Critical Review," unpublished manuscript (University of Pennsylvania, 1964).

8. See Peter Suedfeld, "Theoretical Formulations: II," in John Fubek, ed., *Sensory Deprivation: Fifteen Years of Research* (New York: Appleton-Century-Crofts, 1969).

9. Edward M. Brecher, *Licit and Illicit Drugs* (Boston: Little, Brown, 1972).

10. Jerome Frank, *Persuasion and Healing*, 2nd ed. (New York: Schocken Books, 1975).

11. As cited in Brecher, *Licit and Illicit Drugs*.

12. Charles Tart, *On Being Stoned: A Psychological Study of Marijuana Intoxication* (Palo Alto, Calif.: Science and Behavior Books, 1971).

13. As quoted in *Psychiatric News* 6: 23.

CHAPTER 5

1. From Idries Shah, *The Exploits of the Incomparable Mulla Nasrudin* (New York: E. P. Dutton, 1972), p. 112.

2. A. V. Astin, "Standards of Measurement," *Scientific American*, March 1968, pp. 50–63.

3. J. B. Carroll, ed., *Language, Thought and Reality: Selected Writings of Benjamin Lee Whorf* (Cambridge, Mass.: M.I.T. Press, 1951). See the selection "An American Indian Model of the Universe."

4. Joseph E. Bogen, "The Other Side of the Brain, I, II, III," *Bulletin of the Los Angeles Neurological Societies* 34, no. 3 (July 1969). Reprinted in part in Robert Ornstein, ed., *The Nature of Human Consciousness* (San Francisco: W. H. Freeman; New York: Viking Press, 1973).

5. H. Nichols, "The Psychology of Time," *American Journal of Psychology* 3 (1891): 453–529.

6. Lawrence Durrell, *Clea* (New York: E. P. Dutton, 1960). One of a series of four novels, concerned in large part with time.

7. J. A. Gunn, *The Problem of Time* (London: Allen & Unwin, 1929).

8. See George Miller, "The Magical Number 7 ± 2: Some Limits on Our Capacity for Processing Information," *Psychological Review* 63 (1965): 81–97. L. R. Peterson and M. Y. Peterson, "Short-term Retention of Individual Verbal Items," *Journal of Experimental Psychology* 58 (1959): 193–98.

9. Henri Bergson, *Duration and Simultaneity* (New York: Bobbs-Merrill, 1965).

10. My experiments, summarized in Robert Ornstein, *On the Experience of Time* (Baltimore: Penguin Books, 1969).

11. J. J. Harton, "An Investigation of the Influence of Success and Failure on the Estimation of Time," *Journal of General Psychology* 21 (1939): 51–62.

12. There is a rich and diverse literature on these matters. Tart's volume is an attempt to begin a scientific consideration of drug-users' experience. R. E. Masters and Jean Houston, *Varieties of Psychedelic Experience* (New York: Dell, 1966). Charles T. Tart, *On Being Stoned: A Psychological Study of Marijuana Intoxication* (Palo Alto, Calif.: Science and Behavior Books, 1971).

13. A. Carmon and I. Nachshon, "Effect of Unilateral Brain Damage on Perception of Temporal Order," *Cortex* 7 (1971): 410–18.

14. T. S. Eliot, *Four Quartets* (New York: Harcourt Brace Jovanovich, 1943), pp. 7–8.

15. Dogen, quoted in Alan Watts, *The Way of Zen* (New York: New American Library, 1957), p. 123.

16. Dorothy Lee, "Codification of Reality: Lineal and Nonlineal," *Psychosomatic Medicine* 12, no. 2 (March–April, 1950). Reprinted in Ornstein, ed., *The Nature of Human Consciousness*.

CHAPTER 6

1. This story is from Idries Shah, *The Exploits of the Incomparable Mulla Nasrudin* (New York: E. P. Dutton, 1972), pp. 128–29.

CHAPTER 7

1. This story can be found in many traditions. This version is based on Idries Shah, *Tales of the Dervishes* (New York: E. P. Dutton, 1970), pp. 25–26.

2. J. Robert Oppenheimer, *Science and the Human Understanding* (New York: Simon & Schuster, 1966), p. 69.

3. Carlos Castaneda, *The Teachings of Don Juan: A Yaqui Way of Knowledge* (New York: Ballantine, 1968). This quote is from his *A Separate Reality: Further Conversations with Don Juan* (New York: Simon & Schuster, 1971), p. 36.

4. Idries Shah, *Thinkers of the East* (Baltimore: Penguin, 1972), p. 96.

5. Elmer Green, manuscript in preparation (Topeka, Kansas: The Menninger Foundation). For many other reports, see T. Barber et al., eds., *Biofeedback and Self-Control* (Chicago: Aldine-Atherton, 1971).

6. For a first-person encounter with this "energy," see Gopi Krishna, *Kundalini: The Evolutionary Energy in Man* (Berkeley, Calif.: Shambala, 1970). For the caution, see Idries Shah, "The Fisherman and the Genie," *Tales of the Dervishes*, pp. 117–20.

7. Idries Shah, *The Sufis* (New York: Doubleday, 1971), p. 430.

8. Rafael Lefort, *The Teachers of Gurdjieff* (London: Gollancz, 1968), pp. 62–63.

9. Idries Shah, *Oriental Magic* (London: Octagon, 1968), p. 122.

10. Castaneda, *A Separate Reality*, pp. 262–63.

11. Lefort, *The Teachers of Gurdjieff*, p. 105.

12. Katherine Hulme, *Undiscovered Country* (Boston: Atlantic-Little, Brown, 1966).

13. Idries Shah, *The Way of the Sufi* (New York: E. P. Dutton, 1970), p. 140.

14. Shah, *The Way of the Sufi*, p. 151.

15. Shah, *Thinkers of the East*, p. 122.

16. Adapted from Shah, *The Way of the Sufi*, p. 107.

17. Lefort, *The Teachers of Gurdjieff.*

18. This discussion is based on Kilton Stewart, "Dream Theory in Malaya," in Charles T. Tart, ed., *Altered States of Consciousness* (New York: Doubleday, 1972).

19. See Brenda Milner, "Interhemispheric Differences in the Localization of Psychological Processes in Man," *British Medical Bulletin* 27, no. 3 (1971): 272–77.

20. Shah, *The Way of the Sufi,* p. 16.

21. J. B. Carroll, ed., *Language, Thought and Reality: Selected Writings of Benjamin Lee Whorf* (Cambridge, Mass.: M.I.T. Press, 1951). See the essay "Language, Mind and Reality."

22. Lefort, *The Teachers of Gurdjieff,* p. 57.

23. Idries Shah, *Caravan of Dreams* (Baltimore: Penguin, 1972), pp. 95–96.

24. Dennis Fry, "Some Effects of Music," Institute for Cultural Research Monographs, 13 Soho Square, London, Wl. A paper that opens up the consideration of these matters.

25. Idries Shah, *The Pleasantries of the Incredible Mulla Nasrudin* (New York: E. P. Dutton, 1971), p. 82.

26. Idries Shah, *The Exploits of the Incomparable Mulla Nasrudin* (New York: E. P. Dutton, 1972), p. 20.

27. Shah, *Pleasantries,* p. 67.

28. Shah, *Exploits,* p. 26.

29. Shah, *Caravan of Dreams,* pp. 180–81.

CHAPTER 8

1. Adapted slightly from Idries Shah, *Tales of the Dervishes* (New York: E. P. Dutton, 1970), pp. 84–85.

2. Two less positive views of these traditions are worth considering: Arthur Koestler, *The Lotus and the Robot* (New York: Harper & Row, 1960), and A. Dalal and T. Barber, "Yoga, Yoga Feats, and Hypnosis in the Light of Empirical Research," *American Journal of Clinical Hypnosis* 11 (1969): 155–66.

3. Philip Kapleau, ed., *The Three Pillars of Zen: Teaching, Practice and Enlightenment* (Boston: Beacon Press, 1965), p. 11.

4. Claudio Naranjo and Robert Ornstein, *On the Psychology of Meditation* (Baltimore: Penguin, 1977), pp. 19–74.

5. Walpola Rahula, *What the Buddha Taught* (New York: Grove Press, 1959), p. 70.

6. Kapleau, *The Three Pillars,* p. 79.

7. B. Anand, G. Chhina, and B. Singh, "Studies on Shri Ramananda Yogi During His Stay in an Airtight Box," *Indian Journal of Medical Research* 49 (1961): 82–89.

8. Robert Keith Wallace and Herbert Benson, "The Physiology of Meditation," *Scientific American,* February 1972, pp. 84–90. Reprinted in Robert Ornstein, ed., *The Nature of Human Consciousness* (San Francisco: W. H. Freeman; New York: Viking Press, 1973).

9. Ajit Mookerjee, *Tantra Art: Its Philosophy and Physics* (New Delhi: Ravi Kumar, 1966).

10. Rammurti Mishra, *Fundamentals of Yoga* (New York: Julian Press, 1959), pp. 65–66.

11. This quote is in one of the most beautiful books written on yoga: Frederic Spiegelberg, *Spiritual Practices in India* (New York: Citadel Press, 1962), pp. 46–47.

12. Idries Shah, *Oriental Magic* (London: Octagon, 1968).

13. This and many other articles of interest are collected in Roy W. Davidson, *Documents on Contemporary Dervish Communities* (London: Hoopoe Ltd., 1966), pp. 10–11. The publisher's address is 12 Baker Street, London W1.

14. Cyprian Rice, *The Persian Sufis* (London: Allen & Unwin, 1964), p. 233.

15. Arthur Deikman, "Deautomatization and the Mystic Experience," *Psychiatry* 29 (1966): 329–43. Reprinted in Charles Tart, ed., *Altered States of Consciousness* (New York: Doubleday, 1972), and in Ornstein, ed., *The Nature of Human Consciousness.*

16. E. Kadlovbovsky and G. E. H. Palmer, trans., *Writings from Philokalia, on the Prayer of the Heart* (London: Faber & Faber, 1951).

17. Peter Freuchen, *The Book of the Eskimos* (New York: Fawcett World Library, 1959).

18. Roy M. Pritchard, "Stabilized Images on the Retina," *Scientific American,* June 1961, pp. 72–78. Donald O. Hebb, *The Organization of Behavior* (New York: John Wiley & Sons, 1949).

19. D. Lehmann, G. W. Beeler, and D. H. Fender, "EEG Responses During the Observation of Stabilized and Normal Retinal Images," *Electroencephalography and Clinical Neurophysiology* 22 (1967): 136–42.

20. W. Cohen, "Spatial and Textural Characteristics of the Ganzfeld," *American Journal of Psychology* 70 (1957): 403–10. T. C. Cadwallander, "Cessation of Visual Experience Under Prolonged Uniform Visual Stimulation," *American Psychologist* 13 (1958): 410 (abstract).

21. D. T. Tepas, "The Electrophysiological Correlates of Vision in a Uniform Field," *Visual Problems of the Armed Forces*, ed. M. A. Whitcom (Washington: National Academy of Science, National Research Council, 1962), pp. 21–25.

22. B. Bagchi and M. Wenger, "Electrophysiological Correlates on Some Yogic Exercises," *Electroencephalography and Clinical Neurophysiology* suppl. no. 7 (1957): 132–49. B. Anand, G. Chhina, and B. Singh, "Some Aspects of Electroencephalographic Studies in Yogis," *Electroencephalography and Clinical Neurophysiology* 13 (1961): 452–56. Reprinted in Charles T. Tart, ed., *Altered States of Consciousness*. A. Kasamatsu and T. Hirai, "An Electroencephalographic Study of Zen Meditation (Zazen)," *Folia Psychiatria et Neurologia Japonica* 20 (1966): 315–36. Reprinted in Tart, *Altered States of Consciousness*. Yoshiharu Akishige, *Psychological Studies on Zen*, Bulletin of the Faculty of Literature of Kyushu University, Japan, No. 5 (1968). Dr. Akishige can be written to c/o The Zen Institute, Komazawa University, Komazawa 1, Setagaya-Ku, Tokyo, Japan. Robert Keith Wallace and Herbert Benson, "The Physiology of Meditation," *Scientific American*, February 1972, pp. 84–90.

23. D. Knowles, *The English Mystical Tradition* (London: Burnes & Oates, 1961), p. 57.

24. Kapleau, *The Three Pillars of Zen*, p. 53.

25. Rahula, *What the Buddha Taught*, p. 71.

26. Anand et al., "Electroencephalographic Studies in Yogis."

27. Kasamatsu and Hirai, "Study of Zen Meditation."

28. Arthur Deikman, "Experimental Meditation," *Journal of Nervous and Mental Disorders* 136 (1963): 329–43. Reprinted in Tart, ed., *Altered States of Consciousness*.

29. A. Poulain, *The Graces of Interior Prayer: A Treatise on Mystical Theology* (St. Louis: Herder, 1950), p. 272. Quoted in Deikman, "Deautomatization and the Mystic Experience."

30. Shah, *Tales*, pp. 25–26.

31. William James, *The Varieties of Religious Experience* (New York: New American Library, 1958). Arthur Deikman, "Deautomatization and Mystic Experience."

32. This quote is from a subject in an LSD session. Walter N. Pahnke and William A. Richards, "Implications of LSD and Experimental Mysticism," *Journal of Religion and Health* 5 (1966): 175–208. Reprinted in Tart, ed., *Altered States of Consciousness*.

33. Deikman, "Deautomatization and the Mystic Experience."

34. Wallace and Benson, "Physiology of Meditation."

CHAPTER 9

1. The story is from Idries Shah, *The Pleasantries of the Incredible Mulla Nasrudin* (New York: E. P. Dutton, 1971), p. 28.

CHAPTER 10

1. "There Is More Light Here" is found in Idries Shah, *The Exploits of the Incomparable Mulla Nasrudin* (New York: E. P. Dutton, 1972), pp. 26–27.

2. Elmer Green, manuscript in preparation (Topeka, Kansas: The Menninger Foundation). Alexandra David-Neel, "Magic and Mystery in Tibet" (Baltimore: Penguin, 1971).

3. A. R. Luria, *The Mind of a Mnemonist* (New York: Avon, 1969).

4. *Swansea Medical Reports*, 1971.

5. K. M. Bykov and W. H. Gantt, *The Cerebral Cortex and the Internal Organs* (New York: Chemical Publishing, 1957).

6. Joseph Breuer and Sigmund Freud, *Studies in Hysteria* (Boston: Beacon Press, 1937. Originally published in 1895).

7. J. R. Tarchanoff, "Voluntary Acceleration of the Heart Beat in Man," trans. David Blizard, in *Biofeedback and Self-Regulation, 1972*, ed. Shapiro et al. (Chicago: Aldine-Atherton, 1972).

8. Eric Ogden and Nathan Shock, "Voluntary Hypercirculation," *American Journal of the Medical Sciences* 198 (1939): 329–42.

9. See Neal E. Miller, "Learning of Visceral and Glandular Responses," *Science* 163 (1969): 434–45. Neal E. Miller, "Biofeedback: Evaluation of a

New Technique," in *Biofeedback and Self-Control, 1974,* ed. DiCara et al. (Chicago: Aldine-Atherton, 1975).

10. See Neal E. Miller and Barry Dworkin, "Visceral Learning: Recent Difficulties with Curartized Rats and Significant Problems for Human Research," in *Cardiovascular Psychophysiology,* ed. Obrist et al. (Chicago: Aldine-Atherton, 1974), pp. 312–31.

11. Eugene R. Bleeker and Bernard T. Engel, "Learned Control of Ventricular Rate in Patients with Atrial Fibrillation," *Psychosomatic Medicine* 35, no. 2 (1973): 161–70. Eugene R. Bleeker and Bernard T. Engel, "Learned Control of Cardiac Rate and Cardiac Conduction in the Wolff-Parkinson-White Syndrome," *New England Journal of Medicine* 288 (March 15, 1973): 560–62.

12. Gary E. Schwartz and David Shapiro, "Biofeedback and Essential Hypertension: Current Findings and Theoretical Concerns," *Seminars in Psychiatry* 5, no. 4 (1973): 493–503.

13. David P. Nowlis and J. Kamiya, "The Control of Electroencephalographic Alpha Rhythms Through Auditory Feedback and the Associated Mental Activity," *Psychophysiology* 6, no. 4 (1970): 476–84. Reprinted in Robert Ornstein, ed., *The Nature of Human Consciousness* (San Francisco: W. H. Freeman; New York: Viking Press, 1973).

14. David Galin and Robert Ornstein, "Lateral Specialization of Cognitive Mode: An EEG Study," *Psychophysiology* (1972).

15. Thomas H. Budzynski, Johann Stoyva, and Charles Adler, "Feedback-Induced Muscle Relaxation: Application to Tension Headaches," *Journal of Behavioral Therapy and Experimental Psychiatry* 1 (1970): 205–11. Reprinted in T. Barber et al., eds., *Biofeedback and Self-Control* (Chicago: Aldine-Atherton, 1971).

16. Johann Stoyva and Thomas Budzynski, "Cultivated Low Arousal—An Antistress Response?" in *Limbic and Autonomic Nervous System Research,* ed. Leo DiCara (New York: Plenum, 1974), pp. 48–75.

17. Elmer Green, unpublished manuscript (Topeka, Kansas: The Menninger Foundation, 1975).

CHAPTER 11

1. Nasafi, in Idries Shah, *The Sufis* (New York: Doubleday, 1971), p. 401.

2. Gay Luce, "Biological Rhythms," in *Psychiatry and Medicine* (Bethesda, Md.: National Institute of Mental Health, 1970): 1–80. Much of this

discussion is adapted from Luce's monograph. A more popularized version of this material can be found in her *Body Time* (New York: Pantheon, 1972).

3. Luce, "Biological Rhythms," pp. 1–80.

4. E. E. Von Bount, M. D. Shepherd, J. R. Wall, W. F. Ganong, and M. T. Clegg, "Penetration of Light into the Brain of Mammals," *Annals of the New York Academy of Sciences* 117 (1964): 217–24.

5. Luce, "Biological Rhythms," pp. 1–80.

6. Swami Vishnudevananda, *The Complete Illustrated Book of Yoga* (New York: Bell Publishing, 1960), p. 223.

7. Omar Garrison, *Tantra: The Yoga of Sex* (New York: Julian Press, 1964), pp. 143–45.

8. S. Kimura, M. Ashiba, and I. Matsushima, "Influences of the Air Lacking in Light Ions and the Effect of its Artificial Ionization upon Human Beings in Occupied Rooms," *Japanese Journal of Medical Science* 7 (1939): 1–12.

9. N. Robinson and F. S. Dirnfeld, "The Ionization State of the Atmosphere as a Function of the Meteorological Elements and the Various Sources of Ions," *International Journal of Biometeorology* 6 (1963): 101–10.

10. A. P. Krueger and H. B. Levine, "The Effect of Unipolar Positively Ionized Air on the Course of Coccidioidomicosis in Mice," *International Journal of Biometeorology* 11 (1967): 279–88.

11. Krueger's paper is probably the best review written to date. A. P. Krueger, "Preliminary Consideration of the Biological Significance of Air Ions," *Scientia* 104 (September–October 1969). Reprinted in Robert Ornstein, ed., *The Nature of Human Consciousness* (San Francisco: W. H. Freeman; New York: Viking Press, 1973). See also the more recent review, A. P. Krueger and E. J. Reed, "Biological Impact of Small Air Ions," *Science* 193 (September 24, 1976): 1209–13.

12. S. Kotaka and A. P. Krueger, "Studies on Air Ionized-Induced Growth Increase in Higher Plants," *Advancing Frontiers of Plant Sciences* 20 (1967): 115–208.

13. These studies are referred to in A. P. Krueger, "The Biological Significance of Air Ions," in *Bioclimatology, Biometeorology, and Aeroiontherapy* (Milan, Italy: Carlo Erba Foundation, 1969). Also see the article by Kornbleuth in the same volume.

14. A. L. Tchijevsky, trans., Central Laboratory Sci. Res. Ionification (Publishing House of the Commune, Voronej, 1933). This is merely a report and would need much verification before its contention could be accepted.

15. For the one report that considers a possible mechanism of this effect, see A. P. Krueger, P. C. Andriese, and S. Kotaka, "Small Air Ions: Their Effect on Blood Levels of Serotonin in Terms of Modern Physical Theory," *International Journal of Biometeorology* 12, no. 3 (1968): 225–39.

16. Ida Rolf, "Structural Integration: Gravity, an Unexplored Factor in a More Human Use of Human Beings," *Systematics* 1 (June 1963). David Sobel, "Gravity and Structural Integration," in Robert Ornstein, ed., *The Nature of Human Consciousness* (San Francisco: W. H. Freeman; New York: Viking Press, 1973).

17. Fritz S. Perls, *Gestalt Therapy Verbatim* (Lafayette, Calif.: Real People Press, 1969).

18. Joen Fagan and Irma Lee Shepherd, eds., *Gestalt Therapy Now* (New York: Harper & Row, 1971), p. 38.

19. Idries Shah, *The Sufis* (New York: Doubleday, 1964). See the chapter "Miracles and Magic."

20. M. Ullman and S. Krippner, *Dream Studies and Telepathy: An Experimental Approach,* Parapsychological Monograph no. 12 (1970), Parapsychology Foundation, 29 W. 57th St., New York, New York. M. Ullman, S. Krippner, and S. Feldstein, "Experimentally-Induced Telepathic Dreams: Two Studies Using EEG and REM Monitoring Technique," *International Journal of Neuropsychiatry* 2 (1966): 420–38.

21. Two additional experiments on this mode of communication are reported in Thelma Moss and Thomas Gangerelli, "Telepathy and Emotional Stimuli: A Controlled Experiment," *Journal of Abnormal Psychology* 72 (1967): 341–48, and T. McBain, "Quasi-Sensory Communication: An Investigation Using Semantic Matching and Accentuated Affect," *Journal of Personality and Social Psychology* 14 (1970): 281–91.

22. Russell Targ and Harold Puthoff, "Information Transmission Under Conditions of Sensory Shielding," *Nature* 252, no. 5476 (October 18, 1974): 602–07.

23. Charles T. Tart, *Learning to Use Extrasensory Perception* (Chicago: University of Chicago Press, 1976).

24. Elizabeth Hall, "A Conversation with Idries Shah," *Psychology Today,* July 1975.

ILLUSTRATION CREDITS

INDEX

251